SOCIOLOGICAL OBJECTS

Sociological Objects
Reconfigurations of Social Theory

Edited by

GEOFF COOPER
University of Surrey, UK

ANDREW KING
Kingston University, UK

RUTH RETTIE
Kingston University, UK

LONDON AND NEW YORK

First published 2009 by Ashgate Publishing

2 Park Square, Milton Park, Abingdon, Oxfordshire OX14 4RN
711 Third Avenue, New York, NY 10017

Routledge is an imprint of the Taylor & Francis Group, an informa business

First issued in paperback 2018

Copyright © Geoff Cooper, Andrew King and Ruth Rettie 2009

Geoff Cooper, Andrew King and Ruth Rettie have asserted their moral right under the Copyright, Designs and Patents Act, 1988, to be identified as the editors of this work.

All rights reserved. No part of this book may be reprinted or reproduced or utilised in any form or by any electronic, mechanical, or other means, now known or hereafter invented, including photocopying and recording, or in any information storage or retrieval system, without permission in writing from the publishers.

Notice:
Product or corporate names may be trademarks or registered trademarks, and are used only for identification and explanation without intent to infringe.

British Library Cataloguing in Publication Data
Sociological objects : reconfiguration of social theory
  1. Sociology
  I. Cooper, Geoff II. King, Andrew III. Rettie, Ruth
  301

Library of Congress Cataloging-in-Publication Data
Sociological objects : reconfigurations of social theory / [edited] by Geoff Cooper, Andrew King and Ruth Rettie.
    p. cm.
  Includes index.
  ISBN 978-0-7546-7268-5
  1. Sociology. 2. Sociology--Philosophy. 3. Sociology--Methodology. I. Cooper, Geoff. II. King, Andrew. III. Rettie, Ruth.
  HM585.S595 2009
  301.01--dc22
                                                                                    2008035646

ISBN 13: 978-0-7546-7268-5 (hbk)
ISBN 13: 978-1-138-61545-8 (pbk)

Contents

Notes on Contributors		vii
Preface		xi
1	The Objects of Sociology: An Introduction *Geoff Cooper*	1
PART 1 SOCIAL THINGS		21
2	Durkheim's Globality *David Inglis and Roland Robertson*	25
3	Back to the Things Themselves: On Simmelian Objects *Olli Pyyhtinen*	43
4	Durkheim's Social Facts and the Performative Model: Reconsidering the Objective Nature of Social Phenomena *Irene Rafanell*	59
PART 2 SOCIAL PRACTICES		77
5	Communities of Practice vs. Traditional Communities: The State of Sociology in a Context of Globalization *Anne Warfield Rawls*	81
6	Working Out What Garfinkel Could Possibly be Doing with "Durkheim's Aphorism" *Michael Lynch*	101
7	Mathematical Equations as Durkheimian Social Facts? *Christian Greiffenhagen and Wes Sharrock*	119
PART 3 SOCIAL THEORIES		137
8	Social Theory in Situated Practice: Theoretical Categories in Everyday Discourse *Nanna Mik-Meyer*	139

9	Appropriation, Translation and the Opening of Theory *Anna Tsatsaroni and Geoff Cooper*	159
10	'Identity' after 'The Moment of Theory' *Paul du Gay*	177
11	Concluding Thoughts: Reconfigurations of Social Theory *Andrew King and Ruth Rettie*	191

Index *203*

Notes on Contributors

Geoff Cooper is Reader in Sociology at the University of Surrey. His intellectual interests lie within social theory and science and technology studies, and he has carried out research on the rhetorical structure of disciplines, forms of accountability in changing research cultures, the social shaping of mobile telecommunications, and decisions to invest in nanotechnology. He has published in a number of journals including the *British Journal of Sociology*, *Social Studies of Science*, and *Sociology*, and is currently researching aspects of the relation between lifestyle and energy consumption.

Paul du Gay is Professor of Organizational Behaviour at Warwick Business School and Adjunct Professor in Organization Studies at Copenhagen Business School. His recent publications include *The Values of Bureaucracy* (ed. OUP, 2005), *Organizing Identity: Persons and Organizations 'After Theory'* (Sage, 2007), *Conduct: Sociology and Social Worlds* (eds. with E. McFall and S. Carter, Manchester University Press), and *Identity in Question* (ed. with A. Elliott, Sage, 2008).

Christian Greiffenhagen is a British Academy Postdoctoral Fellow at the University of Manchester, currently conducting ethnographic research on mathematical practice. His doctoral research was a video-based ethnographic study of how a new innovative storyboarding software was embedded in everyday classroom practice and how this reconfigured classroom interaction. His recent publications include 'Unpacking Tasks', *International Journal of Computer Supported Cooperative Work*, 'Mathematical Relativism', *Journal for the Theory of Social Behaviour* (with Wes Sharrock), and 'Kuhn and Conceptual Change', *Science & Education* (with Wendy Sherman).

David Inglis is Professor of Sociology at the University of Aberdeen. He writes in the areas of social theory and the sociology of culture. He has particular research interests in the history of social theory, especially in light of considerations of globalization.

Andrew King is a Lecturer in Sociology at Kingston University, London. He specializes in teaching social theory and its applications. His research covers a range of topics, typically focusing on identity. His doctoral research focused on young people's transitions to adulthood, drawing on ethnomethodology, conversation analysis and post-structuralism. Currently, he is involved in two research projects:

the interaction between learning, space and identity; and the care experiences of older lesbian, gay and bisexual adults.

Michael Lynch is a Professor in the Department of Science and Technology Studies at Cornell University. His research is on practical actions and social interactions in laboratories, criminal courts, and other institutional settings. He is author of *Art and Artifact in Laboratory Science* (1985), *Scientific Practice and Ordinary Action: Ethnomethodology and Social Studies of Science* (1993), and *Truth Machine: The Contentious History of DNA Profiling* (2008, with Simon Cole, Ruth McNally and Kathleen Jordan). He also is Editor of *Social Studies of Science* and President of the Society for Social Studies of Science (2007–2009).

Nanna Mik-Meyer is Associate Professor in the Department of Organization, Copenhagen Business School, and her main research area is within the fields of sociology, organizational/identity research and qualitative methods. She has a PhD from the Department of Sociology, Copenhagen University, and a MA from the Institute of Anthropoloty, Copenhagen Universtity. She has just finished a postdoctoral project at Copenhagen Business School (Department of Management, Politics and Philosophy) on obesity and risk discourse, awarded in January 2006 by the Danish Independent Research Council's Young Researcher's Award.

Olli Pyyhtinen works as a Research and Teaching Associate at the Department of Sociology at the University of Turku, Finland. He is currently completing his PhD thesis on Simmel's social theory and has also translated Simmel into Finnish. His other research interests include materiality, event thinking, social ontology, and art.

Irene Rafanell is a Sociology lecturer at the University of the West of Scotland and an Honorary Fellow of the School of Social and Political Studies at Edinburgh University. She completed her PhD in 2004 at Edinburgh University and her work explores the connections between social theory, social constructionism, sociology of knowledge and the body.

Anne Warfield Rawls is Professor of Sociology at Bentley College. Her research focuses on respecifying ethics, information, work, social order and intelligibility in sociological and interactional terms. Recent publications include *Epistemology and Practice: Durkheim's Elementary Forms* (Cambridge, 2005), Garfinkel's Notion of Time (*Time and Society*, 2005) and *Harold Garfinkel, Ethnomethodology and Workplace Studies* (Organization Studies, 2008). Anne has edited and introduced several books by Garfinkel including *Ethnomethodology's Program: Working Out Durkheim's Aphorism* (2002), *Seeing Sociologically: The Routine Grounds of Social Action* (2007), and *Toward a Sociological Theory of Information* (2008).

Ruth Rettie is a Senior Lecturer at Kingston University. She has degrees in philosophy, an MBA, and a PhD in sociology from the University of Surrey. Her research interests include social theory, STS, mediated interaction, social networking sites, and the role of marketing in shaping consumer attitudes to sustainability. Her doctoral research focused on mobile phone communication. Her research has been published in several disciplines, including sociology, psychology, human computer interaction, and management.

Roland Robertson is Professor of Sociology and Global Society at the University of Aberdeen and is also Distinguished Service Professor of Sociology Emeritus at the University of Pittsburgh. He is the author of numerous books and articles on globalization, social theory, cultural theory, sociology of religion, and political sociology. His work has been translated into over twenty languages and he has held visiting appointments in the USA, Japan, Sweden, England, Brazil, Italy, Austria, and Thailand. He is presently working on a book about the new totalitarianism, centered upon the ideas of exhibitionism, voyeurism, transparency and security.

Wes Sharrock has been at the University of Manchester, where he is now professor of sociology, since 1965. He has research interests in philosophy, philosophy of the social sciences, ethnomethodology, and studies of work. He is currently involved in research on the work of ontology builders in bioinformatics. Recent publications include *Brain, Mind and Human Behavior in Contemporary Cognitive Science* (with Jeff Coulter), Edwin Mellen Press, 2007, *Theory and Method in Sociology* (with John Hughes), Palgrave, 2007, and *There is No Such Thing as a Social Science* (with Phil Hutchinson and Rupert Read), Ashgate, 2008.

Anna Tsatsaroni is Associate Professor of Sociology of Education in the Department of Social and Educational Policy of the University of Peloponnese, Greece. Her research interests are in the sociology of educational knowledge and practices, and in exploring changes in knowledge in crucial subfields of Educational Studies, especially within the context of current reforms. These interests have been pursued in collaboration with colleagues specializing in such subjects as mathematics education and science education. Her publications appear in international Journals such as *The British Journal of Sociology of Education, Social Epistemology, British Educational Research Journal, International Journal of Science and Mathematics Education*, and *Educational Studies in Mathematics*.

Preface

This book had its origins in a one day conference, 'Sociology After Durkheim' held at the University of Surrey, 21 June 2006. The editors are grateful to The Department of Sociology at Surrey, and to the British Sociological Association Theory Study Group for their support of this event.

Chapter 1
The Objects of Sociology: An Introduction

Geoff Cooper

Sociological Objects, Sociological Subjects

What are the objects of sociology? Such a question is characteristic of sociological discourse, which throughout its history has encompassed reflection upon and interrogation of the precise nature, and referents, of particular forms of sociological knowledge. However, although a recurrent question, each repetition is necessarily marked by new relevancies, and the occasions and contexts of its asking in themselves provide some of the resources for formulating answers. To ask what are the objects of sociology, or what is meant by such a question, is therefore both to raise questions about the historical specificity of sociology and the phenomena it studies today, and to relate those questions to the history of the discipline and its questioning.

Already it is apparent that the question is one that opens up others; indeed, simple though it may be, it points towards the consideration of a wide range of possible issues. The objects of sociology may be taken to refer to the goals or purposes of the discipline – what, in the final analysis, should sociology be doing, and what kinds of sociological work are best suited to accomplish these goals? In an important sense, this broad and fundamental question lies beneath or behind the other interpretations of the phrase or question to which the contributions to this book are, perhaps, more directly addressed.

What is, or should be, sociology's object of study? Are there, as Durkheim – a key reference point for this book – appeared to think, social phenomena which provide the discipline with both its own distinctive subject matter and, thereby, much of its legitimacy? Or, as has been argued on more than one occasion and with particular force in recent work, does this vision of sociology rest on some fundamental misconceptions – not least of what is meant by 'social' – and, partly because of its disciplinary aspirations, end up with a restricted field of analysis that is unable to do justice to the heterogeneity of the world?[1] This line of criticism not only suggests that sociologists should broaden their view to encompass different categories of phenomena including – to flag another important dimension of the

---

[1] Recent arguments for a revision to the idea that sociology has its own domain of objects include Latour (2005), and Urry (2000); see also the subsequent discussion of this line of argument by Urry et al. (2007).

term – material objects of various kinds, but may also have implications for how we think about the subject of knowledge, the sociologist.

'Object' carries further meanings that complicate any simple demarcation between object of study and (material) object, particularly if considered in historical terms. For example it is possible to read Latour (2005) as claiming, even if it is not his main point, that a cumulative process of delegation of functions to technologies is underway, which would imply that the inclusion of technologies within social analysis is something that becomes more necessary over time: the object of study is changing, and must include objects. However, this relationship can be seen in quite different ways. Following Foucault, it is possible to look more critically at the way in which human sciences such as sociology are engaged in processes of objectification, where people have become the objects of a disciplinary gaze which configures them in particular ways (Foucault 1977). Objectification within the research process is also an important critical focus of feminist work (Oakley 1981; Smith 1990). In each case, 'object of study' becomes not a neutral term of designation but an indicator of something more complex and problematic.

If we have here, on the one hand, a recommendation to include objects in sociological work and, on the other, a pointing to the ways in which sociology, in its 'traditional' form, has treated people as objects, there are also arguments that some of the phenomena of potential interest to sociologists are becoming more object-like. Lash and Lury (2007) for example argue that new technologically enabled cultural forms of global capitalism imply a move away from representations to 'mediatized' objects which are both material and operational. Interestingly, here and elsewhere, 'the object' co-exists with the language of 'flows' that is deployed in much contemporary theory, notably in Castells' (2000) description of the operation of information in global capitalism, but also in Bauman (2000) and Mol and Law (1994), where similar metaphors are used to aid the description of the current state of modernity on the one hand, and the capturing and conveying of dynamic process on the other.[2] Whilst not opposed, these discursive figures exhibit a degree of tension, and their articulation may in itself imply a transformation of what is meant by 'object'.

These points by no means exhaust the connotations of 'objects'. The appeal to the object can and does become implicated in arguments about or between realism and constructivism, materialism and idealism, objectivism and subjectivism (see for example Daston (2000), where the idea of biographies of objects is used to counter the perceived tendency towards over-subjectivized constructions in social science), even capitalism and socialism if we follow Lukacs' earlier arguments about the processes of reification which are endemic to the former and have shaped, *inter alia*, modern western thought from at least Kant onwards (Lukacs 1971). Further distinctions can be made, for example between objects and things (Heidegger 1971, 2002b; Latour 2004). Nor can these questions about the object

---

[2] See also the presence of 'objects' and 'flows' in Appadurai's (1986) influential treatment of the circulation of commodities.

be safely restricted to the choice of appropriate analytical terminology for a given state of affairs: when Durkheim (1982) urges sociologists to 'treat social facts as things', or Mol and Law (op cit.) propose a language of fluids and flows, are these statements intended, or to be read, as more or less useful analogies or metaphors, as denoting something concrete about the world being described, or perhaps doing other kinds of, performative, discursive work (cf. Garfinkel and Sacks 1970)?[3]

We have then a cluster of issues, many of which centre on the question of the status of the social, have both conceptual and historical dimensions, and frequently imply, if not explicitly invoke, a normative element insofar as a case is made for preferred ways of doing sociology. The latter can be formulated, as already noted, in terms of the sociological subject. Can this subject still be thought in disciplinary terms if, for instance, the heterogeneity of the world requires an approach which cannot be confined within the boundaries of one discipline? What is the (preferred) relation between the knowing subject and sociological object? In what ways can or should professional and lay sociological subjects and their respective understandings be distinguished?[4] Can the objects of sociology be meaningfully considered without reference to the structure of the sociological fields within which they are articulated (Bourdieu et al. 1991; Bernstein 2000)?

These questions can, at least in part, be considered in historical terms. Is sociology, or should it be, changing? One answer to this is that *of course* sociology is changing and should change if it is not to be consigned to irrelevance. But how should we understand this change, particularly in relation to the canonical body of established work? One approach to this issue has been to orient discussion around the idea of some kind of epistemological break as apparently connoted by 'postmodern'. Whilst this paradoxical term has been creatively used precisely to problematize ideas of progress and the progressive accumulation of knowledge through time (Vattimo 1988), it remains the case that it has often, for understandable reasons, been taken to imply just the linear model of history and historical time that it puts into question. In this book, we therefore leave the language of 'post-isms' (Derrida 1990) to one side to look at the ongoing reconfiguration of sociology and social theory. Reconfiguration is taken to include not only new developments in the field, but also the way in which the history of the discipline is itself reformulated, the way that old debates return but are given different inflection, the fact that once discarded figures take on a new relevance. In contrast to the discipline's occasional tendency to assume that current concerns can be unproblematically projected back onto its history – structure and agency arguably being a prominent example (Fuller 1998) – this means both that the history of the discipline is never

---

3   Rafanell's argument, this volume, uses recent conceptualizations of performativity to problematize the apparent dichotomy between objective and subjective; Greiffenhagen and Sharrock also demonstrate difficulties with the way this opposition is often formulated.

4   This is a key issue that runs throughout this book: see in particular the chapters by Greiffenhagen and Sharrock, Mik-Meyer, and du Gay.

given but emerges in different ways from different tellings, and that the relation of sociological work to that history is a continually shifting and contested one.

Geosociology: The Time and Place of Social Theory

An important persistent theme in the work of Deleuze, discussed in detail in Deleuze and Guattari (1994), is that all philosophy is 'geophilosophy' in the sense that it is 'marked by certain features of the time and place in which it is carried out' (Patton 2006: 23). This insight being presumably at least equally applicable to social theory, it may be useful to sketch some of the possibly salient features of the latter's contemporary historical context.

It must be noted however that neither the nature nor the significance of that historical context can be simply assumed. Just as it is a mistake to hypostasize concepts and theories and ignore their historical specificity (Adorno 2000), so it would be problematic to proceed as if history could provide a point of reference that is both external to theory, and therefore able to explain it. Since there is, as we might say, no history outside theory, and no theory outside history, the following observations about historical context are intended to be merely suggestive and necessarily leave open questions of causal significance.

An initial and interesting complication of the task of locating theory in this way derives from the fact that the problematization of 'location' is perhaps one of the key features of the developing world today that needs to be considered. The broad term 'globalization' serves as shorthand for a number of relevant issues here (see Appadurai 2001, for a more comprehensive review). In the first place, the term signifies the expansion of socio-economic processes and relations which take place beyond the limits of the nation state and are seen to weaken the latter's sovereignty, with consequent implications for sociology's unit of analysis, as we shall note. But the term also points in the direction of complications to the very notion of locality. Auge (1995) for example, coins the term 'non-places' to describe the (proliferation of) neutral and formally identical sites such as airports, shopping malls, supermarkets, sites which remain unmarked by their location in a particular town or country and which frame a large part of some people's everyday experience in what he calls 'supermodernity'. Urry (2000) suggests that the phenomenon of mobility, in all its forms, is a defining feature of life today (and that sociology needs to reconfigure itself to get its measure). In both cases, an argument is made that place is losing some of its experiential significance. This argument, in turn, has considerable resonance with Casey's (1997) suggestion that the rationalization of the modern world involves the replacement of place with space, where the former connotes forms of identification – with history, community, home for instance – and the latter the relative neutrality of spatial coordinates. Nancy's (2007) distinction between mondialization and globalization, and his affirmation of the former, makes an analogous point. In short, to ask about the location of social theory in socio-historical terms is already to situate oneself in the midst of highly relevant debates even before any possible answers are suggested.[5] The sociology of place has implications for how we conceptualize the place of sociology.[6]

The term globalization references other important aspects of the contemporary socio-historical context. The networks of information and communication technologies that form a crucial component of the infra-structure of today's global economy, and for some such as Castells (2000) constitute defining features of contemporary societies, clearly deserve serious consideration. Nowotny et al. (2001) for example have argued that the rapid development of new information and communication technologies has not only provided technical preconditions for far reaching social and economic change but 'has had more radical effects that tend to dissolve existing forms of systemic differentiation' (ibid. 32), although they immediately qualify this apparently straightforward claim by noting the analytical difficulty of extricating technology (or science) from the social configurations in which they are located and arguing for a notion of the co-evolution of science and technology on the one hand, society on the other.[7] The idea of a dissolution of differentiation of this kind has been relatively widespread in recent thought, even if understood in terms of different analytical frameworks or social process: for example, the de-differentiation of postmodernization (Crook et al. 1992), or the spread of market logics and criteria into more domains within late capitalism (Habermas 1987b). One indisputable consequence of these technical developments is that much social life, sociology and indeed all academic work now 'take place' in a more information-rich environment than has been the case in the past. Heidegger commented in 1938 that the scholar was being replaced by the researcher who, amongst other things, 'no longer need [ed] a library at home' (Heidegger 2002a: 64); today, a further movement away from the social/intellectual elite whose passing Heidegger regretted is evident in the paradoxical fact that now everybody who is connected to the internet has a kind of library at home, and indeed is encouraged to contribute to and amend the information it contains. For some, such developments contain genuine democratizing potential through their introduction of transparency into the social body (Vattimo 1992); for others, the dominance of (the notion and reality of) information changes knowledge and in particular limits the possibilities of critical thought (Lash 2002; Sandywell 2003). The development of the internet also creates opportunities for reflection back onto the material bases

---

5 For example, Ritzer (2004) argues that 'globalization' obscures processes that would be more truthfully described as 'Americanization'; whilst Burawoy (2007) advances a parallel argument that American sociology presents itself as universal whilst exerting enormous and sometimes detrimental influence on other national sociologies.

6 For a comprehensive review of some different dimensions and aspects of the sociology of place see Gieryn (2000).

7 A similar move is made under the heading of 'co-production', derived from the work of Latour: see Jasanoff (2004).

of knowledge and their history, and the extent to which paper may have provided much more than a neutral medium of transmission (Derrida 2005).[8]

If the technical infrastructures of global capitalism have provided one important backdrop, framework and topic for recent social theory – where the response to the phenomenon might be considered both as analysis and symptom – its dominant politico-economic forms, and in particular the pre-eminence of neo-liberalism have provided another. One result of this has been a renewed interest in analysing the economy and its effects, an interest which has taken many forms: for example, a critique of neo-liberalism, and reaffirmation of the indispensability of the classical sociological tradition for such a task (Smart 2003); sociological analyses of the discourses of late capitalism (Boltanski and Chiapello 2005) and of economics (Granovetter and Swedberg 1992; Slater and Tonkiss 2001); exploration of the complex intersections between technology and economy (Barry and Slater 2005); detailed empirical analyses of markets and their operation (Callon 1998); investigations of the performative effects of the discipline of economics in constituting its own object of study (MacKenzie et al. 2007); or celebrations of the creative properties of contemporary capitalism (Thrift 2005).

There are more reflexive dimensions to consider here, for the erosion of systemic differentiation operates on the university's specificity and relations to other institutions, while market processes and logics continue to become more thoroughly embedded within it. Thus, for example, academic work becomes subject to processes of audit and quality assurance that operate across other sectors (cf. Power 1997) and may be perceived as forms of regulation and management which threaten traditional academic values and forms of practice (see Tsatsaroni and Cooper, this volume). The transformations that are the object of such a critique have prompted some to suggest that a new mode of knowledge production has been inaugurated in which, *inter alia*, research is: not confined to the university but conducted in and between a variety of institutions; problem-oriented rather than discipline-based; and increasingly carried out in the domain of application (Gibbons et al. 1994). According to this view the university ceases to be the bounded entity that it once was (but see Derrida 2004), and the relations between knowledge producers, knowledge 'users' and the public, including the terms in which scientists are accountable, begin to change (Nowotny et al. 2001):[9] for example the ways in which research results are 'disseminated', to use a word which itself becomes suspect. No longer, it is said, are research results released at the end of a project, mainly through the channel of peer reviewed publications; rather we see a less linear process of communication, through a proliferating variety of channels, which takes place between researchers, 'users' and the public throughout a project's life: the increasing presence of PR and marketing departments within the university being one symptom of this.

---

8 Important work on this topic predates the internet: see in particular Eisenstein (1983).

9 Lyotard's earlier (1984) discussion of knowledge production anticipates some of these points.

It is beyond the scope of this chapter to give proper consideration to the validity of these arguments which, in any case, have been sketched here with a very broad brush (but see Godin 1998). However, the fact that these discussions have taken place in the way that they have in recent decades is significant in itself, pointing to an experience or intuition of changes to knowledge production. In such a context, it follows that one of the key issues at stake will be the politics of sociology, in that the question arises (not for the first time) of to whom the discipline should primarily be addressed (Clawson et al. 2007), as does the continually pertinent issue of the extent to which, or ways in which it should critically engage not only with the issues of the day but also with the conditions of its own practice (Gouldner 1970). Similarly, when the status and viability of disciplines *per se* are in question, the continuing relevance of canonical work within the discipline cannot be taken for granted.

That said, if we consider some of the most grossly visible features of the (mediatized) contemporary world, they would appear to offer plenty of purchase for social theory in general, and classical sociology in particular. In relation to understanding developments in the global economy, it is at least arguable that – notwithstanding the long shadow that the last century has thrown across his model for social amelioration – Marx continues to provide the best diagnostic and critical tools (Smart 2003; Harvey 2007). If it would be a mistake to see the rise and political significance of certain forms of faith and religion in term of a simple return or resurgence – for example, because of the complexity of its relations to new forms of technology (Derrida 1998) and to political programmes (de Vries and Sullivan 2006) – it remains the case that the sociology of religion in the work of Weber and Durkheim can still contribute to their understanding.[10] Nor should it be considered that continuing political pertinence is confined to overtly political or even 'macro' forms of sociology (to use a term that has become problematic for some). Sociologies derived from the work of Harvey Sacks (1995) which address the situated use of categories in talk have perhaps never been more necessary at a time when political discourse is dominated by highly contentious and politically consequential category work.[11] One obvious example is 'the war on terror', but we could also note the performative use of the term 'community' to describe certain sections of the population (defined in terms of religious affiliation perhaps), and the way in which that in turn legitimizes discussion of 'its' responsibilities, and configures a certain mode or channel of communication with people who are (*de facto* religious) 'community leaders'.

---

10   Giddens' (1991) characterization of western societies in terms of detraditionalization and reflexivity (with respect to forms of potential authority) is also an important reference point for understanding some of the tensions engendered by new religious forms, although it is an open question as to how far it can explain the latter's emergence.

11   Sacks would not qualify as a classical sociologist according to the usual criteria, but exemplifies the continuing or arguably heightened relevance that well established work can have.

On the other hand, since these socio-political phenomena include new elements and are present in different configurations, the relevance of established sociological approaches can no more be assumed than denied. Moreover, there are of course many more potentially relevant historically specific developments than could be considered or even listed here, each of which constitute a challenge to existing sociological (and social theoretical) knowledge. The rise and continuing presence of feminism as a social and political movement outside the academy has had fundamental implications for practice within it (Smith 2004; Marshall and Witz 2004). The apparent end of the era of empire – but see Hardt and Negri (2001) – has provided a stimulus for forms of contestation over the theoretical frameworks within which the politics of ethnicity, immigration and imperialism should be interpreted. For Verges (2004), for example, the colonial and the postcolonial represent challenges to received, eurocentric, ideas of what constitutes the social; while complementary approaches (see for example Hesse and Sayyid 2005) focus on the ways in which disciplinary understandings (including certain uses of what they call the postcolonial analytic) have themselves been shaped and limited by some of the very forces which they seek to analyse.[12]

Drawing our gaze in another direction are rapid developments within the bio-sciences, which are claimed to have profoundly affected understandings of what it is to be human (Rose 2006) and thereby – according to some (Fuller 2006 for example) – of social science, whose juxtaposition to biology as a competing explanation of human behaviour has always been uncomfortable. One can also note that the biomedical sciences can provide unexpected resources for the social theoretical analysis of recent events: to take one notable example, Derrida (2003) uses the concept of auto-immunity to explain world political developments in the wake of '9/11' (cf. Mitchell 2007). To take a final example, there is the momentous practical problem of environmental damage, the impact of which is likely to be felt within and beyond human societies. For Beck, this is a – perhaps the – prime example of risks which, having entered a qualitatively new phase, have become defining characteristics of contemporary societies (Beck 1992). Moreover, in placing limits not only on socio-political boundaries, but also on the very (human-centred) term environment and indeed, the focus on the human *per se*, such risks may prompt an even more radical reconfiguration of the concepts of society and the social. With this in mind, we turn to look a little more closely at the changing fortunes of these concepts within sociology.

Reconfiguring Social Theory and its Objects

Some of the historical phenomena indicated thus far might be regarded as *prima facie* causes for the recent questioning of the social. Since, for example, it can

---

12 It has also been suggested that political events such as the war in Iraq may necessitate further reframings of postcolonial studies (Gopal and Lazarus 2006).

be argued that sociology's most famous object 'society' has always implicitly if not explicitly referred to the nation state, then the fact of globalization would appear to raise a fundamental question about (what some see as) the discipline's fundamental unit of analysis (see Inglis and Robertson, and Rawls, this volume). Similarly Margaret Thatcher's famously negative assessment of the ontological status of 'society', which has in turn infuriated then fascinated sociologists, can be explained as the rhetorical expression of broadly neo-liberal policies which are premised on a reluctance to regulate or distort the workings of competitive markets with, for example, welfare provision at a societal level. However, there are some problems with direct attribution of this kind. The sheer diversity of problem formulation in this area suggests the need for caution: the social theorists collected in Gane (2004) for example, address challenges to the idea the social with reference to, *inter alia*, liquid modernity, information, mobility, the relation between literary and social theory, cosmopolitanization, globalization, governance, and postcolonialism. It is also notable that some of the most forcefully argued critical accounts, such as Latour's, have been elaborated with comparatively little direct historical reference.

If *direct* attribution to historical events can be problematic, so too is positioning theoretical developments: for the sociological treatment of the twin concepts of 'society' and 'the social', when considered in temporal or historical terms, is twisted and folded.[13] So whilst it is relatively unproblematic to assert that the status of these concepts has come into question in recent years, identifying with any precision either the relative novelty or the theoretical antecedents of contemporary claims and positions requires the unravelling of a densely twisted and knotted skein of arguments. This task is certainly beyond the limits of this brief introduction, but it also poses fundamental conceptual difficulties to any would-be unraveller, since separating out strands of descent has to be done in the absence of any clear consensus about who the relatives were and for what, exactly, they argued.

If the concept of society has been a particular focus of attention in recent years, it is important to remember that its fortunes have always been mixed both within and beyond the discipline. Wagner (2000) maps its course as a 'scientific object' from its relatively recent emergence, perhaps discovery, to its possibly imminent passing away but notes that it has, from the outset, been subject to contestation and reformulation. The word came to be used in the late 18th Century, for the first time, to refer to something that was both broader than small units such a professional associations, and had its own specificity: 'civil society' for example, began to denote something that was distinct from either private households, or political entities such as the state (ibid. 133). Wagner also notes that political revolutions in France and America, with their aspirations to restructure the social body, provided a stimulus to this reformulation, and that the history of the concept, and the debates that they engendered, have had significant political dimensions: for to assert the

---

13   This formulation is taken from Michel Serres: 'time is paradoxical: it folds or twists' (1995: 58).

existence of an entity in between the private household and political institutions is in itself manifestly political.

This distinction between the social and the political is key to Hannah Arendt's (1998) apparently negative view of the social, which is articulated in complex ways with her views on modernization and the rise of 'mass' society and, according to some, widely misunderstood as a consequence (Benhabib 2003). If this 'untenable distinction' (ibid. 138) has potentially adverse consequences for political science, it is the prior idea that the social is a discrete entity that has been the subject of analytical doubts within sociology. Thus, as argued by Pyytinen (this volume), Simmel's preference for terms such as 'sociation' can be understood as anticipating the recent preference for more concrete and process orientated concepts, in contrast to more problematically abstract generalizations such as society.

It would therefore be simplistic and inaccurate to see the current focus on the limitations of the social as a straightforward example of a recent, postmodern, mistrust of grand narratives (Lyotard 1984), for the concept has had a troubled history from its inception. Rather, we are witnessing a reconfiguration of past and present concerns, and their inter-relation. To get a sense of this, it is instructive to look at one particularly tricky analytical knot, as represented by the names Durkheim, Tarde, Latour and Garfinkel.

Tarde has been a relatively neglected figure, and Latour (2002; 2005) not only follows Deleuze and Guattari's (1988) lead in arguing for the force and originality of his thought, but also argues that this neglect has been to the detriment of sociology which, as a discipline, took a wrong turn in taking up his opponent Durkheim's conception of the social and social facts (Durkheim 1982).[14] Tarde's central argument was that any explanation of social phenomena should begin from the individual; that insofar as the idea of social fact could be entertained at all, it must refer to the creation of patterns through imitation; and that imitation necessarily has a psychological basis (Tarde 1969; Lukes 1973: 302–3). Durkheim, by contrast, defended his view that social facts are external, constraining, and emergent properties at the collective level, and saw Tarde's approach as being fundamentally flawed by its methodological individualism and psychologism. To Durkheim's assertion that psychology could not explain the evolution of societies, 'Tarde replied that this could be reduced to the imitation of ideas of genius' (Lukes: 306).[15]

Shifting forward a century, we find Latour giving a characteristically original reading of Tarde which minimizes the significance of what appears to be a central tenet of his thought, namely psychological reductionism (although comparatively little explicit justification is given for side-stepping this apparently central

---

14 For an account of the connections between Deleuze and Latour, see Schatzki (2002).

15 For a fuller account of Tarde and Durkheim's disagreements see Lukes (1973: 302–313), and for an edited transcript of their debate in 1903 at the Ecole Pratique des Hautes Etudes, see Tarde (1969).

difficulty).[16] In doing so, he is able to claim that Tarde is a precursor of his own approach, actor-network theory, in that both see the invocation and use of 'the social' as a kind of category mistake which reads it as a distinctive substance which has effects, rather than as a word for describing diverse forms of association (Latour 2005). Latour's reading is suggestive in the links that it draws, but also brings into focus some common points of weakness, as perceived by their respective critics: for example, Latour's strategy of explaining 'macro' phenomena as resulting from the creative actions of powerful individuals in building up associations (Callon and Latour 1981), which is highly reminiscent of Tarde (1969), has itself been an important target for critical discussion of his work.[17]

However, it is notable that another key point of reference for Latour (2005) is Garfinkel who, in his refusal of a sociological meta-language and insistence on following the actors (to use Latour's terminology), is said to provide a model for Latour's approach.[18] However Garfinkel's most recent work, to the surprise of some ethnomethodologists, presents itself as a realization of what Rawls (1996) calls Durkheim's 'neglected argument', that is, his argument for the social basis of understanding in the later work. Thus Garfinkel, apparently accepting Rawls' reconfiguration of Durkheim as someone who proposed the detailed study of social practice (but see Rawls and Lynch, this volume), claims that when 'correctly understood', ethnomethodology is 'an heir to Durkheim's neglected legacy' (Garfinkel 2002: 94). The idea of a social fact is recast as an ongoing achievement, but the descriptor 'social' is certainly not problematized in the same way as is done by Latour: indeed Garfinkel subtitles his book 'Working out Durkheim's aphorism', the aphorism in question being that 'the objective reality of social facts is sociology's most fundamental phenomenon'.

The complicated relations between classical and contemporary sociology evident in this example provided part of the inspiration for this book, and receive more discussion below, including an interesting elaboration of what is meant by 'working out' (Lynch, this volume). But it is worth noting the role played by creative (mis)readings, to use Lynch's formulation, in both Latour's and Garfinkel's work: fidelity may be difficult to establish, but it also questionable whether it is feasible, or whether translation is a necessary feature of theoretical work (see Tsatsaroni and Cooper, this volume). We might also wish to contextualize certain aspects of the discussion, notably by situating Latour in a French intellectual milieu in which Durkheim's influence is strong (in the work of Bourdieu and his followers

---

16 Latour's creative reading of other authors is well established: see Latour (1993) where he produces an interpretation of Shapin and Shaffer (1985) that neither author fully endorses.

17 See for example Star (1991) on the tendency towards a managerialist perspective in Latour's work, and Amsterdamska's (1990) reservations about the politics of explanation that it implies.

18 To be more precise, half of a model: 'it would be fairly accurate to describe ANT as being half Garfinkel and half Greimas' (Latour 2005: 54).

for example), and in which it makes more sense to attribute to him a wrong turn for the discipline as a whole; whereas, as Fuller notes, sociology's tendency to construct a common tradition of classical sociology is one that acts retrospectively and tends to obscure radical differences between, for example, its key figures such as Durkheim and Weber (Fuller 2006).[19] Moreover, the fact that Latour has recently addressed himself more directly to social theory and sociology (2004; 2005), where his work is starting to have a wider impact (see for example Urry et al. 2007), helps to give this reconfiguration additional significance.

If what we are seeing is in one sense a recurrence of previous debates, the matter does not end there. Why do they recur in particular forms, at particular times? What are the new relevancies that not only demand new concepts, to follow Deleuze (1991), but revitalize discarded ones? (Commodification? Reification? Imitation? Sociation?) We must bear in mind that part of what is happening is a reconstruction of the past – as implied above, it is because of Latour's concern to problematize 'the social' that Durkheim is cast in a particular light, and given a central position which may be deceptive in its implication of disciplinary homogeneity and historical invariability. Moreover, more longstanding criticisms of received views of the social, notably from feminist scholars, still retain their force (Marshall and Witz 2004); while, on the other hand, important work in contemporary social theory proceeds without seeing the need to problematize the social as such.[20]

One further strand that is tied up in this knot is the issue of criticism, in at least two senses. In the first place, to approach the question of sociological pertinence in a contextualized manner is to do something other than simply to criticize or argue about concepts: to quote Deleuze, 'it is never very interesting to criticize a concept: it is better to build the new functions or new fields that make it useless or inadequate' (Deleuze 1991: 94). But in the second place both Garfinkel, in his longstanding insistence that the value of ethnomethodological studies is lost if they are 'done as ironies' (Garfinkel 1984: viii), and Latour (1993; 2004) taking a lead from Serres (1995) and Boltanski and Thevenot (2006), reject the idea that sociology should take a critically debunking stance with respect to the understandings of the people being studied: see du Gay (this volume) for further discussion. If Garfinkel can be said to be following Durkheim's epistemological lead, he is doing so in a radically different way to Bourdieu who affirms the need for a sociology that can both transcend and correct common sense, a position with which Boltanski and Thevenot take issue (see Celikates 2006). If this is seen as a kind of exhaustion of the Kantian idea of critique as Latour (1987) suggests,

---

19 Lemert (2006) treats Durkheim as the key reference point for a wide range of French thinkers whose work goes beyond the limits of sociology.

20 Habermas' formulation of the centrality of communication to the definition and reality of social action might, for all its complexity, serve as an example of this: see Habermas (1987a), Latour's (1993) comments, and Chapter 11. For a spirited defence of the necessity of 'society' see Outhwaite (2006).

it touches on wider questions about the role of theory today. Is this exhaustion analogous to the weakening of theory in philosophy noted and recommended by Vattimo (1988), who simultaneously characterizes modern continental philosophy as a form of Simmelian sociological impressionism (2004)? Does it imply a move away from dogmatism, or is the Kantian sense of critical rather a way of opposing dogmatism (Spivak 1996)? Is the apparent exhaustion of theory simply a belated recognition of Garfinkel's view that theory is not only excessive but largely unnecessary? Or of the fact that it is necessarily limited with respect to unexpected events and phenomena? If so, should it seek new ways of avoiding the tendency towards simplification evident in identity thinking (Adorno 1973) or purification (Latour 1993) in order to do justice to alterity, specificity and heterogeneity?[21] Are there particular metaphors or rhetorical strategies that can facilitate this and thereby rejuvenate theory? Does the recent and relatively widespread recourse to the material object offer a genuine opportunity in this respect (see Dant 1999, for an overview); or should we be more cautious of the longstanding philosophical difficulties that might attend such a move.[22] And how should the efficacy of new concepts and metaphors be assessed: in terms of their philosophical connotations, or the empirical research possibilities that they open up (Barron 2003)?

In other words, reconfiguration, even if it begins from a consideration of the relations between particular figures, inevitably leads us (back) to the fundamental question about the objective of sociology with which we began, and closely associated ones about its character, mode of analysis, and relation to the times in which it is situated.

The Book

If the chapters that follow advisedly eschew necessarily speculative treatment of the larger question of the object(ive) of sociology, the more tightly specified focus of each bears onto it – whether explicitly, implicitly, or sometimes tangentially – and we suggest, and hope the reader agrees, that such an approach has analytical advantages. In themselves, each gives important insights into some of the cluster of relevant issues that have been sketched out here, and some that have not; taken together, they provide a range of sometimes complementary, sometimes conflicting arguments, which operate on a number of levels, with different focal lengths. The

---

21   Gasche (2007) notes that critique has always meant separation, and that the deconstructive emphasis on contamination is in tension with this: in this respect, we suggest, the latter approach has suggestive links with Latour and the position he takes towards purification.

22   Pels et al. (2002) provide detailed consideration of some of the dimensions of this: see especially Woolgar's (2002) measured assessment. For a clear account of the difficulties of achieving a genuinely materialist theory, as perceived by Adorno, see Jarvis (1998).

book has been organized into three parts, but the points of connection run across this division, and other equally coherent layouts would have been possible.

The first part, 'Social Things', addresses the question of sociology's object of analysis and, like many of the chapters in the book, moves back and forth in time to do so. Common themes that run through the section include noting obstacles on certain well trodden paths within the classical tradition, highlighting more recent theoretical routes around them, and pointing to (sometimes relatively neglected) resources within classical sociological theory that can both address features of the contemporary world, such as globalization, and anticipate later theoretical developments.

The second part, 'Social Practices', examines a specific and central category of analytical object as conceptualized by that form of sociology for which it has arguably had most importance, ethnomethodology.[23] This form of analysis is of crucial significance to an understanding of the constitution of sociological objects for a number of reasons, not least its systematic avoidance of theory construction as normally understood, and as such raises questions of central importance for sociology more generally (even if its distinctiveness in this respect has led some to regard it as peripheral). Moreover, as has been indicated, its precise relation to classical sociology has been an explicit subject of recent debate, and has consequences for how sociologists can (re-)read this tradition.

The third part, 'Social Theories', focuses more directly and reflexively upon theory itself, with an emphasis on the fields and contexts in which theory is done today, and the ways in which these might shape or constrain it. The relation between theory and its object of study, which is also the world in which it is located, emerges as a complex one in which theory is continually embedded within, and subject to translation as it moves between disciplines, categories of people, institutions, and historical periods. A final chapter reflects upon some of the strands that have been unravelled or retied during the course of the book.

References

Adorno, T. (1973), *Negative Dialectics* (London: Routledge).
Adorno, T. (2000), 'Subject and Object', in O'Connor (ed.).
Ali, N., Kalra, V.S. and Sayyid, S. (eds) (2005), *A Postcolonial People: South Asians in Britain* (London: Hurst and Company).
Amsterdamska, O. (1990), 'Surely You Are Joking, Monsieur Latour', *Science, Technology and Human Values* 15:4, 495–504.
Appadurai, A. (ed.) (1986), *The Social Life of Things: Commodities in Cultural Perspective* (Cambridge: Cambridge University Press).

---

23 Claims for the central analytical importance of practice today, as made below in chapter five, are not confined to ethnomethodology however: see for example, Schatzki et al. (2001) and, for a more sceptical view, Turner (1994).

Appadurai, A. (ed.) (2001), *Globalization* (Durham and London: Duke University Press).
Arendt, H. (1998), *The Human Condition*, 2nd edition (Chicago: University of Chicago Press).
Auge, M. (1995), *Non-places: Introduction to an Anthropology of Supermodernity* (London: Verso).
Barron, C. (2003), 'A Strong Distinction Between Humans and Non-humans is No Longer Required for Research Purposes: A Debate Between Bruno Latour and Steve Fuller', *History of the Human Sciences* 16:2, 77–99.
Barry, A. and Slater, D. (2005), *The Technological Economy* (Abingdon: Routledge).
Bauman, Z. (2000), *Liquid Modernity* (Cambridge: Polity).
Beck, U. (1992), *Risk Society* (London: Sage).
Benhabib, S. (2003), *The Reluctant Modernism of Hannah Arendt*, new edition (Lanham: Rowman & Littlefield).
Bernstein, B. (2000), *Pedagogy, Symbolic Control and Identity: Theory, Research, Critique*, 2nd edition (New York: Rowman & Littlefield).
Boltanski, L. and Chiapello, E. (2005), *The New Spirit of Capitalism* (London: Verso).
Boltanski, L. and Thevenot, L. (2006), *On Justification: Economies of Worth* (Princeton: Princeton University Press).
Borradori, G. (ed.) (2003), *Philosophy in a Time of Terror* (Chicago: University of Chicago Press).
Bourdieu, P., Chamboredon, J.-C. and Passeron, J.-C. (1991), *The Craft of Sociology: Epistemological Preliminaries* (Berlin: de Gruyter).
Burawoy, M. (2007), 'For Public Sociology', in Clawson et al. (eds).
Cadava, E., Connor, P. and Nancy, J.-L. (eds) (1991), *Who Comes After the Subject?* (London: Routledge).
Callon, M. (ed.) (1998) *The Laws of the Markets* (Oxford: Blackwell).
Callon, M. and Latour, B. (1981), 'Unscrewing the Big Leviathan: How Actors Macrostructure Reality and How Sociologists Help Them to Do So', in Knorr-Cetina and Cicourel (eds).
Carroll, D. (ed.) (1990), *The States of Theory: History, Art and Critical Discourse* (New York: Columbia University Press).
Casey, E. (1997), *The Fate of Place: A Philosophical History* (Berkeley: University of California Press).
Castells, M. (2000), *The Rise of the Network Society*, 2nd edition (Oxford: Blackwell).
Celikates, R. (2006), 'From Critical Social Theory to a Social Theory of Critique: On the Critique of Ideology After the Pragmatic Turn', *Constellations* 13:1, 21–40.
Clawson, D., Zussman, R. and Misra, J. et al. (eds) (2007), *Public Sociology* (Berkeley: University of California Press).
Crook, S., Pakulski, J. and Waters, M. (1992), *Postmodernisation: Change in Advanced Society* (London: Sage).

Dant, T. (1999), *Material Culture in the Social World* (Buckingham: Open University Press).
Daston, L. (ed.) (2000), *Biographies of Scientific Objects* (Chicago: University of Chicago Press).
Deleuze, G. (1991), 'A Philosophical Concept ...', in Cadava et al. (eds).
Deleuze, G. and Guattari, F. (1988), *A Thousand Plateaus* (London: Athlone Press).
Deleuze, G. and Guattari, F. (1994), *What is Philosophy?* (London: Verso).
Derrida, J. (1990), 'Some Statements and Truisms about Neologisms, Newisms, Postisms, Parasitisms, and Other Small Seismisms', in Carroll (ed.).
Derrida, J. (1998), 'Faith and Knowledge: The Two Sources of "Religion" at the Limits of Reason Alone', in Derrida and Vattimo (eds).
Derrida, J. (2003), 'Autoimmunity: Real and Symbolic Suicides – A Dialogue with Jacques Derrida', in Borradori (ed.).
Derrida, J. (2004), 'Mochlos, or the Conflict of the Faculties', in *Eyes of the University: Right to Philosophy* (Stanford: Stanford University Press).
Derrida, J. (2005), 'Paper or Me, You Know ... (New Speculations on a Luxury of the Poor)', in *Paper Machine* (Stanford: Stanford University Press).
Derrida, J. and Vattimo, G. (eds) (1998), *Religion* (Cambridge: Polity).
de Vries, H. and Sullivan, L. (eds) (2006), *Political Theologies: Public Religions in a Post-secular World* (New York: Fordham University Press).
Durkheim, E. (1982), *The Rules of Sociological Method* (London: Macmillan).
Eisenstein, E. (1983), *The Printing Revolution in Early Modern Europe* (Cambridge: Cambridge University Press).
Foucault, M. (1977), *Discipline and Punish: The Birth of the Prison* (Harmondsworth: Allen Lane).
Fuglsang, M. and Sorenson, B. (eds) (2006), *Deleuze and the Social* (Edinburgh: Edinburgh University Press).
Fuller, S. (1998), 'From Content to Context: A Social Epistemology of the Structure-agency Craze', in Sica (ed.).
Fuller, S. (2006), *The New Sociological Imagination* (London: Sage).
Gane, N. (ed.) (2004), *The Future of Social Theory* (London: Continuum).
Garfinkel, H. (1984), *Studies in Ethnomethodology* (Cambridge: Polity).
Garfinkel, H. (2002), *Ethnomethodology's Program: Working out Durkheim's Aphorism* (Lanham: Rowman & Littlefield).
Garfinkel, H. and Sacks, H. (1970), 'On Formal Structures of Practical Action', in McKinney and Tiryakian (eds).
Gasche, R. (2007*)*, *The Honor of Thinking: Critique, Theory, Philosophy* (Stanford: Stanford University Press).
Gibbons, M., Limoges, C. and Nowotny, H. et al. (1994), *The New Production of Knowledge* (London: Sage).
Giddens, A. (1991), *Consequences of Modernity* (Cambridge: Polity).
Gieryn, T. (2000), 'A place for space in sociology', *Annual Review of Sociology* 26, 463–96.

Godin, B. (1998), 'Writing performative history', *Social Studies of Science* 28:3, 465–83.
Gopal, P. and Lazarus, N. (eds) (2004), *After Iraq: Reframing Postcolonial Studies* (London: Lawrence and Wishart).
Gouldner, A. (1970), *The Coming Crisis of Western Sociology* (New York: Basic Books).
Granovetter, M. and Swedberg, R. (eds) (1992), *The Sociology of Economic Life* (Boulder, CO: Westview Press).
Griffiths, A. (ed.) (1987), *Contemporary French Philosophy* (Cambridge: Cambridge University Press).
Habermas, J. (1987a), *The Theory of Communicative Action*, Vol I. (Cambridge: Polity).
Habermas, J. (1987b), *The Theory of Communicative Action*, Vol II. (Cambridge: Polity).
Harding, S. (ed.) (2004), *The Feminist Standpoint Theory Reader* (London: Routledge).
Hardt, M. and Negri, A. (2001), *Empire* (Harvard: Harvard University Press).
Harvey, D. (2007), *Limits to Capital*, updated edition (London: Verso).
Heidegger, M. (1971), 'The Thing', in *Poetry, Language, Thought* (New York: Harper and Row).
Heidegger, M. (2002a), 'The Age of the World Picture', in *Off the Beaten Track* (Cambridge: Cambridge University Press).
Heidegger, M. (2002b), 'The Origin of the Work of Art', in *Off the Beaten Track* (Cambridge: Cambridge University Press).
Hesse, B. and Sayyid, S. (2005), 'Narrating the Postcolonial Political and the Immigrant Imaginary', in Ali et al. (eds).
Jarvis, S. (1998), *Adorno: A Critical Introduction* (Cambridge: Polity).
Jasanoff, S. (ed.) (2004), *States of Knowledge: The Co-production of Science and Social Order* (London: Routledge).
Joyce, P. (ed.) (2002), *The Social in Question: New Bearings in History and the Social Sciences* (London: Routledge).
Knorr-Cetina, K. and Cicourel, A. (eds) (1981), *Advances in Social Theory and Methodology: Toward an Integration of Micro and Macro-sociologies* (London: Routledge and Kegan Paul).
Landry, D. and MacLean, G. (eds) (1996), *The Spivak Reader* (London: Routledge).
Lash, S. (2002), *Critique of Information* (London: Sage).
Lash, S. and Lury, C. (2007), *Global Culture Industry* (Cambridge: Polity).
Latour, B. (1987), 'The Enlightenment Without the Critique: A Word on Michel Serres's Philosophy', in Griffiths (ed.).
Latour, B. (1993), *We Have Never Been Modern* (London: Harvester Wheatsheaf).
Latour, B. (2002), 'Gabriele Tarde and the End of the Social', in Joyce (ed.).
Latour, B. (2004), 'Why has critique run out of steam? From matters of fact to matters of concern', *Critical Inquiry* 30 (Winter), 225–247.

Latour, B. (2005), *Reassembling the Social: An Introduction to Actor-network Theory* (Oxford: Oxford University Press).
Law, J. (ed.) (1991), *A Sociology of Monsters? Essays on Power, Technology and Domination* (London: Routledge).
Lemert, C. (2006) *Durkheim's Ghosts: Cultural Logics and Social Things* (Cambridge: Cambridge University Press).
Lukacs, G. (1971), 'Reification and the Consciousness of the Proletariat', in *History and Class Consciousness* (London: Merlin).
Lukes, S. (1973), *Emile Durkheim: His life and Work* (Harmondsworth: Penguin).
Lyotard, J.-F. (1984), *The Postmodern Condition: A Report on Knowledge* (Manchester: Manchester University Press).
MacKenzie, D., Muiniesa, F. and Siu, L. (eds) (2007), *Do Economists Make Markets? On the Performativity of Economics* (Princeton: Princeton University Press).
Marshall, B. and Witz, A. (eds) (2004,) *Engendering the Social: Feminist Encounters with Sociological Theory* (Maidenhead: Open University Press).
McKinney, J.C. and Tiryakian, E. (eds) (1970), *Theoretical Sociology: Perspectives and Developments* (New York: Appleton-Century-Crofts).
Mitchell, W. (2007), 'Picturing Terror: Derrida's Autoimmunity', *Critical Inquiry* 33:2, 277–90.
Mol, A. and Law, J. (1994), 'Regions, networks and fluids: Anaemia and social topology', *Social Studies of Science* 24:4, 641–71.
Nancy, J.-L. (2007), *The Creation of the World, or Globalization* (Albany: State University of New York Press).
Nowotny, H., Scott, P. and Gibbons, M. (2001), *Re-thinking Science* (Cambridge: Polity).
O'Connor, B. (ed.) (2000), *The Adorno Reader* (Oxford: Blackwell).
Oakley, A. (1981), 'Interviewing Women: A Contradiction in Terms', in Roberts (ed.).
Outhwaite, W. (2006), *The Future of Society* (Oxford: Blackwell).
Patton, P. (2006), 'Order, Exteriority and Flat Multiplicities in the Social', in Fuglsang and Sorenson (eds).
Pels, D., Hetherington, K., and Vandenberghe, F. (eds) (2002), 'Special issue on materiality/sociality', *Theory, Culture and Society* 19:5–6, 1–277.
Power, M. (1997), *The Audit Society: Rituals of Verification* (Oxford: Oxford University Press).
Rawls, A.W. (1996), 'Durkheim's Epistemology: The Neglected Argument', *American Journal of Sociology* 102:2, 430–482.
Ritzer, G. (2004), *The McDonaldization of Society*, revised edition (Thousand Oaks: Sage).
Roberts, H. (ed.) (1981), *Doing Feminist Research* (London: Routledge and Kegan Paul).
Rose, N. (2006), *The Politics of Life Itself: Biomedicine, Power and Subjectivity in the Twenty-first Century* (Princeton: Princeton University Press).

Sacks, H. (1995), *Lectures on Conversation* (Oxford: Blackwell).
Sandywell, B. (2003), 'Metacritique of information: On Scott Lash's "Critique of Information"', *Theory, Culture and Society* 20:1, 109–22.
Schatzki, T. (2002), *The Site of the Social: A Philosophical Account of the Constitution of Social Life and Change* (Pennsylvania: Pennsylvania State University Press).
Schatzki, T., Knorr-Cetina, K. and von Savigny, E. (eds) (2001), *The Practice Turn in Contemporary Theory* (London: Routledge)
Serres, M. with Latour, B. (1995), *Conversations on Science, Culture and Time* (Ann Arbor: University of Michigan Press).
Shapin, S. and Schaffer, S. (1985), *Leviathan and the Air-Pump* (Princeton: Princeton University Press).
Sica, A. (ed.) (1998), *What is Social Theory? The Philosophical Debates* (Oxford: Blackwell).
Slater, D. and Tonkiss, F. (2001), *Market Society* (Cambridge: Polity).
Smart, B. (2003), *Economy, Culture and Society: A Sociological Critique of Neo-liberalism* (Buckingham: Open University Press).
Smith, D. (1990), *The Conceptual Practices of Power: A Feminist Sociology of Knowledge* (Toronto: Toronto University Press).
Smith, D. (2004), 'Women's Perspective as a Radical Critique of Sociology', in Harding (ed.).
Spivak, G. (1996), 'More on Power/Knowledge', in Landry and MacLean (eds).
Star, S.L. (1991), 'Power, Technology and the Phenomenology of Conventions: On Being Allergic to Onions', in Law (ed.).
Tarde, G. (1969), *On Communication and Social Influence* (Chicago: University of Chicago Press).
Thrift, N. (2005), *Knowing Capitalism* (London: Sage).
Turner, S. (1994), *The Social Theory of Practices: Tradition, Tacit Knowledge and Presuppositions* (Cambridge: Polity).
Urry, J. (2000), *Sociology Beyond Societies: Mobilities for the Twenty-first Century* (London: Routledge).
Urry, J., Dingwall, R. and Gough, I. (eds) (2007), 'What is 'social' about social science?', *21st Century Society* 2:1, 95–119.
Vattimo, G. (1988), *The End of Modernity* (Cambridge: Polity).
Vattimo, G. (1992), *The Transparent Society* (Cambridge: Polity).
Vattimo, G. (2004), *Nihilism and Emancipation: Ethics, Politics and Law* (New York: Columbia University Press).
Verges, F. (2004), 'Postcolonial Challenges', in Gane (ed.).
Wagner, P. (2000), '"An Entirely New Object of Consciousness, of Volition, of Thought": The Coming into Being and (Almost) Passing Away of "Society" as a Scientific Object', in Daston (ed.).
Woolgar, S. (2002), 'After Word? – on some dynamics of duality interrogation', *Theory, Culture and Society* 19:5–6, 261–70.

PART 1
Social Things

The chapters in Part 1 all reflect upon the character of social 'things', and in doing so draw upon and reconfigure the work of several classical social theorists: Durkheim (in the cases of Inglis and Robertson, and Rafanell), and Simmel (in the case of Pyyhtinen). Thus, all three chapters consider the legacy of classical social theory, not as a part of an ossified disciplinary canon, but as very much alive and relevant to contemporary issues, debates and concerns.

The continued relevance of Durkheim is evident in the chapter by Inglis and Robertson, who begin by noting the upsurge of interest in questions of globality. They ask: what is the relevance of Durkheim's work for exploring this 'thing'; or as they prefer, what can Durkheim's work add to this type of 'ecumenical analysis'? In answering this question, Inglis and Robertson go against traditional understandings of Durkheim's *oeuvre*, which have tended to view his work as relatively inconsequential on these matters; rather, they suggest that Durkheim can be reconfigured to make a significant contribution to contemporary debates about the nature of globalization.

They begin by considering and questioning the very 'thing' that Durkheim is most commonly associated with: society. They note that Durkheim is frequently criticized for adopting a form of 'methodological nationalism' – namely, equating society with the nation-state. They argue that, in part, this reading reflects Durkheim's own conception of social order, which drew upon Platonic and Aristotelian philosophy. However, they suggest that Durkheim's writings, like those of other classicists such as Marx and Weber, were also highly contextual; in short, Inglis and Robertson contend that although Durkheim *sometimes* equated society to the nation state, at other points in his work he offers a way of conceptualizing society that is much more 'trans-national'.

Perhaps surprisingly, Inglis and Robertson offer a reading of Durkheim's definition of social facts as evidence of his 'trans-national', even global, inclinations. They contrast their reconfiguration of Durkheim with other attempts to find a nascent globality in his work. Durkheim's writings on 'world patriotism', they argue, do not offer the most fertile sources for attaining this 'thing'. Instead, they suggest that Durkheim's first and final books offer more useful resources for discerning a global organic solidarity in his thought. Inglis and Robertson maintain that whilst the former text sets out the 'material conditions' of this solidarity, the latter reveals its 'ideal conditions': a world moral culture. Overall, therefore, Inglis and Robertson demonstrate how reconfiguring Durkheim can be a productive exercise that enables contemporary concerns about globalization to be addressed by uncovering alternative 'things' within his texts.

Pyyhtinen also re-reads the work of a classical theorist, Georg Simmel, to address contemporary concerns: the materiality of 'things'. Pyyhtinen argues that Simmel was one of the first social theorists to view material things as inherently social. Indeed, he argues that for Simmel, the analysis of material things, including concrete objects like money, doors and bridges, is the means by which sociologists can grasp society and social relationships. Rather than treating material things as essentialized, external and constraining upon subjects, Pyyhtinen argues that Simmel offers a means of addressing the dynamism between them; something, he argues, that anticipates central themes in the work of more recent theorists, notably Bruno Latour.

Pyyhtinen is again concerned to demonstrate how a classical social theorist, such as Simmel, is pertinent to contemporary concerns. However, like Inglis and Robertson, he is not uncritical of his chosen theorist: Simmel's work has a number of problems of which the failure to recognize the symmetry of material and social 'things' appears to be the most significant. Simmel, according to Pyyhtinen, places the social above the material. Not only does this reify the social, it replicates a dualism between social and material things; something that Pyyhtinen, following Deleuze and Guattari, argues should be de-ontologized. That said, Pyyhtinen concludes that Simmel's analysis of 'things' remains a significant and rich resource for sociological theorizing.

Both of these chapters illustrate how the work of two classical social theorists remains significant for analysing social things. To an extent, this is reaffirmed in Rafanell's chapter, which reconsiders Durkheim's notion of social objectivity. However, rather than following Inglis and Robertson and attempting to reconfigure Durkheim from 'within', Rafanell draws on the work of Judith Butler and Barry Barnes. Her argument is that performative accounts of social action, rather than being in opposition to Durkheim's position, can instead be utilized to strengthen his account.

Rafanell begins by isolating what she views as the key 'thing' to be taken from Durkheim: that social reality is both collective and objective, or *sui generis*. However, she argues that Durkheim does not account for the ontology of this 'thing'; if collective social reality exists over and above individual activity, as Durkheim implies, how does it emerge?

In attempting to answer this question Rafanell initially draws on Judith Butler's account of performativity, suggesting that Butler, to an extent, is able to demonstrate how an 'objective' social world takes on the appearance of substance and has causal powers. Her notion of gender performativity has been extremely influential and contentious in this respect. However, Rafanell also argues that Butler's account is problematic; in particular, Butler does not fully acknowledge the significance of the collective. Noting that this is a common criticism, Rafanell reasserts that Butler's account of performativity is too individualistic and idealized.

Rafanell then turns to the performative theory incorporated within Barry Barnes' sociology of knowledge, arguing that this provides the 'missing collective' that Butler ignores. She contends that Barnes demonstrates how collective categories and understandings emerge from the negotiations between individual members of a collective. Additionally, by making use of theories of social sanctioning, Rafanell asserts that individuals within a collective are self-referential producers of social realities, and it is practice that gives these realities the appearance of externality. Hence, social objectivity is a 'thing' that is produced performatively by collectives, not something that is somehow beyond them.

The three chapters therefore enable us not only to reconsider, indeed reconfigure, the work of a number of classical social theorists; they also enable us to reconsider the 'things' that are within the remit of sociological analysis.

Chapter 2
Durkheim's Globality

David Inglis and Roland Robertson

Introduction

The present epoch is culturally characterized by strong currents of globality (Robertson 2001; 2007a), in part constituted of forms of thinking which stress the need to understand the world 'as a whole'. Within such imaginaries, the globe is taken as 'one place' which exhibits characteristics of dense connectivity between its geographically disparate parts. Particularly in the last fifteen years or so, social scientific scholarship has come very much to focus on such matters. Regarding particular phenomena, no matter how apparently 'local' or parochial in nature, as being located within global flows, systems or structures, seems today to be an absolutely necessary element of effective social scientific investigation. A veritable plethora of recent books and articles geared towards exhorting social scientists to make the 'global turn' in their thinking, stand as witnesses to the apparent inescapability and ubiquity of 'global' reflections, conceptualizations and imaginings in the contemporary social sciences (e.g. Albrow 1990; Robertson 1992; Urry 2000a; 2000b; 2003). As we have argued elsewhere (Inglis and Robertson 2004; 2005), differing forms of social science that seek to take the 'world as a whole', rather than particular (generally 'nationally'-based) 'societies', as their central unit of analysis, can be grouped under the collective heading of 'ecumenical analytics'. Such forms of analysis are themselves specifically intellectual and academic expressions and refractions of wider 'ecumenical sensibilities', that is, ways of perceiving and feeling, held by different sorts of social actors and social groups, which are based around notions of ever increasing global connectivity and interdependence.

This situation poses important questions as to the relevance – or otherwise – of Durkheim's brand of sociology in the present day. To what degree did Durkheim himself engage with phenomena and forces we today might put under the headings of 'globality' and 'globalization'? How effective and convincing were his analyses in this regard? To what extent can Durkheim-inspired sociological thinking produce useful insights into the conditions of globality in the early 21st century?

It is noteworthy that there is an apparent serious lack of attention in Durkheim's work to 'international', or indeed 'global', phenomena. As far as the present authors are aware, nowhere in his entire corpus does Durkheim explicitly mention, let alone give sustained analytic attention to, such globalizing phenomena as the establishment of World Time, time zones and the Greenwich Meridian, the re-establishment of the Olympic Games, the founding of the Nobel prizes, and suchlike matters.[1] It would perhaps seem that Durkheim failed to respond to the challenges of analysing world-level processes of interchange and connection characteristic of his own epoch. On such a view, Durkheim has to be put into the dock along with other sociological thinkers of the past who generally 'regarded societies as if they were separate entities, each with its own clear boundaries', and who thus failed to take the 'world as a whole' as a serious object of scrutiny (Cohen and Kennedy 2000: 23).

Yet such a view fails to see that there are certain important strains in Durkheim's thinking which at least implicitly deal with such matters. In this chapter we argue that, despite certain limitations, Durkheim's *oeuvre* contains within it, in embryonic form, certain very productive strains of 'global sociology', elements of his thought that should be made more explicit in a self-consciously 'global' age such as ours. To this end, we first consider how the notion of 'society' as a bounded entity has come under much critical fire in recent years. We then turn to examine the degree to which Durkheim's thought is imprisoned within the confines of 'methodological nationalism'. We then begin to reconstruct Durkheim's emergent 'global sociology'. We consider that his remarks on such matters in *The Division of Labour in Society* and *The Elementary Forms of Religious Life* are rather more compelling than those to be found in his writings on 'civilization' and his lectures on 'world patriotism'. By considering his analyses of supranational phenomena in both his first and last books, we reconstruct what we believe Durkheim to have been gesturing towards, namely an account of the interpenetrating relations between 'global organic solidarity' and 'world moral culture'.[2] Overall, we argue that Durkheim's highly interesting, albeit tentative, moves towards a 'global turn' in sociology can serve as useful resources for present-day analysts, not least those who wish to reconfigure what counts as the 'classical' bases and resources of sociological inquiry.

Against 'Society'

Given the 'global turn' much advocated in the social sciences in recent years, the notion of 'society' – understood as a self-enclosed, bounded entity, coterminous with the boundaries of given nation-states – has come under heavy criticism in recent years. This is because it seems highly unsuited for capturing those transnational processes and phenomena that seem so ubiquitous in the present day. Critics of the concept (e.g. Mann 1986; Beck 2000) aver that this notion of

---

1 Durkheim's omission of discussion of such matters is surprising given the Comtean influences in his work. Others influenced by Comte, like the Saint-Simonians, viewed imperial projects such as the building of the Suez Canal, as harbingers of an emerging world social order.

2 For an extended discussion of such matters, see Inglis and Robertson (2008).

'society', for a long time the central plank of (many but not all) sociologists' self-descriptions of what their discipline primarily studied, has now been rendered utterly obsolete. According to such a view, sociology should no longer primarily be concerned with entities such as 'British society' or 'French society', because the equation of the realm of the 'social' with a particular geo-political entity such as the British state, unduly narrows the scope of the former, and obfuscates processes and phenomena that exist 'beyond' or 'above' the confines of the nation-state. One of the earliest exponents of this sort of critique was Herminio Martins, who argued in 1974 that:

> In general, macro-sociological work has largely submitted to national pre-definitions of social realities: a kind of methodological nationalism – which does not necessarily go together with political nationalism on the part of the researcher – imposes itself in practice with national community as the terminal unit and boundary condition for the demarcation of problems and phenomena for social science (Martins 1974: 276).

Why and when might such a 'methodological nationalism' – that is, an equation of the concept of 'society' with territorially bounded nation-states – have come about? For writers such as Martin Albrow (1990), the history of Western sociology is characterized by a major shift that occurred from the later nineteenth century onwards.[3] Prior to that, sociology – as a set of alternative paradigms put forward by figures such as Comte, Saint-Simon, Ward and Spencer – was 'universalistic' in nature, being seen by its various practitioners as 'a science of, and for, humanity, based on timeless principles and verified laws' (1990: 6). But the end of the nineteenth century saw the start of processes in various countries which led both to the institutionalization of the discipline in universities, and to the professionalization of the intellectuals who professed it. The intellectual corollary of these trends towards the emergence of various 'national sociologies' was the appearance of the notion of 'society' as defined above. This understanding of 'society' was, arguably, framed as *the* major object of sociological investigation from the 1920s onwards, at the same time as the discipline was further institutionalized in universities across the major Western countries (Urry 2003).

Indeed, we may regard this process as involving the globalization of the very notion of 'society' itself, rendering it part of an emerging scholarly 'world culture' at this time (Robertson 1992; 1993). Within particular national contexts, distinct departments of 'sociology' were differentiated from other social science departments, on the basis of their apparently unique subject matter, namely 'society' considered 'as a whole'. Textbooks formulated and reinforced this notion, thus tacitly structuring the common-sense of the discipline for generations to come, institutionalizing and rendering apparently 'natural' what was in fact a concept

---

3 For a critical appraisal of Albrow's periodization of the emergence of the 'global' as a sociological object, see Robertson (1993).

that was produced by quite specific socio-historical circumstances. However, this situation of (never total) conceptual hegemony began to be challenged and break down from the 1960s onwards, as is evidenced in the important work of, among others, Johan Galtung, Amitai Etzioni, Gustavo Lagos, Wilbert Moore, Irving Horowitz, Peter Worsley, S.N. Eisenstadt, Immanuel Wallerstein, and Raymond Aron.

On this account of the reasons behind the genesis of the concept of 'society', the equation of the term with the boundaries of nation-states is seen to be primarily an innovation of the twentieth century, particularly from the 1920s onwards. On this view, the 'classical sociologists' of the period stretching from about the 1860s to World War One were not guilty of methodological nationalism, or certainly were much less guilty than their twentieth century successors.[4] However, for one of the major social theorists of the present day, namely Ulrich Beck (2000), it is in fact the case that these thinkers too were wedded to methodologically nationalist dispositions. He poses his case in this manner:

> The association between sociology and nation-state was so extensive that the image of "modern", organized individual societies – which became definitive with the national model of political organisation – itself became an absolutely necessary concept in and through the founding work of classical social scientists. Beyond all their differences, such theorists as Emile Durkheim, Max Weber and even Karl Marx shared a territorial definition of modern society, and thus a model of society centred on the national-state, which has today been shaken by globality and globalization (Beck 2000: 24).

On this account, the problematic definition of 'society' under discussion here actually has its roots in the ideas of figures such as Durkheim, Weber and even Marx. This would seem to suggest that their respective intellectual projects are no longer 'fit for purpose' in the present day. How convincing are Beck's claims in this regard?

Beck's allegations against the classical sociologists have themselves been subjected to criticism. According to Peter Wagner (2000), the very complex genealogy and etymology of the idea of 'society' as it was deployed in – mostly French and German – sociology in the later nineteenth century, is such that no simple account, like Beck's, can be rendered of the connections between notions of social order in general, and more specific, territorially-oriented understandings of it. Consequently, Beck's claims very much simplify a complex conceptual terrain. Similarly, for Daniel Chernilo (2006), Beck has set up various straw men with the aim of contrasting their alleged naive territorially-oriented assumptions with his model of 'cosmopolitan sociology' oriented towards the comprehension of 'world

---

4 The conventional periodization here encompasses the period generally taught in undergraduates courses on 'classical sociological theory', that is, from the period of Marx through to the deaths of Max Weber and Durkheim.

risk society'. A more historically accurate depiction of the analytical orientations of the sociological thinkers in question would show, for example, that Max Weber's account of social action is not at all contained within the concept of 'society' in general, let alone a territorially-defined understanding of the term (Gane 2005). Beck's claim that there are strong currents of methodological nationalism in Marx also seems lacking in nuance. While Marx did of course emphasize the strength of the bourgeois national states in impeding socialist revolution, his statements as regards 'the need of a constantly expanding market for its products chases the bourgeoisie over the whole surface of the globe' (Marx and Engels 1968 [1848]: 38) very much suggest that Marx's vision is at least as much 'global' in nature, because of its perception of the globalizing tendencies of bourgeois socio-economic order, as it is focussed upon the power of 'national' economies and governments (see Renton 2001, passim.).

In light of these assessments of Beck's claims, we think that it is most sensible to say that the work of the classical thinkers is very much *multi-faceted*. This means acknowledging that what they wrote and thought in any given context depends on what specific aims they were trying to achieve and what audiences they were writing for. Regarded in that light, we may say that *sometimes* their specific writings are (or seem to contemporary exegetes to be) more methodologically nationalist, while *sometimes* their writings are less oriented in that direction, and *sometimes* may even be critical of such dispositions. This position also involves acknowledging that they also *sometimes* wrote about phenomena that we nowadays might want to refer to with the words 'globality' and 'globalization'.[5]

Durkheim and 'Society'

Contemporary critiques of the notion of 'society' of the sort depicted above apparently bear heavily upon Durkheimian sociology. Extending the sorts of claims made by Beck, one could argue that it is his notion of 'society' – and the teaching of it in undergraduate programmes – that has animated and sustained the concept's use in sociological discourse over the last hundred years within the context of many 'national sociologies'. If this understanding of 'society' has been strongly methodologically nationalist until relatively recently, can the 'blame' be laid at Durkheim's door?

One possible way of answering that question in the affirmative could be constructed in the following way (see Inglis and Robertson 2004, for a full treatment of this position). One could argue that Durkheim remained too wedded

---

5   This point applies much more to Durkheim and Marx than it does to Weber. The latter was content to operate at the level of engaging in analytic comparisons of different culture-units – for example, Protestant Europe as opposed to Confucian China – rather than examining the actual historical processes whereby such units had come into relations of complex connectivity with each other.

to ancient antecedents in social science, most specifically his obvious debts to both Plato and Aristotle, and their focus on 'the problem of social order: the nature and sources of social integration, coherence and solidarity' (Gouldner 1970: 94). Here one could point to Durkheim's conception of sociology as the science of practically-oriented social reform, which takes as its object of diagnosis the 'national society' (of France), and which in part derives its inspiration from ancient Greek sources. Both Plato's *Republic* (2003) and Durkheim's *The Division of Labour in Society* (1964 [1893]) were written by their authors in periods of perceived social dislocation, and both are concerned with the need for moral and spiritual reconstruction of the social-political entity under consideration. Both Plato and Durkheim outline the conditions of possibility of a 'healthy' social-political order; both identify pathological forms of that order; and both set out the means whereby these problems could be rectified (Pickering 1984). Similarly, if we compare Aristotle (1999) and Durkheim, we see that both share the conviction that one does not just identify analytically the nature of the 'good life', one must also try to foster empirically the creation of such a state of affairs. How the *polis* or the (national) 'society' should be organized so as to increase the sum of human happiness, is arguably at the centre of both the Aristotelian and Durkheimian projects (McCarthy 2003). Thus when Durkheim conceives of sociology as a science of social reform, the conceptualization of 'society' that goes with this view of sociology, is highly analogous to the *polis* conceived of by both Plato and Aristotle, in that both 'society' and *polis* are taken to be territorial units bounded by political borders, and that the social order contained within those borders can be subjected to the reforming policies of the state apparatus which controls the modes of human existence within those borders.

However, as argued above, the classical sociologists *sometimes* are more methodologically nationalist, while at other times are less so or not at all. We would argue that this understanding applies as much to Durkheim as it does to, say, Marx. Certainly, 'society' as an object of state-driven reform is a methodologically nationalist concept, for the obvious reason that the state itself in Durkheim's time is – and is thought to be – a 'national' entity, patrolling its own delimited geographical territory. But there is more to Durkheim's sociology, and thus also as to what he means by 'society', than this reform-oriented, directly 'political' conception (remembering here the root of the modern word 'political' in the Greek term *polis*). 'Society' in Durkheim's thought has – or can have – other connotations too. This can be regarded either as ambiguity in Durkheim's thinking, or as due to the latter's rich and productive polysemic texture. Consider, for example, the following statements about the key issue of 'social facts', to be found in *The Rules of Sociological Method*:

> Here, then, is a category of facts with very distinctive characteristics: it consists of ways of acting, thinking and feeling, external to the individual, and endowed with a power of coercion, by reason of which they control him ... since their source is not in the individual, their substratum can be no other than society,

either the political society as a whole or some one of the partial groups it includes such as religious denominations, political, literary and occupational associations, etc. (1982 [1895]: 3).

The key word here is the 'either' in the fifth line. We are told that the source and location of the 'social facts' that constrain individual persons is *either* 'political society' (an entity coterminous with the boundaries of a particular political unit, here the nation-state) *or* 'some one of the partial groups it includes such as religious denominations, political, literary and occupational associations, etc.'. Thus 'society' *can* be taken to refer to a national, politically-organized entity, but it need not be defined in this way only. It can also refer to the modes of social order created by what are being depicted here as 'sub-national' entities too. This comes across in the words that immediately follow the ones quoted above:

If I do not submit to the conventions of society, if in my dress I do not conform to the customs observed in my country and in my class, the ridicule I provoke, the social isolation in which I am kept, produce, although in an attenuated form, the same effects as punishment ... I am not obliged to speak French with my fellow-countrymen nor to use the legal currency, but I cannot possibly do otherwise ... (ibid. 5).

The constraining nature of social facts created by, and characteristic of, 'national society' can be seen in what happens if one does not speak the national language or use the national currency. But the customs one must observe are said to be characteristic not just of 'my country' but also of 'my class', where class is taken to be a sub-national form and source of social order (in the sense that each class has its own mores that individuals within it are constrained to adhere to). Thus it is clear from these examples that if 'society' refers to modes and sources of social order, for Durkheim it can take both 'national-political' and 'sub-national-political forms'. But if for Durkheim 'society' need not necessarily be equated with social order existing inside state-controlled territory, can it also refer to forms of social order that, instead of being 'sub-national' in character are in fact 'trans-national', in that they exist somehow 'above' or 'across' or 'beyond' the boundaries of the national-political society? The answer to that question can be gained through a reconsideration of some of Durkheim's other works, and of passages in them that have often not been given the attention they are due.

Durkheim Beyond the Nation-State

One obvious location for those wishing to reconstruct Durkheim's views on supra-national phenomena are his writings on the notion of 'civilization'. His understanding of the latter term indicates that he is indeed analytically aware of such matters. In a famous essay co-authored with Marcel Mauss, he notes that 'social phenomena that are not strictly attached to a determinate social organism do exist; they extend into areas that reach beyond the national territory or they develop over periods of time that exceed the history of a single society. They have a life which is in some ways supranational' (Durkheim and Mauss 1998 [1913]: 152).

Durkheim is here thinking about 'supranational' languages, technologies, aesthetic forms and suchlike. In this essay, Durkheim (ibid. 153) argues that 'supranational' cultural forms 'result from ... process [es] involving more than [one] determinate society' – that is, supranational forms can arise not just by being generated in one bounded locale and spreading to others, but can be generated and spread by inter-unit interaction itself. However, in this context he also contends that 'international life is merely social life of a higher kind' than that which pertains in bounded units, that is, that any 'civilization' has as its 'substratum ... a plurality of interrelated political bodies acting upon one another' (ibid. 154). In other words, bounded social-political entities are the primary units of social life and order, and any more supranational entity is derivative of them. Moreover, in his writings on civilization the interactions between different civilizational units themselves are not engaged with. It is left to Mauss, in a piece from 1929, to talk of a burgeoning 'international civilization' in the present day, which is primarily, but not exclusively (e.g. the contemporary success of 'primitive art' in the West), Western in genesis and is spreading all across the planet (Mauss 1998 [1929]). In essence, then, Durkheim's own reflections on 'civilization' do indicate a certain movement in the direction of the analysis of 'supranational' phenomena, but these are regarded as derivate of allegedly more fundamental bounded socio-political units, supranational phenomena being seen as ultimately derivative of these. The suggestion then is that the basic ontological building-blocks of human social order are 'societies' in the national-political sense of the word.

In recent years, various scholars (Fine 2003; Turner 2006; Chernilo 2007) seeking to rehabilitate Durkheim's reputation in an age of self-conscious globality have fastened onto his (somewhat limited and scattered) remarks on 'world patriotism'. The background to such remarks are some of the more Comtean and 'international socialist' dimensions of his thinking, which one might plausibly think would provide fertile grounds for Durkheimian ruminations on transnational phenomena. This is indeed true, at least to some degree. These sorts of themes are summed up in an address Durkheim gave at the Paris Universal Exposition of 1900:

> Doubtless, we have towards the country in its present form, and of which we in fact form part, obligations that we do not have the right to cast off. But beyond this country, there is another in the process of formation, enveloping our national country: that of Europe, or humanity (cited at Lukes 1973: 350).

Here we encounter what Turner (2006: 133) depicts as Durkheim's 'notion of a cosmopolitan sociology [designed] to challenge the nationalist assumptions of his day'. The main source of further evidence as to Durkheim's adumbration of such a position derives from the series of lectures on politics and morality he gave in Bordeaux between 1890 and 1900, and which were repeated at the Sorbonne in 1904 and 1912. These lectures were published posthumously as *Professional Ethics and Civic Morals* (Durkheim 1992). In the lectures Durkheim gives some (relatively brief) consideration to the apparently contradictory notion of 'world patriotism'. This does not involve modes of affiliation to a putative 'world state'. He does in fact note the possibility that at some point in the future there could arise a situation where 'humanity in its entirety [was] organized as a [single] society'. However, he goes on to note that 'such an idea, while not altogether beyond realization, must be set in so distant a future that we can leave it out of our present reckoning' (1992: 74). He then goes on to develop the concept of 'world patriotism' from within what he takes to be the realities of the contemporary international system of states, whilst endeavouring to raise this system to what he sees as a higher moral and ethical level. In the 'world patriotism' model, each state would encourage the highest moral sentiments among all of its citizens. Thus each national polity seeks 'not to expand, or to lengthen its borders, but to set its own house in order and to make the widest appeal to its members for a moral life on an ever higher level' (ibid.). If this happened, then 'civic duties would be only a particular form of the general obligations of humanity' (ibid.). Here Durkheim points toward some kind of 'world culture', constituted of certain – as yet undetermined – moral and ethical codes, which are both contributed to by particular nation-states and which are, when these codes have become part of an acknowledged 'world culture', adopted by each state, but with specific national inflections, as regards the education of citizens.

Turner (1990: 347) has argued that for obvious reasons compelled by the international political situation, at the outbreak of World War I Durkheim in part turned away from such 'cosmopolitan' reflections towards 'the idea of nationalism as a modern version of more traditional sources of the *conscience collective*'. This is true, but only to a certain degree. In actual fact, the onset of the war did not force Durkheim to drop the world patriotism position. Instead, he adapted it for somewhat new purposes, deploying it as a useful resource for anti-German propaganda. In the 1915 pamphlet *Germany Above All* (Durkheim 1915), the German state's aggressive activities are depicted as being driven by a chauvinistic nationalism that is the direct antithesis of 'world patriotism', and which is morally pernicious exactly because it goes against the norms of the empirically existing, if rudimentary, contemporary version of world-level moral culture. German elites of the 19th century were contributors to this moral culture, being people 'who belonged without any reservation to the same moral community as we ourselves in France and the other Allied countries' (ibid. 4). Conversely, their instigation of hostilities and their brutal treatment of combatants and civilians signalled a total rejection of their moral responsibilities as members of the world 'moral community'.

Certain positions in present-day social theory are quite akin to these remarks of Durkheim. There are some interesting glimpses in the ideas of world patriotism of something approaching the 'world culture' thesis put forward in recent years by Lechner and Boli (2005) among others (Robertson 2007). On this view, certain general values, such as a belief in the sacrosanct nature of human rights, come over time to pertain within – and across – every 'national' territory in the world, while at the same time there exist specifically 'national' (or regional) colourings of these ('glocal' norms and values, in Robertson's (1992) terms). Given the scholarly attention it has received in recent years, the notion of 'world patriotism', one might think it was precisely here that any attempt to claim a Durkheimian legacy in 'global sociology' might be primarily based. However, it remains the case that Durkheim's remarks about such issues are both sketchy and also operate more at the level of normative political philosophy than of sociological analyses of concrete empirical contexts. In our view, other texts written by Durkheim yield more sociologically compelling accounts of supranational phenomena than do the world patriotism comments, and it is to these that we now turn.

Durkheim and Globality

One can turn to both Durkheim's first book, *The Division of Labour in Society* (1964 [1893]) and his last, *The Elementary Forms of Religious Life* (2001 [1912]), to see other ways in which he treated, albeit tentatively, the nature of supranational phenomena. In *The Division of Labour in Society* we find Durkheim sometimes gesturing towards the possibility that 'organic solidarity' – the complex division of labour of modernity – is a condition that tends to exist not only *within* particular nation-states but also *between* them. When Durkheim (1964 [1893]: 369) notes that within one society under conditions of organic solidarity, 'the fusion of the different segments [of production] draws [hitherto separate] markets together into one which embraces almost all [of national] society', he goes on to add that this process 'even extends beyond [national frontiers] ... and tends to become universal, for the frontiers which separate peoples break down at the same time as those [boundaries disappear] which separate the segments of each of them [within a given polity]. The result is that each industry produces for consumers spread over the whole surface of the country or even of the entire world'.

Thus on this view, 'national-level' organic solidarity develops at the same time as 'international-level' organic solidarity. One could read Durkheim to mean that within the overall social process that is the development of organic solidarity, there are both 'national' and 'international' dimensions, and the two develop in tandem with each other. On such a reading, organic solidarity has a 'natural' tendency not only to be international in scope, but in fact to be trans-national, for each industry and its corresponding market potentially stretches across the whole world, rather than being primarily located in national terms. Given this, it is perhaps not too much to claim, as does Barkdull (1995: 678), that 'Durkheim anticipated a global organic society', in the sense that trans-national tendencies seem to be endemic to the development of organic solidarity itself.

Intriguingly, Durkheim also says in this context that 'it can be affirmed that an economic or any other function can be divided between two societies only if they participate from certain points of view in the same common life, and, consequently, *belong to the same society*' (1964 [1893]: 280, italics added). How can 'two societies' nonetheless 'belong to the same society'? In our view, the answer would seem to be that organic solidarity depends on different national entities, which are in relations of commercial interdependence with each other, sharing – at least at some level and to some degree – the same set of values and norms. The latter involves the 'non-contractual elements' in the contracts operative between the different national units, a system of values which generates norms which in turn guide each unit's interactions with the other. If then we imagine a situation where, at the material level production, trade and consumption are characterized by an organically solidary condition pertaining among all states in the world, then the 'proper' functioning of this system would require some sort of 'world culture' to make it 'work', because all national units would have to subscribe to certain values, in particular the respecting of the terms of contracts entered into, and also would have to operate on a mundane basis according to the regulative norms generated by those values.

This latter point returns us to the notion of 'world culture' (involving, for instance, universally acknowledged laws of contract) which Durkheim gestured towards in his depiction of 'world patriotism'. Thus when Durkheim claims that 'two societies' can 'belong to the same society', he is using two different definitions of 'society' – the first referring to a territorially-bounded political unit, and the second to the 'world moral culture' sketched out above. Our reconstruction of Durkheim's statements can be rendered as follows:

> When a (large) number of specific 'societies' (definition 1 of 'society' – a social-political entity located within a given state's territory) are in complex, organically solidary relations with each other, the condition of inter- and transnational organic solidarity thus created is itself a 'society', a (potentially) 'global society' (definition 2 of 'society' – a planet-spanning social order, characterised by world-encompassing organic solidarity). The operations of the latter are regulated by a 'world moral culture' (akin to Durkheim's notion of 'world patriotism'), which is itself 'glocal' in nature, insofar as its elements initially are contributed by particular 'societies' (of the definition 1 type) and, once they are part of 'world culture', are taken on board and given particular colourings by, and within, each individual 'society' (again of the definition 1 type).

If this is a plausible account of what Durkheim was gesturing towards, the task remains to further flesh out the nature of the 'world moral culture' that is the 'ideal' side of organically solidary 'global society'. We contend that this can be done by (re)considering the highly suggestive final chapters of *The Elementary*

Forms. While there are apparent analytic differences between his first and last books, nonetheless we feel that the relevant sections in *The Division of Labour* may be taken as setting out the nature of the 'material conditions' of global organic solidarity, *The Elementary Forms* sketches out the 'ideal conditions' – the cultural and ideational elements – of that form of social order. These elements are both generated by global organic solidarity and in turn make the ongoing working of the latter possible.

In one respect, *The Elementary Forms* seems like an unpromising source for searching for elements of 'global sociology'. It may be seen as the most dramatic and fully realized of a series of attempts in France at that time to pursue the idea of 'society' as an apparently secular replacement for 'religion' (Pecora 2006: 109). The social bonds understood to be fostered by religion could be retained for the purposes of promoting feelings of community and solidarity within the territory of the French state, while purging these of any Christian traces. Thus 'political theology' (Pecora, ibid.) of *The Elementary Forms* involves viewing 'society' as a bounded political unit, because it is an apparently secular replacement for forms of religion that had in the past bound together particular sorts of groups of people – clans, tribes, nations and suchlike.

However it is our contention that the later chapters of the book depart quite notably from the emphasis of the earlier chapters, the latter involving 'society', as a primarily 'religious' entity, being a bounded, territorial, 'political' unit. Instead, in the later chapters Durkheim focuses in on 'religious universalism', a condition whereby a belief system claims to have validity over more than one 'national' group.[6] The key point is that Durkheim claims that this condition is not just found in the 'world religions', but also 'at the summit' of Australian aboriginal religion too. For Durkheim, in aboriginal Australia particular gods are recognized by multiple tribes, and so 'their cult is, in a sense, *international*' (2001 [1912]: 321, italics added). On this viewpoint, neighbouring tribes cannot avoid social contact with each other, and over time they become more systematically interlinked, primarily through commerce and group inter-marriage. Thus they enter into a situation where they become ever more conscious of what they have in common:

---

6 One should note the strong structural and thematic similarities between *The Elementary Forms* and another notable work of sociology of religion, namely Fustel de Coulanges' *The Ancient City* (1980 [1864]). Both works follow exceptionally similar narrative paths, possibly suggesting a certain amount of homage to Fustel's book on Durkheim's part (Robertson 1977). Both texts initially concern themselves with the socio-cultural conditions of bounded entities, the pre-Roman empire *polis* and aboriginal 'society'. Both these social orders are seen as having religious beliefs at their very roots. But both texts in their closing chapters pursue somewhat different lines of inquiry from what has gone before. In Fustel's case, there is an account of the usurpation of the *polis* by the more complex and more 'global' social form that is the Roman empire. In like manner, Durkheim shifts from analysis of particular tribal religions to the emergence, under conditions of emerging organic solidarity between tribes, of the 'international gods' described further below.

'mutual [cultural] borrowings ... serve to reinforce' this sense of 'international' commonality (ibid.).

Given the increasing interpenetration of hitherto distinct tribes at the 'material' level (and here we are probably dealing with what Durkheim thinks is a very rudimentary form of organic solidarity), the 'international gods' mentioned above are created in two ways. First, at the completely ideational level, each tribe's notion of a god fuses with the ideas of the other tribes they are in systematic contact with, and the resulting 'international god' is made manifest in the minds of all participants. In this sense the 'international gods' are the results of a 'hybridization' of distinct tribal (as it were, 'national') traditions. Second, for Durkheim the 'international gods' are very much gods of initiation ceremonies. Thus they are generated through initiation rituals held at 'intertribal assemblies'. Durkheim contends that at these assemblies 'sacred beings were ... formed that were not fixed to any geographically fixed society'. The territory they correspond to, and in a sense are produced by, is inter-tribal (that is, 'international'), does not have clear borders, and conceptually is 'spread over an unlimited area'. The gods that correspond to this territory thus 'have the same character [as the territory itself]; their sphere of influence is not circumscribed; they glide above the particular tribes and above space. They are the great international gods' (2001 [1912]: 321).

In the earlier chapters of *The Elementary Forms*, Durkheim had argued that the social structure of a given bounded 'society' produces a body of religious beliefs which express that very structure. In the later chapters, an analogous argument is pursued, but this time at another level: 'international society' produces a body of beliefs as to 'international gods' which reflect its nature too. If 'national' religions are the necessary preconditions for effective social functioning within a given politically-bounded 'society', so the functioning of 'international society' would also seem to depend on its 'religious' expressions and values, both as regards the guiding of individual actions through norms, and also in the definition of 'reality' through its cognitive lenses. One might expect that an 'international religion' carries out its constructing of reality in ways that are more 'cosmopolitan' than those of 'national' religions, especially given that the former is, at least in some ways, a 'hybrid' entity.

Durkheim does not elaborate on any of these points. But judging by his remarks at the end of the book, he did want to draw conclusions from aboriginal 'international religion' as to the emerging world-spanning social conditions of his own epoch. In the present day, he notes, 'there is no people, no state, that is not involved with another society that is more or less unlimited and includes all peoples ... There is no national life that is not dominated by an inherently international collective life. As we go forward in history, these international groupings take on greater importance and scope ...' (2001 [1912]: 322). If this is the case at the 'material' levels of trade and politics, then this situation must have a corollary at the cultural level, at the level of the secular religion which is concomitant with the development, and necessary for the operation, of world-wide organic solidarity. If the latter is not just international in nature, but in fact is truly 'global' – involving a 'society that is more or less unlimited and includes all peoples' – then so too must be the religious-cultural nexus that is both produced by it and upon which it depends.

Would a 'world culture', corresponding to and ordering world organic solidarity, be merely an exportation of Western values, based around respect for the individual and for the binding nature of contracts, around the globe? Durkheim gives us no explicit answer to such a question. But the point made above about 'international gods' being hybrid products, drawing upon different cultural traditions and synthesizing them, might suggest something more complex than a simple account of 'Westernization'. What is clear, though, is that Durkheim feels that such a culture is as yet in his own time still embryonic: 'the great things of the past ... no longer excite the same ardour in us ... or because they no longer answer to our current aspirations, and yet nothing has come along to replace them ... we do not yet see clearly what this should be nor how it might be realized' (2001 [1912]: 322). Durkheim's point is that only principles which emerge from present-day circumstances can meet present-day needs. If social reality is increasingly not just internationalized but in fact globalized, then it is those latter conditions themselves which will produce cultural forms appropriate for them. His overall conclusion is optimistic: 'there are no immortal gospels and there is no reason to believe that humanity is henceforth incapable of conceiving new ones' (2001 [1912]: 323). Durkheim possibly takes 'humanity' here to be a phenomenon not just in the abstract, but as an entity that is becoming a concretely existing reality through the means of the spread of organically solidary relations throughout the world, and its corollary, the values of world culture. If so, then it might be 'humanity' per se, rather than distinct 'national' segments of it, which he regarded as creating the values expressed in world moral culture.[7]

Conclusion

In this chapter we have traced out what we take to be the major lineaments of what can be taken as Durkheim's 'global sociology'. His apparently strong focus on 'society' as a bounded political unit might seem to make his work appear antediluvian, given present-day concerns to do with trans- and supra-national forces and forms. Yet if one re-reads his *oeuvre* with an eye to recovering and pulling together the points within it where global phenomena do hove into view, one can indeed begin to discern an embryonic account – or set of accounts – of global organic solidarity and its interweaving with world moral culture. While Durkheim's moves in these directions were tentative, nonetheless we believe there is a discernible thread in his writings, from the earlier work through to the magnum

---

7 This has to be offset against Durkheim's remark (1988 [1913]: 153) that 'one might say that the human milieu, the integral humanity of which Comte hoped to make a science, is only a construction of the spirit', rather than a concrete entity in itself.

opus of *The Elementary Forms*, that engages with transnational phenomena and conditions of globality. In the early twenty-first century, it is now possible not just to reconstruct, but in fact to resurrect, Durkheim's emergent sociology of globality. Contained within it are tantalizing glimpses of what he took to be the elementary forms of global social life, hints that present-day analysts should recognize as important precursors to their own attempts to think sociologically about the world as a whole. Scattered throughout Durkheim's *oeuvre* are ideas that are rich and productive enough to act as the bases for neo-Durkheimian accounts of global social solidarity, and its opposites, accounts that surely should be taken just as seriously as those proffered by Marx as to the genesis and nature of globalization and globality.

Acknowledgement

This chapter is in part based on material that first appeared in David Inglis and Roland Robertson (2008), 'The Elementary Forms of Globality: Durkheim and the Emergence and Nature of Global Life', *Journal of Classical Sociology* 8:1, 5–25.

References

Albrow, M. (1990), 'Introduction', in Martin Albrow and Elizabeth King (eds), *Globalization, Knowledge and Society* (London: Sage/International Sociological Association).

Aristotle (1999), *Politics*, trans. David Keyt (Oxford: Clarendon Press).

Barkdull, J. (1995), 'Waltz, Durkheim, and International Relations', *American Political Science Review* 89:3, 669–680.

Beck, U. (2000), *What is Globalization?* trans. Patrick Camiller (Cambridge: Polity).

Chernilo, D. (2006), 'Social Theory's Methodological Nationalism', *European Journal of Social Theory* 9:1, 5–22.

Chernilo, D. (2007), 'A Quest for Universalism: Re-assessing the Nature of Classical Social Theory's Cosmopolitanism', *European Journal of Social Theory* 10:1, 17–35.

Cohen, R. and Kennedy, P. (2000), *Global Sociology* (Basingstoke: Palgrave Macmillan).

Durkheim, E. (1915), *Germany Above All: German Mentality and War* (Paris: Librairie Armand Colin).

Durkheim, E. (1964 [1893]), *The Division of Labour in Society*, trans. George Simpson (New York: Free Press).

Durkheim, E. (1982 [1895]), *The Rules of Sociological Method*, trans. W.D. Halls (New York: Free Press).

Durkheim, E. (1992), *Professional Ethics and Civic Morals*, trans. Cornelia Brookfield (London: Routledge).

Durkheim, E. (2001 [1912]), *The Elementary Forms of Religious Life*, trans. Carol Gosman (New York: Oxford University Press).

Durkheim, E. and Mauss, M. (1998 [1913]), 'Note on the Notion of Civilization', in Rundell and Mennell (eds).

Fine, R. (2003), 'Taking the "Ism" Out of Cosmopolitanism: An Essay in Reconstruction', *European Journal of Social Theory* 6:4, 451–470.

Fustel de Coulanges, N.S.D. (1980), *The Ancient City: A Study on the Religion, Laws, and Institutions of Greece and Rome* (Baltimore: Johns Hopkins University Press).

Gane, N. (2005), 'Max Weber as Social Theorist: Class, Status, Party', *European Journal of Social Theory* 8:2, 211–226.

Gouldner, A.W. (1970), *The Coming Crisis of Western Sociology* (New York: Basic Books).

Inglis, D. and Robertson, R. (2004), 'Beyond the Gates of the *Polis*: Reworking the Classical Roots of Classical Sociology', *Journal of Classical Sociology* 4:2, 165–189.

Inglis, D. and Robertson, R. (2005), 'The Ecumenical Analytic: "Globalization", Reflexivity and the Revolution in Greek Historiography', *European Journal of Social Theory* 8:2, 99–122.

Inglis, D. and Robertson, R. (2008), 'The Elementary Forms of Globality: Durkheim and the Emergence and Nature of Global Life', *Journal of Classical Sociology* 8:1, 5–25.

Lechner, F. and Boli, J. (2005), *World Culture* (Oxford: Blackwell).

Lukes, S. (1973), *Emile Durkheim: His Life and Work. A Historical and Critical Survey* (London: Allen Lane The Penguin Press).

Mann, M. (1986), 'The Sources of Social Power', Vol. I, *A History of Power from the Beginning to A.D. 1760* (Cambridge: Cambridge University Press).

Martins, H. (1974), 'Time and Theory in Sociology', in Rex (ed.).

Martins, H. (ed.) (1993), *Knowledge and Passion: Essays in Honour of John Rex* (London: I.B. Tauris).

Marx, K. and Engels, F. (1968 [1848]), 'Manifesto of the Communist Party', in *Marx-Engels Selected Works* (Moscow: Progress Publishers).

Mauss, M. (1998 [1929]), 'Civilizations: Elements and Forms', in Rundell and Mennell (eds), 155–159.

McCarthy, G.E. (2003), *Classical Horizons: The Origins of Sociology in Ancient Greece* (Albany: State University of New York Press).

Pecora, V.J. (2006), *Secularization and Cultural Criticism: Religion, Nation and Modernity* (Chicago: The University of Chicago Press).

Pickering, W.S.F. (1984), *Durkheim's Sociology of Religion: Themes and Theories* (London: Routledge and Kegan Paul).

Plato (2003), *The Republic*, trans. Desmond Lee (Harmondsworth: Penguin).

Renton, D. (2001), *Marx on Globalization* (London: Lawrence and Wishart).

Rex, J. (ed.) (1974), *Approaches to Sociology: An Introduction to Major Trends in British Sociology* (London: Routledge and Kegan Paul).

Ritzer, G (ed.) (2007), *The Blackwell Encyclopaedia of Sociology*, Vol. 4 (Oxford: Blackwell).
Robertson, R. (1977), 'Individualism, Societalism, Worldliness, Universalism: Thematizing Theoretical Sociology of Religion', *Sociological Analysis* 38, 281–308.
Robertson, R. (1992), *Globalization: Social Theory and Global Culture* (London: Sage).
Robertson, R. (1993), 'Globalization and Sociological Theory' in Martins (ed.).
Robertson, R. (2001), 'Globality', in Smelser and Baltes (eds).
Robertson, R. (2007a), 'Globality' in Robertson and Scholte (eds).
Robertson, R. (2007b), 'Globalization, Culture and', in Ritzer (ed.).
Robertson, R. and Inglis, D. (2004), 'The Global *Animus*: In the Tracks of World-Consciousness', *Globalizations* 1:1, 38–49.
Robertson, R. and Scholte, J.A. (eds) (2007), *Encyclopaedia of Globalization*, Vol. 2 (London: MTM/Routledge).
Rundell, J. and Mennell, S. (eds) (1998), *Classical Readings in Culture and Civilization* (London: Routledge).
Smelser, N.J. and Baltes, P.B. (eds) (2001) *International Encyclopaedia of the Social and Behavioural Sciences*, Vol. 9 (Oxford: Elsevier/Pergamon Press).
Turner, B.S. (1990), 'The Two Faces of Sociology: Global or National', *Theory, Culture & Society* 7:3–4, 317–32.
Turner, B.S. (2006) 'Classical Sociology and Cosmopolitanism: A Critical Defence of the Social' *British Journal of Sociology* 57:1, 133–151.
Urry, J. (2000a), 'Mobile Sociology', *British Journal of Sociology* 51:1, 185–203.
Urry, J. (2000b), *Sociology Beyond Societies* (London: Routledge).
Urry, J. (2003), *Global Complexity* (Cambridge: Polity).
Wagner, P. (2000), *A History and Theory of the Social Sciences: Not All That Is Solid Melts Into Air* (London: Sage).

Chapter 3
Back to the Things Themselves: On Simmelian Objects

Olli Pyyhtinen

Introduction

Since the days of its foundation, sociology has rested on a seemingly safe distinction between the social and the non-social, the human and the non-human. As a latecomer in the family of sciences, sociology had to struggle to find a distinct subject matter of its own: for Emile Durkheim, for instance, this was found in 'social facts', for Max Weber in 'social action' and for Georg Simmel in 'social forms'. Notwithstanding their crucial differences, all these notions were employed in order to specify what is *purely* social, 'the social' as such – the quest for a genuine sociological phenomenon which would legitimize sociology as an independent science called for serious work of 'purification'.

Because the core of 'the social' has been defined above all by demarcating it from what is not-social, a by-product of this has been that sociologists have forgotten the material side of social phenomena far too easily. Its absence culminates in the paradox that while the social has been made into a 'thing', as if 'stuff' – Durkheim's (1982, 14) famous aphorism, 'consider social facts as things', providing the paradigmatic example of such a view – things themselves have been overlooked. As Bruno Latour (2005, 82) puts it, sociologists seem to 'consider, for the most part, an object-less social world': their images of social reality lack our companionship with, passion for and attachment to things. The 'masses' are missing from sociological investigation (Latour 1992).

Recently social theory has begun to stress materiality more fully by paying attention to the materiality of power, to material culture and to materialized nonhuman 'actants', for instance. However, there were attempts to integrate the material world into the theoretical reflections on the social already in classical sociology. In this chapter, I suggest that it was above all Simmel who introduced objects to social theory and, by way of few examples, make a modest attempt to show how he did this.

Interpretations of Simmel's work rarely highlight his thought on the material world.[1] This is not that surprising since, to be sure, Simmel's programmatic texts that seek to lay the foundations of sociology, and for which he is also best known, lack

---

[1] For exceptions see e.g. Miller (1987) and Appadurai (1988).

almost all reference to the material world. However, Simmel's writings theorizing cultural objects[2] such as money, the bridge, the door, the handle, the ruin, the picture frame, exhibition architecture and the letter address the material domain very explicitly. And what is important is that instead of perceiving materiality as simply exterior to the social, Simmel paid attention to the ways it is intertwined both with social relationships and with the experience of subjects.

The chapter is divided into four sections. The first section scrutinizes Simmel's outlook on things. Simmel's work is concrete in the sense that he takes things seriously in their profaneness and superficiality. Yet there's an unremitting tension between *part* and *whole* in his take: on the one hand, Simmel portrays things as they are, subject to their own individual laws; on the other, they are treated either as mere clues to more profound realities or as only receiving their qualities and form by virtue of relations to other entities. This tension will be taken up and expanded on in the two following sections; the second section discusses money as a mediator and enactment of relations, while the third section picks Simmel's essay on the bridge and the door as an example of the way he often sets out to drop a plumb line from the surface of things to metaphysical realities. Then I will move on to discuss the relation of subject and object in Simmel's theorizing of culture. It will be maintained that, for Simmel, the development of subjects and the subjective modes of experience are deeply interrelated with cultural objects. This argument will be followed by a critical assessment of some of the shortcomings of Simmel's theorizing. I will conclude the chapter by suggesting why, notwithstanding all the criticism posed, it is still educational and relevant to turn to Simmel when thinking things sociologically.

Simmelian Exposé of Things

Simmel does not consider the preoccupation with the most superficial things as a task too worthless for any self-respecting theorist. He did not fear getting his hands dirty with what seems 'banal' and 'repulsive' (see Simmel 1992b, 198), but rather very consciously concerned himself with the most common and 'profane' phenomena in his work, such as the above mentioned cultural objects.

In this respect, Simmel can be said to have accomplished in philosophy a shift in focus from what is universal, eternal and deeply significant to concrete objects.[3] According to Theodor Adorno, that shift 'remained canonical for

---

2   By cultural objects, to be precise, Simmel means not only material things which can be seen and touched, but also categories, norms, ideas, worldviews, works of art, scientific findings, social formations, institutions and so on. However, I will restrict myself here only to the investigation of material things. The terms 'things' and 'objects' will be used interchangeably.

3   Here again, by 'objects' is meant not only material things, but many other kinds of concrete objects of study as well, such as fashion, secrecy, the stranger, style, coquetry, and

anyone dissatisfied with the chattering of epistemology or intellectual history' (Adorno 1984, 558; trans. Frisby 1997, 24). Whereas philosophy had traditionally contemplated at most the Ideas of things, now it set out to grasp the things themselves. In fact, Simmel's effort to grasp things and theorize them perhaps carries out in practice, paradoxically, Edmund Husserl's slogan 'back to the things themselves' more fully than Husserl himself ever did in his work. Husserl, with only few exceptions, as Gary Backhaus (2003, 203–204) notes, was too concerned with the general methodological explication of the program of phenomenology to actually investigate the things he insisted on going back to from the outset. Of course, the battle cry has a completely different sense with the two thinkers. Whereas in Husserl, the emphasis is on thinking without presuppositions on the basis of things, in the case of Simmel we can understand it literally as an endeavour to think things, to take concrete objects as one's objects of study.

In thinking things, Simmel contrasts his own approach especially to those of Plato and Hegel. Unlike Plato, Simmel does not regard the surface level of things as being only apparent and more or less imperfect reflections of the world of Ideas. Plato's doctrine exemplifies for Simmel (1996a, 101) the 'typical tragedy of the spirit: the being has to be loved, because as such it nevertheless is the reality of the idea, and it has to be hated, because it is precisely reality and not as such the idea'. Neither does Simmel try to elevate superficialities 'to the level of philosophical nobility' as he regards Hegel to have done (Simmel 2003, 309; trans. 2005, 3). Simmel (1989a, 367–8) criticizes Hegel for losing sight of the objects themselves when seeking their general rule and metaphysical base.

Contrary to Plato and Hegel, Simmel's philosophy is *concrete* in the sense that it takes things seriously in their plain superficiality. As he writes in the preface to *Rembrandt*: 'Philosophical concepts ... ought to give to the surface of existence what they are able to give' (Simmel 2003, 309; trans. 2005, 3) instead of trying to make it 'fit into a philosophical system' (Simmel 2003, 310; trans. 2005, 3). Abstract philosophical systems keep too wide a distance from concrete phenomena as they only try to save the latter from 'isolation and lack of spirituality' (Simmel 1989b, 12; trans. 2004, 55). By contrast, Simmel (2003, 309; trans. 2005, 3) thinks it would be better to leave the surface 'simply as it is and subject to its own immediate laws'.

Yet it is not in their plain immediacy that Simmel examines objects. He is interested in them above all to get a glimpse of a totality – either that of modern society, which has become too complex to be grasped in a single vision as such in all its entirety and in every detail (see Simmel 1992a, 31; Hetzel 2001, 72), or, ultimately, the totality of existence, which is 'accessible to no one and can act upon no one' (Simmel 1996a, 17). This is 'the miracle of banality' (cf. Rammstedt 1991, 142n) in Simmel's essays: an object is always revealed to be more than it appears to be. Simmel, as Georg Lukács (1993, 172; trans. 1991, 145) put it, views 'the

---

so on. However, for the sake of the argument, let us circumscribe the use of the term in the following for material things only.

smallest and the most inessential phenomenon of daily life so sharply *sub specie philosophiae* that it becomes transparent and behind its transparence an eternal formal coherence of philosophical meaning becomes perceptible'. Thus, Simmel's view of objects is marked by a tension between part and whole, the specific and the general, the temporary and the eternal: while trying to leave objects subject to their individual laws, as individual wholes and unities unto themselves, Simmel perceives them at the same time as expressions of metaphysical realities or enactments of a set of relations. For Simmel, objects are often treated as backdoor entrances to more general problems, whether sociological or philosophical. He tries to get hold of the 'large' by the 'small'. I will first examine the way Simmel thinks money makes visible the relative unity of society and, after that, his view of the bridge and the door as expressions of profound metaphysical meanings.

Money and Simmel's Methodological Fetishism

Simmel questioned the heuristic value of the all-encompassing and hypostasized notion of 'society' (see Simmel 1992a, 14; 1992b, 53–4, 56; Frisby 1992, 10; Hetzel 2001, 73). Society – as, for Simmel, does any unity – consists in dynamic reciprocal relations between its elements: society is, ultimately, nothing but interactions of its 'parts' (Simmel 1989a, 129–30). It is 'present wherever several individuals enter interaction' (Simmel 1992b, 54; cf. 1992a, 17; 1995, 54–5; 1999, 69). Society is an 'immanent infinity' reminiscent of that of the circle which 'develops only in complete mutuality, by which each part [...] determines the position of other parts' (Simmel 1989b, 121; trans. 2004, 119).

In the analysis of modern society, money, as it is theorized in *Philosophie des Geldes* (1989b [1900]; trans. 'The Philosophy of Money' 2004 [1978]), holds for Simmel a special place. It is the prime theoretical means to study the complex relative unity of our society. The resulting image of modern society would be bound to remain vague and abstract were one to start from the social and cultural context of money itself. However, by following the movement and circulation of money, Simmel (1989b, 13; trans. 2004, 56) argues, 'the unity of things [...] becomes practical and vital for us' – not one of substantial, absolute oneness, but constituted by shifting and dynamic relations. By drawing on Appadurai's (1985, 5) formulation, one could thus say that Simmel's approach is imbued by a sort of 'methodological fetishism': it is informed by an idea that 'it is the things-in-motion that illuminate their human and social context'. Accordingly, for Simmel money is not merely a 'prism' through which to examine social relations (Papilloud 2002, 97). On the contrary, he stresses that, with its circulation, money weaves the web of society (Frisby 1984b, 51). Money is one of the focal points and articulations of modern society:

> On the one hand, money functions as a system of articulations in this organism [i.e. society], enabling its elements to be shifted, establishing a relationship of

mutual dependence of the elements, and transmitting all impulses through the system. On the other hand, money can be compared to the bloodstream whose continuous circulation permeates all the intricacies of the body's organs and unifies their functions by feeding them all to an equal extent (Simmel 1989b, 652; trans. 2004, 469).

Via money, we are at once dependent on the whole of society. Simmel (1989b, 305; trans. 2004, 236) argues that, 'at present ... the whole aspect of life, the relationships of human beings with one another and with objective culture are coloured by monetary interests'. Consequently, money presents itself as an excellent means to study society's 'movements' and 'transformations' (Papilloud 2002, 97).

Money is also a good example of the fact that Simmel does not treat objects in their brute tangible materiality. His take is far from sheer 'materialism'. The ability of money to relate things together is not based simply on its material components and effects in the physical world. On the contrary, Simmel examines money as a form of interaction, as an effect or enactment of dynamic relations. It is precisely because 'its qualities are invested in the social organizations and the supra-subjective norms' that money has been able to express and foster, *despite* its materiality and not due to it, the relational unity of the (social) world (Simmel 1989b, 264; trans. 2004, 210). 'Money has value not on account what it is, but on account of the ends that it serves', Simmel (1989b, 251; trans. 2004, 201) writes.

The Bridge and the Door

Instead of limiting his analysis to the horizontal level of the network of social interactions by following its different strands and links lengthwise, more often than not Simmel also sets out to penetrate its surface depthwise. He is convinced that the superficialities of life can be related to its metaphysical depths. The image of the 'plumb line' connecting the surface level and the deep metaphysical currents constantly recurs in his writings. As Simmel writes for instance in a passage of his famous 'metropolis' essay ('Die Großstädte und das Geistesleben'):

> [F]rom each point of the surface of being, however much it may appear to have merely grown in and out of this surface, a plumb line can be dropped into the soul's depth such that all of the most banal superficialities are in the end bound to the final determinations of the meaning and style of life via indications of direction (Simmel 1995a, 120; trans. Scott and Staubmann 2005, xiii).

In the preface to *Rembrandt* (2003, 309; trans. 2005: 3), Simmel defines the effort to drop a plumb line into the profound metaphysical realities beneath the immediacy of things as the 'essential task of philosophy'. Things present themselves as theoretical means to explore the depths of life. Simmel thinks that each fragment already contains the totality of existence from its own perspective: 'from every point, the *whole* beauty, the *whole* sense of the unity of the world radiates for the gaze that is sharp enough' (Simmel 1992a, 199). In *Hauptprobleme der Philosophie*, Simmel phrases this into a paradox: 'The world has been given to us as a sum of fragments, and philosophy strives to set a totality in the place of the fragment; it succeeds in this insofar as it is able to set a fragment in the place of the totality' (Simmel 1996a, 32).

The essay 'Brücke und Tür' (2001)[4] provides a good example of how Simmel thinks physical shapes and material realities can themselves be connected to deep metaphysical meanings. Bridge and door are of interest for Simmel especially because in his view they *materialize something metaphysical*. They render ultimate meanings that are not perceptible as such into something material, concrete and visual.

The bridge epitomizes for Simmel (2001, 56) our 'will-to-connect': it overcomes spatial separation, connects and relates what is separate. And, as an artefact it also makes this interrelation immediately visible: it freezes movement into something enduring by giving it 'a permanent figure' (ibid.). This is what for Simmel distinguishes humans fundamentally from animals. Animals also overcome distance, he admits, but it is only humans who are able to stabilize the fluctuating movement from here to there into something lasting (ibid.): into *objects* – paths[5] and bridges.

It is symptomatic that Simmel does not develop the idea sociologically to any extent in the essay. And very unfortunate too, since the stabilizing function achieved by objects, as the work of, for instance, Michel Serres (1995, 87–8) and Bruno Latour (1986; 1996) famously emphasize, is of relevance for our lives above all in a social sense. Even though the contrast made between humans and animals was flawed in the sense that the social life of animals is not completely devoid of objects, this does not undo the main point of the argument: that human sociality is not made of social elements alone. It is not 'purely' social, but the social bonds make themselves durable by materializing into extra-social elements – objects. As for the bridge, it is a material mediator of the social in the most concrete sense, literally connecting humans with one another as it traverses distance. Surprisingly, from a sociological point of view, Heidegger has observed the way the bridge creates connections and relates in a much more interesting and adequate manner than Simmel does. In 'Building Dwelling Thinking', Heidegger writes (and in so doing becomes, very briefly, an actor-network-theory sociologist):

---

4 In English 'Bridge and Door', translated by Mark Ritter, and published in *Theory, Culture and Society* 11:1, February 1994, pp. 5–10 (reprinted in *Simmel on Culture*, 1997, pp. 170–174), and 'The Bridge and the Door', translated by Michael Kaern for *Qualitative Sociology* 17:4, 1994, pp. 397–413.

5 The path is for Simmel a prior form of the bridge.

The city bridge leads from the precincts of the castle to the cathedral square; the river bridge near the country town brings wagons and horse teams to the surrounding villages. The old stone bridge's humble brook crossing gives to the harvest wagon its passage from the fields into the village and carries the lumber cart from the field path to the road. The highway bridge is tied into the network of long-distance traffic, paced as calculated for maximum yield. Always and ever differently the bridge escorts the lingering and hastening ways of men to and from, so that they may get to other banks and in the end, as mortals, to the other side (Heidegger 2001, 150).

Whereas the bridge, with regard to the separated–connected axis, puts the accent on connecting, on the spanning of a gap, the door demonstrates for Simmel 'in a more explicit manner ... that the acts of separating and connecting are but two sides of the same act' (Simmel 2001, 57). Because of the possibility of its being closed, the door marks off a limited and finite space. It demarcates the space of the 'human' out of the endless continuity and infinity of all space. Yet in the very same act of demarcation the door also cancels this partition into the inside and the outside (ibid. 58), since there is always the possibility – even when the door is locked – of 'overstepping' the boundary: opening the door and just stepping out.

Notwithstanding its more speculative aspects, the significance of Simmel's theorizing of the bridge and the door, as well as of money, is that it tries to think objects as being essentially connected to the human condition. Things, relatively enduring and permanent forms, are placed at the heart of humanity. We may discover something fundamental about what it is to be human by looking at something that is not human, i.e. an object: human subjects are not only in and by themselves but their experience and very existence are crucially tied to objects. Because of this, we can also perceive objects themselves, such as money, as being characteristically human: they are not only human-made but may also have effects on humans and replace some human actions (e.g. money replaces subjective valuation with an objective yardstick). Even though Simmel's metaphysical explorations of objects may indeed be aesthetically quite enchanting, it is thus his theorizing on how objects affect and participate in our social lives which proves theoretically the most rewarding.

Dynamics of Subject and Object

Jürgen Habermas (1986, 10) has stated that it is above all Simmel's neo-Kantian concept of culture which makes him distant from us. To be sure, the romanticized humanist or, to be more exact, *Bildungsbürgerliche* ideals of freedom and the refinement of the personality it carries within itself do make it a little outdated. Yet as regards the role of things in subjective experience as well as in the emergence and the stabilization of the social, the manner in which Simmel theorizes culture as a relation between subject and object is still worth consideration.

For Simmel, a subject is not something which exists solely by and in itself. On the contrary, it is a product of relations to multiple 'others', both subjects and objects. Whereas the relation between 'I' and 'you' is Simmel's basic scheme of conceptualizing the relations between two subjects and ultimately society itself (see Simmel 1992b, 42–61; cf. 1999, 160–162), he explores the relations between subject and object as components of culture. He approaches culture as 'the process pending between the soul and its forms' (Habermas 1986, 11). For Simmel, subjective modes of experience are deeply interrelated with cultural objects. Objects, 'such as tools, means of transport, the products of science, technology and art', increasingly 'determine and surround our lives' (Simmel 1989b, 620; trans. 2004, 448).

What is interesting in Simmel's theorizing is that instead of serving as his point of departure, subject and object are rather his destination: he does not commence from fully-fledged subjects and objects, but looks at how subjects and objects come into existence by mutually determining one another. The development of selfhood always involves 'something external' to the subject itself (Simmel 1993, 367–8). The cornerstone of Simmel's conception of culture is the idea that subjects could not exist as subjects were it not for the creation and assimilation of objects. Objects are obligatory points of passage and essential materials for the making of ourselves. The creation of objects is for Simmel the reverse side of becoming a subject: the subject forms its selfhood by producing and giving form to objects. That is, in order to become who one is, the subject has to take a detour through the historico-cultural world. Simmel maintains that it is by cultivating things that we cultivate ourselves (Simmel 1989b, 618) or, to put it the other way, that 'we develop ourselves only by developing things' (ibid. 622; trans. 2004, 449). Thus, according to Simmel, 'culture, in a unique way, sets the contents of life at a point of intersection of subject and object' (Simmel 1993, 371; trans. 1997, 45). The cultural processes of subjectification and objectification go hand in hand: 'Whatever difficulties metaphysics may find in the relationship between the objective determination of things and the subjective freedom of the individual, as aspects of culture their development runs parallel' (Simmel 1989b, 403; trans. 2004, 302–3). Objects play a crucial part in our subjective and social lives.[6]

Accordingly, Latour (2004, 81) has given Simmel recognition for being perhaps the only social scientist he knows who has treated objects as 'neither all powerful nor powerless'. Latour specifies this by contrasting Simmel to Marx. Marx too paid attention to material objects, but in Marx, objects are either capable of too much – the notion of material infrastructure suggesting that material elements are able to cause social relations to happen – or capable of too little – as when they are regarded as merely reified social relations (ibid.). Latour, however, does not say what the account 'neither all powerful nor powerless' would mean in a positive sense. I think it is best interpreted in terms of the 'double' nature of

---

6 It can be noted in passing that, in this respect, the Greeks had a convenient name for 'thing': *pragmata*, that with which one fraternizes with concern (see Heidegger 1972, 68).

Simmelian objects. That is, the objects Simmel treats are at once *constructed* (i.e. human-made) and *objective* (i.e. independent from subjective observations and having effects on us). They have a considerable impact 'upon our psychological and emotional states as well as our social being' (Frisby 1997, 24). Besides connecting various individuals, spaces, objects and actions to one another and thus considerably extending the circle of our lives, money, for instance, has according to Simmel significant psychological effects (such as cynicism and blasé attitude) resulting from the reduction of concrete and incomparable values to the mediating value of money (Simmel 1989b, 332–7).

Yet, while maintaining that the subject attains a selfhood only through and in relation to objects, Simmel also assumes that subjects are genuinely threatened by the autonomy of objects. This prevents Simmel from seeing how *closely* social formations and the lives of subjects are in fact always already tied to and inscribed into things; he holds that the culture of subjects and that of objects are increasingly growing apart from one another. Simmel describes this process with his renowned notion 'the tragedy of culture'. Basically, the concept entails the idea that the objects of our own making 'follow an immanent developmental logic in the intermediate form of objectivity ... and thereby become alienated from both their origin and their purpose' (Simmel 1996b, 408; trans. 1997, 70). According to Simmel, 'historical development tends increasingly to widen the gap between concrete creative cultural achievements and the level of individual culture'. Objective culture has 'become substantially ... independent of subjective culture', because objects 'become more perfect, more intellectual, they follow more and more obediently their own inner logic of material expediency' (Simmel 1993, 372; 1997, 45). As a result, we become dominated by objects of our own creation. As William Outhwaite (2006, 63) puts this, 'we set up an organization and make ourselves its puppets; we adopt an innovative artistic convention and find ourselves unacceptably constrained by it'.

Against Simmel's cultural criticism which presents an image of atrophied subjects under the sway of the hypertrophy of the culture of objects, it would be possible to argue for the increasing mixing and folding into each other of subjects and objects, as for instance Latour (e.g. 1999; 2005) has done in his work. One might argue that the real problem for the people who design, say, technological objects is not that they become autonomous of the subject, but on the contrary *how to make them autonomous*, how to give them opportunities to start acting independently and by themselves, without support. As for users, things go smoothly as long as objects continue to act independently. Problems start – after one has learned from the manual how the device actually works – only when objects stop working in the instant of breakdown. So, even though Simmel's cultural criticism may be right in claiming that objects have become more and more independent and begun to dominate our lives, in the sense that we cannot assimilate them all and make them work for the benefit of our own self-improvement, it nevertheless misses the many ways subjects and objects are both profoundly and subtly crumpled and folded into one another. The subject, of which objects are a constituent part just as it is a part of them, cannot possibly be threatened by those objects, since they already belong to its mode of existence – without things, it could not be the way it is (Latour 1993, 136–8).

Hence, the fact that Simmel apprehends objects primarily from the viewpoint of *mastery* – our mastery over them and, as in the notion of the tragedy of culture, their mastery over us – does not permit him to fully appreciate our complex entanglements with them. Of course, as stated above, in *Philosophie des Geldes* Simmel does make the observation that in modernity, the whole aspect of life and the relationships of individuals with one another and with the culture of things are coloured by money. Nevertheless, we need more detailed explorations of both what people do with material things (i.e. on the uses of things) *and* what things make us, people, do.

As for the first point, Simmel takes the use of objects as far too self-evident and given. Instead of paying attention to specific ways of using objects he contents himself to merely stating their instrumentality: 'A chair exists so that one can sit on it, a glass in order that one can fill it with wine and take it in one's hand' (Simmel 1993, 379; trans. 1997, 214).[7] Likewise, Simmel remarks that the purpose of the handle of a jug is to be 'taken in one's hand', so that the jug, an island-like aesthetic object in a Kantian sense, is thus 'drawn into the bustle of practical life' (Simmel 1996b, 278–9) – a jug can be 'grasped, raised, tipped up' by its handle (ibid. 279). This misses the specific ways that things inscribe into our everyday lives and the amount of energy, time and attention the care of and the handling that things require. They need constant care and upkeep. A large part of our daily activities consists of various dealings with things. As Orvar Lofgren (1997, 103) puts it: 'We shuffle things back and forth, rearrange them, recycle them. Every day, new objects enter our homes and old ones go out the back door.' Our homes are stations and terminals for a whole variety of commodities from technology to food, books and furniture, as well as too often also being points of transit on the way to the waste tip.

As for the second point, for Simmel objects and things cannot have similar agentic effects to humans within interactive networks. Of course, again in *Philosophie des Geldes* Simmel states that money creates a whole new relationship between freedom and bond: it liberates us from personal bondages by replacing payment in kind by money payment. Yet much more careful considerations are needed on the specific ways in which things create potentials for our actions and increase our capabilities, affect us and move us both in place and from place to place, articulate our rationalities, politics, passions, and wills, participate in our world-making, and so on. With Simmel, there is always an *a priori asymmetry* between the capabilities of humans and non-humans: while permitting them *some* agency effects, Simmel would never grant that non-humans have the *same*

---

7 For the sake of fairness let it be noted, however, that Simmel makes this point in order to contrast works of art to applied arts and other utility articles, and not to reflect on the uses of objects.

powers of effecting as an active human. Simmel carries a Kantian heritage in that ultimately, in his view, the knowable world out there is produced and organized by the mental activity of the subject. Only the human subject is endowed with the powers to generate and cause it.

As a result of this asymmetry, while emphasizing the interdependence of the material and the social, Simmel nonetheless pictures their mixes as some sort of zero sum game: the more natural or material a phenomenon is the less cultural or social it is and the more cultural or social a phenomenon is the less natural or material it is. His essay on the sociology of the meal, for instance, is a good example of this. Although Simmel acknowledges the interdependence of social processes and the material world, in the text the social is depicted as being placed higher in the hierarchical order than materiality. Even though in the meal the physiology of eating is connected with the sphere of social interaction, i.e., 'with a frequency of being together, with a habit of being gathered together' (Simmel 2001, 140; trans. 1997, 130), compared to the materiality of the meal, its social dimension is for Simmel a domain of higher order: 'the shared meal elevates an event of physiological primitiveness ... into the sphere of social interaction, and hence of supra-personal significance'. That is, the meal 'permits the merely physical externality of feeding ... to rest upon the principle of an infinitely higher ranking order' (Simmel 2001, 142; trans. 1997, 131). Without thereby being completely detached from its material basis, the sociality of the meal nonetheless designates a triumph over the naturalism of eating (Simmel 2001, 142, 147): while being bound to materiality, the shared meal elevates us beyond its own materiality. Materiality is considered solely as the content of the social form, the meal.

His dualistic conviction renders Simmel's reflections on the social–material question insufficient if read solely by themselves. Indeed, the value of more recent work on the articulation of the social and the material – for example, in studies making use of actor-network-theory – lies precisely in its break from this kind of dualistic thinking. For instance, Steve Woolgar (2002, 268) suggests that, rather than picturing the relation between the social and the material as 'a zero sum game ... we might instead consider that the entanglement between the two is mutually stimulating. The more material the more social?' The point has been made by others as well (see e.g. Serres 1995, 87–8; Latour 1996, 229; 1999, 114, 146), but the idea is, basically, the same: the more mediated and the more attached to materiality the social is the more existent it becomes. The social is not 'pure' and self-referential but substantially supported by extra-social elements such as material objects.

Thus, in order to be able to conceptualize the social–material question adequately we would have to abandon Simmel's dualistic mode of thought. Whereas for Simmel dualism is his basic scheme, *the* form in which any unity (and not only a social or cultural one) is ever capable of existing (see Simmel 1999, 233; cf. 1992a, 391; 1995b, 9, 121, 225), perhaps we should rather, to use the expression of Deleuze and Guattari's (1987, 21), consider dualisms as 'an entirely necessary enemy'. Not being able to escape the confines of language, we have to keep on producing and re-producing dualisms when it comes to linguistic expressions: but this is completely different to ontologizing dualisms. In fact, in de-ontologizing dualisms in order to remain sensitive to the mixed nature of beings and the world, using and even multiplying dualisms may indeed prove to be the only viable strategy. To challenge and undo one dualism via invoking another as Deleuze and Guattari suggest – perhaps this is also the way to finally pass the futile ontological dichotomy of the social and the material that has made so much sociology indifferent to things and objects over the years.

Conclusion

Notwithstanding the above criticism, there are elements in Simmel's work which might provide valuable insights when thinking things and object-relations. First of all, what makes his theorizing fertile is the nature of Simmelian objects. Instead of making them matter either too much – when conceived of as imposing their all-powerful causal laws upon us – or not enough – when seen as merely a projection or reification of social forces – Simmel examines objects at once as human-made and as having a huge impact upon our experience and our social lives. For Simmel, the subjective modes of experience are always deeply interrelated with objects, and certain objects, most evidently money, may operate as mediators of the social. His treatment of the dynamics between subject and object draws attention to things as essential materials in the making of ourselves. Neither could we exist as subjects nor could our fluctuating social interactions be stabilized into durable social bonds were it not for objects.

Secondly, Simmel's work introduces a remarkably wide range of objects to sociological reflection. Thereby Simmel's writings open up a space for exploring many different materialities and material worlds instead of just one. Above I have not tried to address this in a systematic fashion but have settled for only giving a couple of examples. Not that the choice of examples has been completely arbitrary. No example is ever purely individual, as if it would exist merely in itself, but any ex-ample always appears also alongside itself (cf. the German term *Bei-spiel*), expressing that which is individual in what is common to more than one individual case. Accordingly, I think that, by looking at the chosen examples, money, the bridge and the door, it is possible to suggest a more general preliminary model – a method which, to be sure, is not that distant to Simmel's.

Money and the bridge could be considered as examples of things which assemble, gather, connect and relate, but examples in that they are not the only things which operate as mediators and links. As a means of exchange, money relates the most diverse objects and the most distant places and people with each other. As for the bridge, it spans the gap both between people and between places in the most concrete manner, by connecting what was previously separate. As it happens, conceived of in this way, money and the bridge both express the etymological meaning of 'thing' (Ger. *Ding*, Scand. *ting*, OE. *Thang*): 'meeting', 'gathering', 'assembly', especially deliberative or juridical assembly, court, council (see Pels, Hetherington and Vandenberghe 2002, 3). Besides being assemblages and gatherings, they themselves also gather, assemble and relate.

However, besides things that connect and relate, there are also things that separate: walls, barriers, things that some have and others do not. The door demonstrates that there is no separating without connecting and no connecting without separating. The two are nothing but two sides of the same coin. Another example could be a fashionable outfit, as it draws a boundary between those who are fashionable and those who are not, while emphasizing social obedience among the former (Simmel 1996b, 186–218). And of course money, of all the things, is something which not only connects and relates but also separates people into those who have it and those who do not.

Thirdly, and lastly, from a methodological point of view, Simmel's approach is crucial in that it explores social interactions through objects. This was termed the *methodological fetishism* of his analysis of money, a move that turns attention to the things themselves: it is precisely by following the motion and circulation of money that Simmel is able to illuminate its socio-cultural and human context – modern society. This should convince us that assigning things a notable part in the study of social relations does not render our investigations non-sociological. On the contrary, it forces us to broaden our conception of 'the social' itself: the social *is* in other ways as well besides social – it is inscribed into, supported by and stabilized with the help of material objects. Although in his programmatic texts Simmel sought pure social forms, his theorizing on cultural objects places material heterogeneity at the heart of the social and of culture. For the social theory of material objects, Simmel's work thus continues to provide a rich source from which to draw.

References

Adorno, T.W. (1984), *Noten zur Literatur*, Gesammelthe Schriften 11 (Frankfurt am Main: Suhrkamp).
Appadurai A. (1988), 'Introduction: Commodities and the Politics of Value', in Appadurai (ed.).
Appadurai, A. (ed.) (1988) *The Social Life of Things*: *Commodities in Cultural Perspective* (Cambridge: Cambridge University Press).
Backhaus, G. (2003), 'Simmel's Philosophy of History and Its Relation to Phenomenology: Introduction', *Human Studies* 26:2, 203–8.
Dahme, H.-J. and Rammstedt, O. (eds) (1984) *Georg Simmel und die Moderne. Neue Interpretationen und Materialien* (Frankfurt am Main: Suhrkamp).
Deleuze, G. and Guattari, F. (1987), *A Thousand Plateaus: Capitalism and Schizophrenia*, trans. Brian Massumi (Minneapolis and London: University of Minnesota Press).

Durkheim, E. (1982), *Rules of Sociological Method*, trans. Halls (New York: The Free Press).
Frisby, D. (1984), 'Georg Simmels Theorie der Moderne', in Dahme and Rammstedt (eds).
Frisby, D. (1997), 'Introduction to the Texts', in Frisby and Featherstone (eds).
Frisby, D. and Featherstone, M. (eds) (1997), *Simmel on Culture: Selected Writings* (London: Sage).
Gane, N. (ed.) (2004), *The Future of Social Theory* (London: Continuum).
Gamm, G., Hetzel, A. and Lilienthal, M. (eds) (2001), *Hauptwerke der Sozialphilosophie* (Stuttgart: Reclam).
Gassen, K. and Landmann, M. (eds) (1993), *Buch des Dankes an Georg Simmel. Briefe, Erinnerungen, Bibliographie*, 2 Aufl. (Berlin: Duncker & Humblot). (In English: (1991), 'Georg Simmel', *Theory, Culture & Society* 8:3, 145–50.)
Habermas, J. (1998), 'Simmel als Zeitdiagnostiker', in Simmel, *Philosophische Kultur. Über das Abentauer, die Geschlechter und die Krise der Moderne* (Berlin: Wagenbach).
Heidegger, M. (1972), *Sein und Zeit*. Zwölfte, unveränderte Auflage (Niemeyer, Tübingen).
Heidegger, M. (2001), 'Building Dwelling Thinking', in Heidegger, *Poetry, Language, Thought*, trans. A. Hofstadter (New York: Perennia).
Hetzel, A. (2001), 'Georg Simmel: *Philosophie des Geldes* (1900)', in Gamm, Hetzel and Lilienthal (eds).
Latour, B. (1986), 'The Powers of Association', in Law (ed.).
Latour, B. (1992), 'Where are the Missing Masses? Sociology of a Door', <http://www.bruno-latour.fr/articles/article/050.html>.
Latour, B. (1993), *We Have Never Been Modern* (Cambridge, MA: Harvard University Press).
Latour, B. (1996), 'On Interobjectivity', *Mind, Culture & Activity* 3:4, 228–45.
Latour, B. (1999), *Pandora's Hope. Essays on the Reality of Science Studies* (Cambridge, MA: Harvard University Press).
Latour, B. (2004), 'Bruno Latour: The Social as Association' (with Nicholas Gane), in Gane (ed.).
Latour, B. (2005), *Reassembling the Social. An Introduction to Actor-Network-Theory* (Oxford: Oxford University Press).
Law, J. (ed.) (1986), *Power, Action and Belief* (London: Routledge).
Lukács, G. (1993), 'Georg Simmel' in Gassen and Landmann (eds).
Lofgren, O. (1997), 'Scenes From a Troubled Marriage: Swedish Ethnology and Material Culture Studies', *Journal of Material Culture* 2:1, 95–113.
Miller, D. (1987), *Material Culture and Mass Consumption* (Oxford: Blackwell).
Outhwaite, W. (2006), *The Future of Society* (Oxford: Blackwell).
Papilloud, C. (2002), 'Critical Relations. Anthropology of Exchange in Georg Simmel and Marcel Mauss', *Simmel Studies* 12:1, 85–107.

Pels, D., Hetherington, K. and Vandenberghe, F. (2002), 'The Status of the Object. Performances, Mediations, and Techniques', *Theory, Culture & Society* 19:5/6, 1–21.
Rammstedt, O. (1991), 'On Simmel's Aesthetics: Argumentation in the Journal Jugend, 1897–1906', *Theory, Culture & Society* 8:3, 125–44.
Scott, A. and Staubmann, H. (2005), 'Editors' Introduction', xi–xix in G. Simmel, *Rembrandt*, trans. A. Scott and H. Staubmann (New York: Routledge).
Serres, M. (1995), *Genesis* (Michigan: The University of Michigan Press).
Simmel, G. (1989a), *Aufsätze und Abhandlungen 1887–1890; Über sociale Differenzierung, Die Probleme der Geschichtsphilosophie*. Georg Simmel Gesamtausgabe Band 2 (Frankfurt am Main: Suhrkamp).
Simmel, G. (1989b), *Philosophie des Geldes*. Georg Simmel Gesamtausgabe Band 6 (Frankfurt am Main: Suhrkamp).
Simmel, G. (1991), *Schopenhauer and Nietzsche*, trans. H. Loiskandl, D. Weinstein and M. Weinstein (Urbana and Chicago: University of Illinois Press).
Simmel, G. (1992a), *Soziologie. Untersuchungen über die Formen der Vergesellschaftung*. Georg Simmel Gesamtausgabe Band 11 (Frankfurt am Main: Suhrkamp).
Simmel, G. (1992b), *Aufsätze und Abhandlungen 1894–1900*. Georg Simmel Gesamtausgabe Band 5 (Frankfurt am Main: Suhrkamp).
Simmel, G. (1993), *Aufsätze und Abhandlungen 1901–1908 Band II*. Georg Simmel Gesamtausgabe Band 8 (Frankfurt am Main: Suhrkamp).
Simmel, G. (1994), 'The Bridge and the Door', trans. M. Kaern, *Qualitative Sociology* 17:4, 407–12.
Simmel, G. (1995a), *Aufsätze und Abhandlungen 1901–1908 Band I*. Georg Simmel Gesamtausgabe Band 7 (Frankfurt am Main: Suhrkamp).
Simmel, G. (1995b), *Philosophie der Mode; Die Religion; Kant und Goethe; Schopenhauer und Nietzsche*. Georg Simmel Gesamtausgabe Band 10 (Frankfurt am Main: Suhrkamp).
Simmel, G. (1996a), *Hauptprobleme der Philosophie*, in Georg Simmel Gesamtausgabe Band 14 (Frankfurt am Main: Suhrkamp), 7–157.
Simmel, G. (1996b), *Philosophische Kultur*, 159–459 in Georg Simmel Gesamtausgabe Band 14 (Frankfurt am Main: Suhrkamp).
Simmel, G. (1997), *Simmel on Culture. Selected Writings*, edited by D. Frisby and M. Featherstone (London: Sage).
Simmel, G. (1999), *Der Krieg und die geistigen Entscheidungen; Grundfragen der Soziologie; Wom Wesen des historischen Verstehens; Der Konflikt der modernen Kultur; Lebensanschauung*. Georg Simmel Gesamtausgabe Band 16 (Frankfurt am Main: Suhrkamp).
Simmel, G. (2001), *Aufsätze und Abhandlungen 1909–1918 Band I*. Georg Simmel Gesamtausgabe Band 12 (Frankfurt am Main: Suhrkamp).
Simmel, G. (2003), *Goethe; Deutschlands innere Wandlung; Das Problem der historischen Zeit; Rembrandt*. Georg Simmel Gesamtausgabe Band 15 (Frankfurt am Main: Suhrkamp).

Simmel, G. (2004), *The Philosophy of Money*, third enlarged edition, trans. D. Frisby and T. Bottomore (New York: Routledge).
Simmel, G. (2005), *Rembrandt. An Essay in the Philosophy of Art*, trans. A. Scott and H. Staubmann (London: Routledge).
Woolgar, S. (2002), 'After Word? – On Some Dynamics of Duality Interrogation: Or: Why Bonfires Are Not Enough', *Theory, Culture & Society* 19:5/6, 261–70.

Chapter 4
Durkheim's Social Facts and the Performative Model: Reconsidering the Objective Nature of Social Phenomena

Irene Rafanell

Introduction

Durkheim's challenge that social phenomena should be understood as objective 'facts' has incited many social theorists to analytically ground this insight. Durkheim's positivist stance maintains that the 'social' can be analysed as objective phenomena outside the subjective life of individuals. For Durkheim, social phenomena are understood as encompassing a whole collective action, thus existing beyond individual activity. He argues that social life is more than the aggregate of individuals' activities. Central to Durkheim's positivist stance is his emphasis on the causal and determining powers of social facts over individual activity. While he does not dismiss micro-activity – placing social sanctioning at the core of his account of the determining powers of social phenomena – Durkheim's focus is not interaction, but rather the existence of macro-phenomena beyond individual activity: the structural level of social reality.

Structuralist models have been questioned since their very inception.[1] Recent post-structuralist commentaries argue that structuralist approaches tacitly support an essentialist ahistorical bias and emphasize the micro-dynamics of individual activities as underpinning structural reality. Such stances have been widely attacked for dissolving the 'social' altogether by denying its objective reality. Judith Butler's prominent post-structuralist model, based on a combination of Foucauldian and performative stances, is widely taken to be an example of such an approach. Butler has resolutely criticized structuralist models (such as feminism's support of a macro-reality like patriarchy) for reifying an analytical construction into a universal given; and has herself been fiercely criticized. Her model has been accused of discounting the world of 'things' in favour of the world of 'words' (Jackson and Jackie 1998); in other words, of being a form of

---

1 Notably by authors emphasizing interactive micro-dynamics among individuals as central to the emergence of the social. These include Weber and others who have built on his emphasis on micro-interaction as the basis of meaning formation (Ethnomethodology, Symbolic Interactionism and Giddens, for example).

idealism; of neglecting the existence and constraining force of materiality (Bordo 1992) or being a form of indeterminism; and thus of being a form of voluntarism (Bourdieu 2001) where individuals are totally free from external forces. Such criticisms tacitly tap into the most significant argument advanced by Durkheim: that we should see the social as objective phenomena that exist independently of, and determine, individuals' activities.

In contrast with such critics, I do not locate Durkheim in opposition to post-structuralist models. It is my contention that the post-structuralist stance reinforces Durkheim's notion of social objectivity and thus further accounts for the causal impact of social phenomena over individual activity. Conversely, Durkheim's account emphasizes the constitutive power of the collective – something that has not only been widely disregarded, but which also supports post-structuralist positions. In constructing this argument I draw on the work of Barry Barnes, a widely overlooked social theorist who, I argue, provides the analytical tools to build a connection between Durkheim and post-structuralist models.

I begin by identifying what I see as the main element of Durkheim's notion of social facts: their collective nature. Although collective agreement is central to Durkheim's account, he weakened his position by not fully developing this notion. The shortcomings of his position are more clearly revealed by comparing Durkheim's tenets with the post-structuralist arguments of Butler's performative model and the main criticisms it has generated. Focusing on the criticism helps frame the discussion insofar as it shows how her use of the concept of performativity has been misinterpreted – mainly because the collective nature of the performative process has not been fully understood. I argue that Butler herself leaves this aspect underdeveloped, thus forestalling fuller examination of the constitutive power of individuals' activity; and that such analysis is helpful in understanding Durkheim's notion of the collective.

In my view, the true constitutive nature of the performative force of individuals' activity is more clearly developed by Barnes' *performative theory of social institutions.* Barnes' account enables us to appreciate the collective nature of social life; and I propose that combining the performative positions of Butler and Barnes allows us to move beyond models that reify social phenomena outside individuals' actions, by suggesting an ontology of the 'objective' nature of social facts rooted in the micro-activity of individuals' interactions. Such conceptual tools not only provide further insights into Durkheim's positivist prescription, but discredit the accusations that the performative models are a form of idealism that fail to recognize the existence of objective macro-phenomena.

I conclude that the performative approach allows for a fuller understanding of the dialectics between objective social reality and the world of individual activity – and thus further elucidate an answer to the question of how it is possible for human activity to produce a world of 'things'. The ultimate aim of this exercise is to advance the argument that the dichotomy between structures (things) and discourse (words, practices) is a false one. In doing so I attempt to further ground two core aspects of Durkheim's position: the objective and the collective nature of social facts.

The Main Elements of Durkheim's 'Social Facts'

I will start by isolating three main features of Durkheim's argument. His view that the social has a reality *sui generis* is demonstrated by:

a. Its collective nature: "What constitute social facts are the beliefs, tendencies and practices of the group taken collectively" (Durkheim 1982, 54);
b. Its constraining – thus causal and determining – powers over individual activity: "A social fact is any way of acting (…) capable of exerting over the individual an external constraint" (ibid. 59);
c. Its independent status from individual activity: "[a social fact is that] which is general over the whole of a given society whilst having an existence of its own, independent of its individual manifestations" (ibid. 59).

The most prominent feature of Durkheim's definition is its *collective* nature. Social facts are not the possessions of individuals, but of collectives. They are collective accomplishments *beyond* single individuals that exert coercive force upon them. According to Durkheim, this coercive force generates two fundamental aspects of social life: agreement, and consequently the constitution of the collective 'good'. The *collective* and the *constraining* constitute two core aspects of Durkheim's view of social reality. The third element emphasizes that these collective and constraining phenomena acquire an existence in their own right by becoming *independent* of their individual manifestations.

This last point has generated much criticism. Durkheim has been accused of proposing an overtly structuralist account that allows no place for individual agency; or, as Bourdieu put it, a "hypostatization of the social" that is "a false solution to the problem" of individual action (Bourdieu 2000, 155). Bourdieu's criticism is useful in highlighting one of the most problematic aspects of Durkheim's view: reconciling the premise that social facts are collective accomplishments with the idea that they are independent of individual's activity. This apparent paradox is the key question to be addressed when attempting to argue that social reality has an objective status. Is it possible to talk of social phenomena as the result of a community of individuals, which also possesses an independent ontological status beyond them? In other words, how can phenomena emanating from individuals' practices acquire a life of their own, as it were, and become a constraining (and thus determinant) force on the very persons from whom they originated?

Durkheim further states that social facts "function independently of the use [individuals] make of them" and that they "possess the remarkable property of existing outside the consciousness of the individual" (Durkheim 1982, 51). I believe that these two statements reveal the fundamental shortcoming in his position. If, as he claims, the existence of social facts can be identified by their effects on individual practices – mostly via social sanctioning mechanisms imposed upon the individual by others – individuals' consciousness must surely play some role in maintaining collective properties, if only because individuals must understand, accept and abide by the sanctions imposed by others. While social facts are not immediately evident to individual consciousness, they cannot be conceived as functioning independently of the use that is made of them. This is the main source of weakness in Durkheim's position that we are under "an illusion [if] we believe that we ourselves have produced what has been imposed upon us externally" (Durkheim 1982, 53). It is not the structuralist position revealed in his desire to present the social as an objective phenomenon that is contentious, but the fact that he maintains that those structures are not the product of individual activity. This argument fails to provide an understanding of how these structures emerge in the first place.

I will now turn to two radical social constructionist accounts that I believe provide useful tools for grounding Durkheim's notion of social objectivity. They are Butler's *performative theory of sex and gender*, and Barnes' *performative theory of social institution*. Using the conceptual tools of these two positions, I will argue that, as Durkheim suggests, the 'social' must be conceived as a reality outside a single individual's activities; but that contrary to him, such reality acquires this status *precisely* as the result of such activity.

Butler's Ontological Argument

Butler's performative account of sex/gender identity, and her critique of feminist theory as an ontology tacitly subscribing to a 'metaphysics of substance' (Butler 1990, 18) is particularly significant for my argument. Although her critique addresses nature – specifically, the physicality of bodies – her account also relates to social phenomena, particularly the development of the individual's subjective sense of a sexed identity. Butler's anti-structuralist account has had a mixed reception in sociological quarters. Her emphasis on the performative (constitutive) force of linguistic utterances has been widely criticized, mostly for endorsing a form of radical idealism. Exploring the nature of these criticisms should reveal both parties' analytical shortcomings, and help reframe Durkheim's ontological commitment.

Butler's performative model is based on two key features. It is first and foremost a discursive approach based on the Austinian argument that some linguistic utterances, termed 'performative', are constitutive (Austin 1970); that is, some speech acts have the power to 'bring into being' that which they name. In her case study on the embodiment of sex and gender identities, Butler uses Austin's claim to argue that "there is no reference to a pure body which is not at the same time a further formation of that body" (Butler 1993, 10). According to her constructionist framework, bodies are only intelligible through the categories used to describe them, and end up fitting the categories used to refer to them rather than the other way around. More specifically, the repetition of certain gendered practices (both verbal and non-verbal) lays the foundations for the formation of sexed bodies. Butler argues that the 'materiality' of sex is not something that exists prior to our knowledge of it. Quite the reverse, in fact, because our categories and practices construct the 'materiality' of bodies as sex entities, sex identity is the 'performative' effect of repeated acts.[2]

Butler develops the performative force of linguistic utterances in different ways, arguing that language 'interprets' rather than describes, and that in interpreting we formulate the characteristics of the object we refer to. Drawing on Foucault, Butler further notes that this process of 'interpretation' is conditioned by multiple factors beyond biological matter – factors related to the social world and the relations and processes encountered within it. The Foucauldian framework not only allows Butler to further her constructivist stance, but also provides a crucial political dimension to her discursive model. By incorporating Foucault's claim of the 'productive' force of power relations, her model can be said to place power, conflicts of interests and group hierarchies at the centre of her model. Thus, particular speech acts are performative in the sense of 'producing' social phenomena, not only because of the Austinian linguistic effect, but also because they are embedded in particular social relationships governing and constituting differentiated, competing and hierarchical social groups and 'regimes of truths'.[3]

Butler's model has attracted much criticism, which can be divided into three main categories. First are the accusations that she neglects the physical reality of the body. Bordo is a case in point, arguing that Butler's 'discursive linguistic foundationalism', which reads the body as 'text', neglects the constraints of the materiality of the body (Bordo 1992, 170). Secondly, Butler's model is dismissed on the grounds that it neglects the constraining force of the 'materiality' of social reality. As Jackson and Jackie put it, Butler's model discounts the world of 'things' – as in the materiality of structures – in favour of 'words' (Jackson and Jackie 1998, 25). Thirdly, a group of critics concur with Bourdieu's charge that Butler is proposing a form of 'radical voluntarism'. Despite the fact that Bourdieu's critique addresses the notion of agency rather than structure, both he and Jackson and Jackie note Butler's failure to acknowledge that categories and practices are "deeply rooted in things (structures)", and that "roles cannot be played at will by individuals" (Bourdieu 2000, 141).

Both Bourdieu and Jackson and Jackie refer to social structures as 'things' (as opposed to 'words'), in terms reminiscent of Durkheim's ontology. Such terminology reflects the philosophical controversy between idealism and realism. In their use of the concept of 'materialist' structures, Bourdieu and Jackson

---

2 Butler's counter-intuitive account is clarified by a considerable amount of natural sciences research that reveals the conventional nature of the categories used to describe the physical world. The work of Fausto-Stirling (1992) is a very pertinent case in point supporting Butler's claim. This molecular biologist reveals that a closer, non-culturally prejudiced study of humans' genetic material exposes the inadequacy of the existing two sex categorizations; and she proposes that we should talk of a five-sex system.

3 As I have argued elsewhere, power relationships are part and parcel of the performative process in Butler's model (see Rafanell 2004).

and Jackie seem to attempt to ground their ontological commitment in a realist position (Jackson and Jackie 1998, 25; Bourdieu 2000, 103). Their use of the term 'materialist' seems to straddle the Marxian structuralist notion of historical materialism and a realist commitment to understand the world as independent of our perception of it. The connections between these two positions are not straightforward, and Bourdieu and Jackson and Jackie do not explicitly clarify the meaning of the notion of materialism, which is a fundamental aspect of the present discussion. These authors seem to suggest that social structures should be understood as existing independently of the actor's perceptions of them: as 'material' and thus 'objective', in the same way that physical entities are commonly seen to exist.

However, the exact nature of such ontological claims needs to be more explicitly clarified if we are to follow Durkheim's sociological precepts. This analytical clarification is of paramount importance in a sociological enterprise. Without it, sociological positions merely provide reificatory stances that are closer to Platonic idealism than to realist commitment, and which are consequently unable to support the positivist and causalistic features central to sociological enterprise. Indeed, this is Durkheim's central sociological tenet: to determine the existence of the social independent of individual activity and, fundamentally, to establish its causal impact on individual practices and beliefs.

Contrary to Butler's critics, I suggest that her central concern is not to dismiss the intentions and efforts of a materialist sociology, but to provide a more nuanced analytical account of the constitution of the 'materiality' of the social world, its 'objective' nature and, in particular, to provide an understanding of its causal powers. I argue that Butler's critique of mainstream feminism reveals another form of idealism: one that subscribes to a 'metaphysics of substance'. In other words, Butler's analysis draws attention to the fact that mainstream feminism has fallen prey to the illusion of language: that naming a category as a noun – i.e. a substantive – creates the illusion that a material object exists as such *before* the naming.[4]

Performativity versus Performance

The mutual criticism between Butler and the aforementioned feminists is central to the Durkheimian premise of understanding the objective nature of social reality. Both structuralist and discursive models attempt to argue that social reality has

---

4 "(...) the notion of sex appears within hegemonic language as *substance*, as, metaphysically speaking, a self-identical being" (Butler 1990, 18). The critique of the notion of 'metaphysics of substance' in Butler's thought appears to be directly related to the Derridian critique of a 'metaphysics of presence', one that understands that reality 'exists' or 'is' prior to our descriptions of it. Essentialist and universalizing understandings of the nature of the social world would thus subscribe to a metaphysics of 'presence'.

some kind of *external* quality that is particularly evident in its 'compelling' and 'coercive' force over individual activity. Indeed, this is the basis for certain criticisms of the ontology of Butler's performative model: that it neglects the causal and determinant nature of the social world. Roles, says Bourdieu, are deeply rooted in 'things' and cannot be played at will.[5] Given that Butler's work is mainly dedicated to exploring the constraining forces of power relationships, particularly the heterosexual matrix embedded in our culture, it seems surprising that most readings of her model accuse her of denying the determining force of the social. I suggest that this criticism originates from a common misreading of Butler's performative notion as performance. Her model is read as if the performative activity was that of independent individuals and not the operation of interacting members of a collective. Despite her protests at this confusion (Butler 1993, 94; 1994), I believe that the reason for such misinterpretation is that Butler's analytical construction neither fully develops nor properly acknowledges the role of the collective in the constitutive dynamics of performative activity. Butler notes that the "act that one performs ... is clearly not one's act alone"; rather, actors follow a script that "requires individual actors to be actualized and reproduced as a reality once again" (Butler 1988, 526). But nowhere in her work do we find a clear indication of how such a script emerges as a collective good, how it impacts on individuals, or how it gets actualized and reproduced by their single individual actions.

To develop this particular point I will now turn to another performative model: the social constructionist account given by the sociologist of knowledge, Barry Barnes. The intention of this summary is to demonstrate that, when read in the correct analytical light, discursive constructionist accounts can fulfil both Durkheimian precepts. Firstly, that social reality exists outside the individual, in the form of a collective 'consciousness' that is nonetheless a product of individual activity. Secondly, that viewing social facts as *collective goods* allows us to understand the determining and constraining power of social facts over individual practices and beliefs. Within this view, structuralist and discursive accounts are neither incompatible nor irreconcilable.

The Performative Theory of Social Institutions: A Collectivist Account

Barnes' account of the sociology of knowledge is particularly useful in unpacking the dichotomy between the collective and the individual.[6] He draws attention to the nature and bases of knowledge production, and hence of the constitution of social life, by placing the collective at the centre of social dynamics. He notes that the reference of a particular linguistic predicate (of an object) is a reality that

---

5 Bourdieu explicitly reads Butler as if she suggests that actors 'perform' roles (Bourdieu 2001).
6 Barnes' account is developed in a series of texts (see 1982, 1995 and notably 1983).

is constituted by the *social* practice of making references to it; thus highlighting the fact that the performative capacity of individual referencing activities is only active in the practices of a collective of individuals. Or, as Barnes put it, "persons individually learning, and confirming what they learn, *collectively* create its reference" (Barnes 1983, 533).[7] Barnes' account can be summarized by stressing two central arguments: a) that the categories we use to refer to a specific object are part and parcel of the further constitution of that object; and b) that this effect is the result of a 'social' practice: single individual performative activity is always produced within a collective of individuals confirming and aligning with each others' individual acts.

Barnes' argument thus coincides with Butler's performative emphasis on the constitutional force of linguistic utterances. What Barnes provides in addition to Butler's model, is the emphasis on the central role of the collective. Barnes' model helps us understand that the performative effect cannot be that of single isolated individuals, but rather that of a collective of individuals interacting and, in the process of aligning themselves with each other, constituting the collective knowledge active within a community.

To fully capture the importance of this argument, we need to review some central details of his performative model. The notion of self-referentiality is central to Barnes' *performative theory of social institutions*, which introduces the notion of social and individual life as a collective accomplishment. Here the word 'collective' acquires a specific meaning that requires explication.

Social life as a 'Self-Referential Bootstrapped Induction'

In the sociology of knowledge, the notion of self-referentiality relates to debates about issues of reference and reference creation: "the relationship between our speech and that which is spoken of" (Barnes 1983, 525). Barnes' account develops an ontological understanding of the nature of the 'social' based on the mechanics of individuals' production of knowledge. He views learning, using and creating knowledge categories as central to the constitution of social life, and his account of the process of categorizing reality enables us to understand social life as collective systems of knowledge.

In examining the nature of social categories, Barnes explores category ascription in general. In order to do so he devises an (idealized) analytical distinction between categories that refer to the physical world (Natural kind terms, or NK) and the social world (Social kind terms, or SK). This distinction is not intended to reflect an empirical division in the social world as such; rather, his intention is to analyse how individuals learn and apply categories, and to reveal a process of self-referentiality within these referencing dynamics that denotes a clear social construction behind human knowledge and practices in general.

---

7   My italics.

In detailing this operation Barnes provides crucial insights into the understanding of the constitution of social life. Let us begin by analysing the use of Natural kind terms (NK), which refer to entities external to the human categories that describe them (e.g. mountain, tiger or electron). Imagine that individuals contain cognitive machinery that divides their category production into two phases. First, a 'pattern-recognizing' phase (PR), in which the external physical object (P) is recognized according to an *already* internalized pattern; and second a 'pattern attachment' activity (PA) in which a label (N) is attached to describe the external object. An important aspect of this representation is that individuals are seen as fundamentally acting inductively. In the PR stage it is essential to have observable material in order to be able to proceed with the PA phase. Here there is a clear causal relationship between external object and individuals' category ascription activity. This external object can be conceived as an 'alter-referent', an object that exists 'out there' prior to the category ascription process. However, contact with (P) is always mediated with already internalized categories (N) generated during the community's negotiations over correct usage. Such labels are thus to be conceived as self-referential in nature: label N is what the community refers to as the label N. Although it is embedded in the whole process, the social aspect (self-referential feature) of NK terms refers more to the PA phase than the PR phase.

However, SK terms exhibit a fundamental difference to NK terms. The categorization process for SK terms (marriage, authority, leadership, etc.) may equally be described as preceding the PR and PA stages. The crucial difference with SK is that the entity cannot be recognized until it has been labelled: a married person must be pronounced married before they can be recognized as such, and a leader has to be known as a leader to be taken as such.[8] Therefore, while the reality recognized (P) in NK is different from the label attached (N), demonstrating the independent existence of the 'alter-referent'; in SK terms the reality to which they refer is the same as the label attached. It does not exist outside the self-referential process, but comes to exist *precisely* in and through the referential process. Thus, the entities categorized by SK terms can be understood as being purely social, with no external reality independent of the social dynamics that constitute them and no empirical features clearly recognizable independently of our labeling practices.[9] This crucial difference between these two types of category ascription are what allows Barnes to spell out social life as a *purely* self-referential process;

---

8 This is not so much a circular process as a different way of conceiving the arrow of causation: social practice precedes the emergence of the social category.

9 I consider physical artefacts such as rings, badges, uniforms and other material aspects that endow individuals with specific social statuses as a form of self-referential entities, given that they possess a symbolic status, and thus a semiotic force, precisely because the collective ascribes it to them.

one that is 'bootstrapped' in the sense that there is no aid outside the activity of the collective.[10]

It is important to clarify a further point here in reference to SK terms. Pure self-referentiality does not preclude causality. Rather, in SK terms, causality exists in a different form than in NK terms. While in the latter causality is clearly evident from our direct contact with an physical external entity, in SK terms, causality exists in the form of specific social dynamics: hearing other people's labels, perceiving their behaviour, doing something because of it and being susceptible to the positive or negative reactions of others profoundly influences individual practices. According to this model, individual behaviour cannot be understood as free of constraints. However, the constraints are not those of an external pre-existing structure, but those of the immediate interactive collective.

Individual Inferences as Collective Accomplishments

To further clarify the significance of this emphasis on the collective, it is useful to concentrate on the emergence of SK terms. In SK terms there are no ultimate external features to guide our category ascription, so we rely on received categories or labels. These are either provided by an external authority or, as is most commonly the case, the categories are just there, active within a community of users and transmitted to one another by interaction, often ostensively. So, rather than understanding category production and ascription as the dynamics of isolated individuals learning from authoritative sources – and then individually and unproblematically using these categories in future contexts[11] – individuals' (inductively) learn from an existing pool of knowledge. Such learning is constantly permeated by the dynamics of negotiation, modification, agreement or disagreement, corresponding to a variety of factors that are ever-present in individuals' biographies (their particular cultural background, socio-economic status, ideological tendencies, characteriological propensities, and so on). However, such dynamics should not be seen as solely individual in nature, as individuals are connected to one another through constant, interactive processes of learning, negotiating and sharing knowledge.

Claiming that individuals infer from a collectively held pool of knowledge is not to suggest that this will ensure identical outcomes among a variety of individuals. The knowledge held by a collective is not the product of the aggregated inferences of isolated individuals, but the outcome of the dynamics of negotiated agreement among them. This is a key point in this analytical framework: knowledge acquires collective status only if it is accepted by other members of the collective. One

---

10   As Barnes and Bloor make clear in their writings about Natural Science, NK terms are also self-referential. The purpose of my commentary here is to emphasize the different self-referential nature of SK terms.

11   Searle provides a model which resonates with this description: once a label has been agreed by the collective, the content or meaning is fixed and it is unproblematically used by individuals in an isolated fashion (Searle 1995, 166).

of the most insightful observations offered by Barnes is that reality only *under-determines* knowledge; what fully establishes knowledge is the work of the collective. In other words, it is only by checking our individual inferences with other members of a collective that we can generate stable content and meaning of a category. Or, as David Bloor puts it:

> Collectively held normative standards come from the consensus generated by a number of interacting rule followers, and it is maintained by collectively monitoring, controlling and sanctioning their individual tendencies (Bloor 1997, 17).

Collective monitoring is a central aspect of the production of social life. The internalization of collective customs through socialization is an essential part of a process that undoubtedly generates a disposition to act in certain ways and not others, but which cannot override heterogeneity.[12] Central to the performative model of social institutions is the acknowledgement that while individuals are differing and heterogeneous beings, they are essentially mutually susceptible to the opinions and reactions of others.[13] Social monitoring is central to achieving consensus, and thus to forming patterns of behaviour. This particular point reveals how social constructionist models meet the Durkheimian precepts that social facts are collective in nature, and effect a constraining force upon individuals.

The existence of ubiquitous social sanctioning has been widely acknowledged in sociological literature.[14] The performative model adds to these accounts by explicitly detailing how sanctioning mechanisms are profoundly implicated in the constitution of collective phenomena. As Bloor notes: "we need methods for sanctioning and modifying our individual dispositions *to keep them in line*. This is mediated by verbal commentary, criticism and evaluation; e.g. by saying you can or you must" (Bloor 2001, 101).[15] Sanctioning dynamics address two crucial aspects: the generation of consensus among individuals in a collective – and thus the creation of collective good; and the constitution of this collectively held good as an 'objective-like' reality. Let me explain these two points by exploring the dynamics of social sanctioning presented by Scheff and Kusch.

---

12 Bourdieu's model is a case in point: a position that suggests that collective agreement is the product of individual socialization. An extended discussion of the problematic nature of this argument can be found in Rafanell (2002).

13 A considerable amount of research in different disciplines asserts that mutual susceptibility is essential to human nature. Particularly suggestive in this respect are the experiments carried out by psychologists like Selbya and Bradley (2003). Their data reveal the intersubjective nature of infant development and behaviour development as the product of group interaction.

14 Notably by interactionist accounts like that of Goffman (1956); Collins (1975; 1981); and Scheff (1988; 1990).

15 My italics.

Scheff makes a convincing argument of how collectives tend to punish dissent and reward conformity (Scheff 1988; 1990). His 'deference-emotion system' model stresses that conformity to norms is rewarded by deference and feelings of pride, while non-conformity is punished by lack of deference and feelings of shame. Scheff expands Goffman's tenet of the significance of face-to-face interaction and impression management by maintaining that the propensity to be susceptible to others' evaluation appears to be universal. Scheff argues that emotions like pride and shame effectively become mechanisms of social control and build conformity by generating self-monitoring processes. This deference-emotion system acts between and within interactants, efficiently aligning their individual thoughts, feelings and actions. Conformity with the collective leads to positive rewards and a sense of individual pride, generating a tendency to conform and further establish commonly held normative standards and beliefs.

That the collective good is achieved by sanctioning individual practices is further articulated in Kusch's argument that knowledge that the community takes for granted – particularly the commonly shared beliefs and undisputed practices that become platitudinal knowledge – is one of the most protected aspects of a community (Kusch 1999). He notes that collectives are inherently drawn to protect their systems of platitudes, not least because they form the basis of successful co-ordination and create the possibility of shared activity. Crucially, platitudes frequently function as standards of rationality and normativity. Violation of these standards is often punished with judgements of irrationality or accusations of 'improper' activity, while conformity with generally accepted platitudes tends to be rewarded. It is well known that individual statements (or practices) that contradict commonly held notions create feelings of perplexity among the other members of the collective. Any radical deviation will result in serious exclusion from social or even civil rights. This world of platitudes is permanently reinforced by the constant checking and resetting of individual differences in accordance with it.[16] Kusch notes that discrepancies between individual behaviour and the universe of platitudes are usually ascribed to human 'fault' rather than possible error in the platitude assumptions. This is because platitudes are commonly granted the ontological status of pre-existing, self-evident, immutable truths, external to individual activity. Because they are perceived as such, rather than as culturally conventional products, platitudes are constantly reinforced by individual practices. Thus, every single individual action that coincides with the platitudinal world further re-constitutes the universe of platitudes. Scheff and Kusch's emphasis on the role of the collective in the formation of collective goods helps further discern the Durkheimian premise of the social understood as an objective reality.

---

16 "Any human interaction is partly about checking or synchronising our plausible action explanations" (Kusch 1999, 328).

Concluding Remarks: The 'Objective' Status of Social Reality Reconstructed

The work of Scheff and Kusch expands the performative model by further grounding an ontological definition of social reality as internal to the practices of a collective of individuals, but perceived by them as external. Whilst Scheff presents internal mechanisms for achieving agreement within a collective, Kusch allows us to see how phenomena achieved by collective agreement are perceived as 'external', or objective. The strength of the performative model is that it allows us to understand social reality as a phenomenon that acquires causal status over individual activity, and is yet the product of these same individuals' activity. It thus becomes 'objective' to single individuals without being 'external' to their activity. Socially constituted reality acts with the same constraining force as an independently existing reality, although ontologically speaking it is dependent on the processes of collectively shared individual acts of categorization: if *all* humans stopped their self-referential activity, social reality would also cease to exist. This counter-intuitive argument can be clarified by comparing it with a hologram (Barnes 1993, 214), where the final image is the collective product of all the individual light beams. The disappearance of a single beam will change the final image very little, but removing a substantial number or all of the beams will radically change the image or make it disappear. This 'materialization' of social reality relies on the existence of multiple projecting points. It is a phenomenon that is 'internal' to the self-referential activity of individuals.

Thus, following the performative model, social phenomena can be understood as neither material things outside individuals' activity, nor 'mythical posits' outside space and time. On the contrary, they acquire a material status as *artefacts*, as it were: phenomena constructed by humans but perceived as objective materiality. Individuals inductively learned knowledge is constantly checked against others inductive inferences, and in the process alignment and consensus emerge. Social life is both 'inductive' and 'tautological' (Barnes 1983): inductive for the single individual, and tautological insofar as it is the product of the performative effect of a community of self-referring individuals. There is, therefore, nothing external to the community of referring agents, yet from the actors' point of view there appears to be an external reality that guides their inferences.

This view is often so internalized that it is treated as 'natural'. This is a key argument of the social constructionist account of the performative model of the strong programme: that social reality appears as external, reified, as it were, to the single individual that participates in its construction: "consensus makes norms *objective*, that is, a source of external and impersonal constraint on the individual" (Bloor 1997, 17). Individuals in large social institutions cannot intuitively be aware of the crucial role their activity plays in constituting and sustaining them. To single individuals, this constructed reality becomes *reified*, with the constraining and determining power of an external reality.[17]

The performative model provides us with the analytical tools needed to ground the form of structuralism advocated by Durkheim and the discursive constructionism developed by Butler. Barnes' performative approach helps elucidate and reconstruct Butler's argument that it is the use of language's substantives that produces the illusion that there is a 'substance' to which the language refers (Butler 1993). In Bloor's terms, it is a psychological side-effect of language and collective agreement that there is an external reality guiding our knowledge when the only reality guiding us is the collective force: "We are only compelled by rules in so far as we, collectively, compel one another" (Bloor 1997, 22). The strong programmers' ontological definition of the 'social' is thus a particular form of linguistic idealism that does not dismiss the existence of a reality 'out there'; rather, it conceives it as "a reality having no existence independent of our collective references to it" (Bloor 1997, 35).

Thus, Barnes' emphasis on the collective allows us to reconstruct Butler's model (and respond to her critics) as a constructionist approach that does not dismiss macro-structural phenomena. It allows us to see that Butler's weakness lies in failing to acknowledge that the performative activity only acquires its constitutive power when performed by a collective of mutually susceptible and interconnected individuals. Like Butler, Barnes' argument supports a form of a linguistic idealism: it is through the referring activity of individuals that social life is constituted. Unlike Butler, however, Barnes provides analytical tools to understand how this referring activity is a fundamentally collective achievement. The inferences of single individuals are only performative when connected within a collective. Individual inferences are derived from a collective system of knowledge that has no outside 'reality'; rather, it is an internal reality that is the product of the sum of the inferences of an aggregate of individuals learning, sharing and aligning their individual knowledge in and through interaction with one another.

Barnes' argument therefore allows for a genuine dialectical model between collective and individual phenomena that does not prioritize one or the other. Collectively produced phenomena are continuously generated as a result of being perpetually maintained by individuals; they are not the product of any reified external entity like norms, rules, psychological features or 'material' structures. Indeed, as Bourdieu claims, roles cannot be played at will by individuals; it is the collective alignment among individuals that leads them to experience social influences as 'compelling and irresistible', and as existing outside their practice. To reflect on Durkheim's argument: social facts are the beliefs, tendencies and practices of a group taken collectively; as such they acquire an existence in their own right, and yet are not independent of individual activity.

---

17 I developed this model regarding the constitution of sex/gender habits in Rafanell (2004).

Thus, social facts should be understood as social institutions. I have attempted to show that the discursive constructivist position of the performative model does not preclude the existence of macro-structures, but rather provides a sound ontological approach to them. What the performative model allows us to explain is that social structures can be discursively produced and yet acquire an objective status. Durkheim argues that it is via the constraining force that social facts exert over individual activity that we can perceive their objective status. For Durkheim, this is what makes social facts acquire a "sort of consistency which separates them out" (Durkheim 1982, 53) from individual activity. The performative approach allows us to see how social facts acquire an external status as more than the sum of an aggregate of single individuals' activity. As a collective achievement, they end up functioning as the background knowledge from which individuals make their inductive inferences, and as such they behave as external objects.

Crucially however, the performative model provides analytical tools to reconfigure Durkheim's externalist position. Social facts do not "function independently of the use we make of them" (Durkheim 1982, 53); rather, they exist precisely as a result of this use. As Butler puts it: "I accept that every speaking being is born into a symbolic [structural] order that is 'always' already there, but the status of this 'always-already-thereness' is also always in the process of being made and remade. It can't continue to exist without the ritualistic productions whereby it is continuously reinstalled" (Butler 1994, 36).

However, as noted above, Butler's performative model lays itself open to misinterpretation by neglecting to state that the performative constitutive force is not the effect of single individuals, but that of a collective. Barnes' model provides the precise analytical tools needed to clarify the role of the collective in performative dynamics. Central to these dynamics are mutual susceptibility and a tendency to align ourselves with other members of our immediate communities.

Consensus among individuals makes commonly shared knowledge appear 'objective' to individuals and social phenomena 'structurable'. The objectifying process also stems from the fact that self-referentiality is necessarily invisible to the single individual – particularly in large social institutions (the heterosexual matrix being a paradigmatic case in point). Individuals cannot be aware of the crucial role of self-referential dynamics in meaning formation. At the individual level, the reality constituted through interaction and self-referentiality act as a "reality out there" – it becomes objectified, reified as a 'thing' with power over individual practices. The performative model thus confirms Durkheim's insight that individuals feel compelled by a reality that transcends them, but which must not be seen as being beyond the collective of individuals and its constitutive practices.

Therefore, the ontological reality *sui generis* that Durkheim advocates can be reconfigured as a particular reality that is the product of the performative effect of the self-referential activity of a community of individuals. This model allows us to understand structural reality without falling into ahistoric and essentializing reifications of social phenomena that often unwittingly represent social reality as possessing a natural kind of materiality – either reified as a platonic entity outside the activity of individuals, or possessing the materiality of a tangible object.

Although the model of performative approaches elaborated here could be said to adopt a form of idealism, it does differ from radical idealist theories that totally discount the causality of reality. Indeed, the performative model stresses that reality has a necessary causal impact on individual acts of knowledge and practices. If we return to Barnes' explanation of pattern-matching and pattern-recognition, these operations depend on the properties of the external entity: in the case of SK, an existing background pool of knowledge, norms, beliefs, etc. is central to the ostensive learning necessary for individuals to become fully functioning social beings. Indeed, the notion of performativity as an activity that *brings about what it names* makes the performativists' linguistic idealism highly compatible with a 'robust realism'.[18]

The analytical tools of the performative model provide a way forward for conceptualizing an ontology of social reality that achieves a true synthesis between the structural world and individual activity, and thus strengthens Durkheim's ontological precepts about social reality. It is not enough to acknowledge that human activity has 'social' causes; we must explain what we mean by 'social'. Materialist sociologists should not be wary of discursive constructionism, but embrace it as a way forward in further sociologizing the 'social'. The social cannot be conceived as independent of individual activity. On the contrary, it is as a reality emerging from the continuous activity of a collective of individuals, linked by shared knowledge and mutual susceptibility, that the social acquires its own reality *sui generis*.

Acknowledgments

Thanks to David Bloor, Ivan Crozier, Hugo Gorringe, and Donald Mackenzie and the anonymous referees for their valuable feedback on the different drafts of this chapter.

References

Austin, J.L. (1970), *How to Do Things with Words: The William James Lectures Delivered at Harvard University in 1955* (Oxford: Clarendon Press).
Barnes, B. (1982), 'On the Conventional Character of Knowledge and Cognition', in Knorr-Cetina and Mulkay (eds).
Barnes, B. (1983), 'Social Life as Bootstrapped Induction', *Sociology* 17:4, 524–545.

---

18 See Bloor (1995) for an extended explanation of the point that a linguistic idealistic account can also be committed to a 'robust realism'. Rafanell (2004) proposes that the body can be profoundly implicated in the performative process and not only in verbal activity.

Barnes, B. (1993), 'Power', in Bellamy (ed.).
Barnes, B. (1995), *The Elements of Social Theory* (London: UCL Press).
Bellamy, R. (ed.) (1993) *Theories and Concepts of Politics* (Manchester: Manchester University Press).
Bloor, D. (1995), 'Idealism and the Social Character of Meaning', mimeo (unpublished transcript), Science Studies Unit, University of Edinburgh, 1–25.
Bloor, D. (1997), *Wittgenstein, Rules and Institutions* (London: Routledge).
Bloor, D. (2001), 'Wittgenstein and the Priority of Practice', in Schatzki, Knorr-Cetina and Savigny (eds).
Bordo, S. (1992), 'Review Essay: Postmodern Subjects, Postmodern Bodies', *Feminist Studies* 18:1, 159–175.
Bourdieu, P. (2000), *Pascalian Meditations* (Cambridge: Polity Press).
Bourdieu, P. (2001 [1998]), *Masculine Domination* (Cambridge: Blackwell).
Brubaker, R. and Cooper, F. (2000), 'Beyond "Identity"', *Theory and Society* 29:1, 1–47.
Butler, J. (1988), 'Performative Acts and Gender Constitution. An Essay in Phenomenology and Feminist Theory', *Theatre Journal* 40:4, 519–353.
Butler, J. (1990), *Gender Trouble: Feminism and the Subversion of Identity* (London: Routledge).
Butler, J. (1993), *Bodies That Matter: On the Discursive Limits of Sex* (New York: Routledge).
Butler, J. (1994), 'Gender as Performance. An Interview with Judith Butler', *Radical Philosophy* 67, 32–39.
Collins, R. (1975), *Conflict Sociology: Toward and Explanatory Science* (New York: Academic Press).
Collins, R. (1981), 'On the Microfoundations of Macrosociology', *American Journal of Sociology* 86:5, 984–1014.
Durkheim, E. (1982), 'What is a Social Fact', in Lukes (ed.).
Fausto-Sterling, A. (1992), *Myths of Gender: Biological Theories About Men and Women* (New York: Basic Books).
Goffman, E. (1956), 'Embarrassment and Social Organisation', *American Journal of Sociology* LXII:3, 264–271.
Jackson, S. and Jackie, J. (1998), *Contemporary Feminist Theories* (Edinburgh: Edinburgh University Press).
Knorr-Cetina, K.D. and Mulkay, M. (eds) (1982), *Science Observed. Perspectives on the Social Study of Science* (London: Sage).
Kusch, M. (1999), *Psychological Knowledge: A Social History and Philosophy* (London: Routledge).
Lukes, S. (ed.) (1982), *Durkheim: The Rules of Sociological Method and Selected Texts on Sociology and its Method* (London: Macmillan).
Rafanell, I. (2002), 'The Social Genesis of Individual Practices: an Individualistic Versus a Collectivist Account', *Edinburgh Working Papers in Sociology* (Sociology Department: University of Edinburgh).

Rafanell, I. (2004), *The Sexed and Gendered Body as a Social Institution: A Critical Reconstruction of Two Social Constructionist Models* (unpublished PhD, University of Edinburgh).

Schatzki, T.R., Knorr-Cetina, K. and Savigny, E. (eds) (2001), *The Practice Turn in Contemporary Theory* (London: Routledge).

Scheff, T. (1988), 'Shame and Conformity: The Deference-Emotion System', *American Sociological Review* 53, 395–406.

Scheff, T. (1990), *Microsociology: Discourse, Emotion, and Social Structure* (Chicago and London: The University of Chicago Press).

Searle, J.R. (1995), *The Construction of Social Reality* (London: Penguin Books).

Selbya, J.M. and Bradley, B.S. (2003), 'Infants in Groups: A Paradigm for the Study of Early Social Experience', *Human Development* 46, 197–221.

PART 2
Social Practices

The authors in Part 2 all share an ethnomethodological perspective and an emphasis on social practices. As Rawls notes, practices are an intrinsically sociological phenomenon and studies of communities of practice have their origin in sociology. All three chapters take Durkheim as a key point of reference but differ in their assessments of the significance of his work for the analysis and understanding of the nature of social practices.

Rawls continues the theme of globalization addressed by Inglis and Robertson in Part 1. She argues that globalization is progressively creating highly differentiated modern societies in which, in the absence of shared beliefs and values, solidarity is based on social practices. Traditional communities are being replaced by shared, situated practices or 'communities of practice'. Whereas classical sociology recognized the primacy of participation in social processes, contemporary sociologists tend to focus on conceptually based institutions, structures, motives and goals. Rawls claims that this emphasis on conceptual abstractions, and the corresponding neglect of the concrete details of situated practices, obscures the relationship between sociology and its object; conceptualization conceals the essential details of practice, rendering them invisible. Failure to recognize shared situated practice as sociology's object therefore threatens the position of sociology in the modern, globalized world.

Rawls contests the customary classification of Durkheim, based on his earlier empirical work, and claims that he has been misread, and misidentified with positivism. On the contrary, she claims, Durkheim recognized that practices warrant detailed study, and that essential details can be lost through generalization and classification. Moreover, he foresaw the increasing importance of shared practice for sociology as traditional belief-based societies give way to modern societies, founded in shared practices. Rawls highlights links between Durkheim's emphasis on the details of situated practices and Garfinkel's ethnomethodology, but argues that ethnomethodology goes further and shows how orderliness and intelligibility are produced by members in ongoing and recognizable ways.

Whereas Rawls portrays Garfinkel as developing Durkheim's emphasis on situated practice, Lynch argues that Garfinkel's work is in fundamental respects radically distinct from classical sociology. His reading of Durkheim is rather different to that of Rawls: *The Rules of Sociological Method* 'epitomize an extreme program of sociological positivism' (this volume: 101). Contesting Rawls' view that Garfinkel's work is a direct development of Durkheim, Lynch explores the apparent contradiction between the tenets of ethnomethodology and Garfinkel's claim that ethnomethodology is 'centred' on a restatement of Durkheim's aphorism 'the objective reality of social facts is sociology's fundamental principle'. Garfinkel's book *Ethnomethodology's Program* is subtitled 'Working Out Durkheim's Aphorism': in his chapter, Lynch is 'working out' the connection between Garfinkel and Durkheim's aphorism.

Lynch's account is informed by his seminars and tutorials with Garfinkel over ten years (1972–1982). During this period Garfinkel used Durkheim's aphorism, but, Lynch suggests, more as a resource or as an indexical 'coathanger', than with a view to authentic exposition. Garfinkel, like Durkheim, is concerned with social facts even if the examples he uses differ: the end of a queue, a recurrent traffic jam, a routine greeting sequence for instance. From an ethnomethodological perspective, their key characteristic is not their external objectivity, nor their inaccessibility to those without professional sociological training, but rather their ongoing production by those involved. Garfinkel and Durkheim agree that social facts are things, but for Garfinkel the nature of social facts and their role within sociology are rather different. Social facts (such as queues) act as tutorials for ethnomethodologists, helping them to 'retune their sensibilities' by exposing the taken for granted but unseen nature of social phenomena. Garfinkel, Lynch suggests, does not simply refer to Durkheim's social facts, but uses them as situated tutorials to 'work out' and respecify what social facts are.

Greiffenhagen and Sharrock continue the focus on social facts, suggesting that debates about whether or not there are social facts should be reframed as disagreements about the *nature* of social facts. Inflationary readings of social facts stress their ontological status as things, and link this to the development of a professional, scientific sociology. In contrast deflationary readings, their preferred approach, depict social facts as commonplace understandings, accessible to ordinary members of society. This distinction highlights an important strand of argument that runs through the readings of Durkheim given by Rawls, Lynch and others in this book.

Greiffenhagen and Sharrock critique Bloor's attempt to demonstrate that mathematical statements are social facts. Bloor's conception of social facts is inflationary; he is not simply asserting that different cultures can use different arithmetical conventions, but arguing that a sociological explanation of knowledge is applicable to mathematics. Greiffenhagen and Sharrock develop an alternative, deflationary approach, differentiating between necessity within a system and the necessity of a system. A question such as 'Must $2 + 2 = 4$?' can be asked either within the 'default' mathematical system or about the 'default system'. Within the system it is necessarily (and logically) true, but outside the system the question is either false, because there are alternative arithmetics, or meaningless. Bloor assumes that mathematical statements are social facts in an inflationary sense, and analyses the source of their necessity and facticity; in contrast, Greiffenhagen and Sharrock treat mathematical expressions as rules. These create necessity within a system, but the adoption of the system itself is, nevertheless, conventional rather than necessary. Extending their argument, Greiffenhagen and Sharrock challenge the inflationary assumption that social practices are sustained by justification. They argue that the coercive force of social practices derives not from their status as facts, but from the practical necessity that arises from their institutionalization in local customs.

Construing social facts as rules undermines their truth functional status as facts, but also explains why they are accepted as certain without justification. These rules are not learnt as justified, true propositions (Greiffenhagen and Sharrock), or through conceptual abstraction (Rawls) but acquired directly as practices through situated tutorials (Lynch). The three chapters thus all, in different ways, show why social practices are an important focus for sociology. Indeed, whilst Rawls' chapter is the only one which – intriguingly – frames its argument with reference to the historical significance of practice, all of them suggest that a certain orientation to practice raises important questions about what we might call the default system for doing sociology, and some of its problems.

Chapter 5
Communities of Practice vs. Traditional Communities: The State of Sociology in a Context of Globalization

Anne Warfield Rawls

As the economic system has globalized, producing exchange and production relations across vast spatial and cultural distances, older social forms, which work best in a context of familiarity, are giving way to a more fluid situatedness in which social "skills", have become more important than a commitment to traditional communities of belief and/or culture. David Reisman noted in *The Lonely Crowd* (1950) that this increased focus on practice was producing a distinctive modern character responsive to the immediate demands of situations rather than deeply held beliefs. Communities of practice and situated moralities of self are progressively replacing traditional communities and their values in many areas of modern life. The challenge this presents to academia, and to sociology in particular, is a serious one. The social logic of practices is really nothing like the social logic of concepts, narratives and beliefs. Consequently, academic disciplines that treat social orders as belief and concept based, and concepts as the limit of what can be known, giving pride of place to aggregation, interpretation and narrative, are failing to come to terms with situated practices as they are emerging in a modern global context. The impression of contingency and moral erosion is created where it does not in fact exist.

It can thus appear, as social forms change in a context of globalization, that sociology is losing its object as it loses its shared beliefs. But, in fact, the opposite is the case. The original sociological object, consisting of situated practices that operate independently from beliefs, is coming back into view after a long hiatus. Emile Durkheim anticipated this historical moment in 1893, arguing, in *The Division of Labor in Society*, that the social facts of practice would become the central sociological object in highly differentiated modern societies as traditional beliefs eroded, and founding a school of sociology to study those social facts in empirical detail (Rawls 2003). Beginning in the 1940s Harold Garfinkel elaborated on this insight, intensifying the focus on practice and for the first time demonstrating empirically that the coherence of practices lay, not in rules, or more formal aspects of organization, but rather, in the ability to produce social forms for one another that are recognizable in their details (Garfinkel 2006 [1948], 2008 [1952]; Rawls 2002a, 2006, 2008a).

Garfinkel's (1952, 1963, 1967) arguments with regard to "trust" and the need for mutual orientation to the "routine grounds" of ordinary activity ushered in an impressive range of studies, across many disciplines, all focused on situated communities of practice. The work of Reisman (1950) and Erving Goffman (1959) on the implications of a reliance on practice for the social construction of self and character had a similarly broad impact on developing approaches to situated personhood.

The study of communities of practice not only has its origin in sociology, but practices are themselves inherently sociological phenomena. This has created a need for and an interest in sociology among those who study situated practices. The achievement of situated order and mutual understanding and shared objects through practice, requires a great deal of coordinated social effort. That coordination takes a specific and empirically specifiable form (Garfinkel 1964, 1967, 2002; Sacks 1992; Garfinkel and Sacks 1970). The boundaries of social "objects" have socially enacted gestalt properties (Garfinkel 2008 [1952]). The commitment and cooperation required to recognize such "objects" occasion the development of new moralities of practice (Rawls 1987, 1989, 1990, 2002b; Goffman 1959).

Trust becomes a necessary feature of interpersonal relations in new and more immediate ways. It is no longer an attitude toward persons, but a necessary shared commitment to and competence with practice that is constitutive of sensemaking, identity and objects. This is a change with consequences not only for the shape of practice and the development of self and personal character, but also for the form that needs to be taken by those social institutions within which selves and practices will be accountable matters (Garfinkel 1967; Reisman 1950; Goffman 1962; Mills 1940; Rawls 1989).

The adaptability required by a rapidly changing social and economic environment requires that persons be willing to give up plans and motives based on goals (whether individual or shared), for a more fluid process, analogous to being able to "see" a next move as a possibility in a sequential series of moves; seeing possibilities in the emerging, but "recognizable", looks of things (Garfinkel 2002; Livingston 1987). Consequently, as Suchman (1999 [1987]) has shown research based on measuring the relationship between plans, motives and the goals they seek, becomes obsolete. Moves in a sequence of action are motivated by the developing contours of sequences, not by "motives" in the conventional sense. Even where more traditional types of external motivation do exist, they cannot order sequences (Garfinkel 2006 [1948]). They bring actors to those sequences, but while they may afford an "agenda", they do not supply the sequential means for achieving it.

In the more fluid and unfamiliar context of global exchange relations, the individual confronting the need to interact in unfamiliar situations with relative strangers increasingly relies on practices with which they can make sense in the absence of shared beliefs and values. In this context, situated practices provide possibilities for "seeing", for those who learn to look, and whose competence to do so can be trusted, that are closed to more traditional belief based approaches

(Garfinkel 2006 [1948]; Heath and Luff 2000; Harper 1998; Rawls 2008b). Reason itself, like morality, tends to become more completely situated in practice under such conditions (Durkheim 1933 [1893]; Rawls 1996, 2004).

This change in the form of global social relations places sociology in a unique position. Traditional notions of epistemology, reason, morality, intelligibility and social order are all giving way. First postmodernism and post-structuralism and now pragmatism challenge their validity even as questions. The situated self and situated meaning challenge the conception of the reasoning individual central to philosophy and economics (Durkheim 1933 [1893]; Garfinkel 1988, 2006 [1948]; Rawls 1996, 1998, 2004). Situated dilemmas of interpersonal relations challenge the theory of the person in psychology (Goffman 1959, 1963; Garfinkel 1956, 1967; Reisman 1950). In all cases the immediacy of the social dimension involved has been heightened. A long theoretical tradition with regard to a sociology of practice offers over a century of theory and research on which to ground the new studies, most of which were inspired by pioneering sociological research in the first place.

In a context of globalization, sociology becomes the key to understanding the integration of technology into modern life. Because people must use technologies in social settings of both work and play their use always has a social dimension. The contours of objects, including technical objects, are social (Garfinkel 2008 [1952]). Technologies must be integrated into the recognizable contours of practice. Whatever the computer, internet, cell phone, or Xerox machine require people to do must be compatible with the way people "see" things, the way they construct sequences of action, and recognize the boundaries of social events/ objects within those sequences. Thus, engineers and computer scientists must now take the sequential construction of the recognizable gestalts of social objects into account.

Not only are practices becoming more important in social life, but new technologies make it necessary for people to interface with more complex practices than before (Orr 1996; Heath and Luff 2000; Suchman 1999 [1987]; Mondada 2005). Unskilled workers must master increasingly complex technological dimensions of work, and do so in cooperation with others, while at the same time maintaining higher levels of quality in a context of increased competition (Duguid and Brown 2000; Hughes et al. 2003). Consumers using cell phones, computers and other high tech aids to everyday life are similarly challenged (Suchman 1999 [1987]; Manning 1979; Drew and Heritage 1992; Sellen and Harper 2001). While social behaviour is infinitely adaptable, when the demands of technologies conflict with fundamental prerequisites for mutually coordinated practice, the research shows that technologies, not practices, give way. It is only through the enactment of recognizable practices that actions and objects come to have mutual intelligibility (Garfinkel 1967, 2002, 2006 [1948], 2008 [1952]; Sacks 1992; Rawls 1989, 1990, 2008a; Button 1993; Button and Sharrock 1994). Therefore, the demands of practice must be understood by those who design new technologies if they are to succeed.

For all these reasons, situated practices have become the "new" essential object in the study of social relations, rendering a conventional sociology of conceptually based institutions and structures, motives and goals, obsolete. Societies as they existed in the past are no longer the essential units of social solidarity. The communities of practice that have taken their place cannot be studied through indicators that reduce practices to concepts, rendering their details invisible.

Statistical and Interpretive Sociologies

Unfortunately, the reigning commitment to reducing everything to conceptual terms has come to stand between sociology and its object. As a consequence, even studies of practice, in trying to ground themselves sociologically, generally do so in conventional conceptual and interpretive terms that do not provide an adequate foundation. There is a problem with trying to specify the boundaries of phenomenal field objects conceptually. To take a simple example, it is not possible to use the concept of a queue (or line), to find your place in any actual queue. The instruction "take your place in the queue" cannot be followed successfully if one does not know that "your place" is the "next place" at the "back" of the queue. Similarly the instruction "go to the back of the queue" means nothing if one cannot "recognize" the back of the queue. The back of the queue is a developing field of possibilities whose boundaries are recognizable only by reference to just those situated practices through which it is being constituted moment by moment, movement by movement. The recognition work required by situated practice is always detailed local work that must be coordinated between parties. It cannot be done in the abstract, or by individuals alone.

In spite of this, interpretive approaches are often confused with studies of practice and offered as a corrective for reductive approaches. But, the assumption that social orders are negotiated by a process of interpretation, moment by moment, is as problematic as the more conventional approach to social orders as the result of individual action based on plans and goals. The interpretive approach treats social orders as conceptual, the individual as an interpreter, and substitutes "indicators" of order for actual orders. An interpretive approach cannot explain *how* people manage the coordination of extremely complex social orders from second to second without misunderstanding – which they do more often than not. Such studies tend to identify practices with contingency and concepts as ways of managing contingency. Research on practices, however, shows that practices are ways of managing contingency, whereas a reliance on concepts, or treating practices as concepts, produces contingency, rather than reducing it.

Developing phenomenal fields require a full focus of attention, as oriented objects must continually be recognizably constituted for others. Turn by turn, participants must manage a sequence of moves for and with one another that display/create, without ambiguity, a shared orientation toward a particular developing social object. Because of the complexity involved, differences in orientation also manifest themselves turn by turn, moment by moment, and misunderstandings are quickly evident, and just as quickly repaired. There is no time for interpretation to occur as a planning element in directing practices. Where interpretation does occur, generally at points where turns are unexpected or unclear, interaction is temporarily turned from its ongoing course back onto itself. The process of producing an interpretation is itself a practice, also involving a developing phenomenal field, and its production cannot be explained as simply involving another act of interpretation without invoking an infinite regress.

Narrative and interpretation provide retrospective accounts of the interactional troubles that they follow. While they are ordered in their own right, in being retrospective and conceptual, they focus attention away from the details of social order that they are usually thought to provide indicators of. Furthermore, because their function is to explain *troubles*, narrative accounts inevitably highlight what went *wrong*, not what went *right*. Studies that focus on retrospective accounts will therefore produce the *appearance* that social interaction involves ongoing interpretation in a context of *contingency* in which detail is unimportant. It is not surprising then that the interpretive view concludes that social order is something of a fictive cover drawn over a reality of ongoing contingency.

Studies of practices in their details by Garfinkel and those inspired by his work show that communities of practice are orderly in ongoing detailed and recognizable ways. There appears to be more contingency and interpretation than there actually is. Persons tend to remember and focus on moments of uncertainty and contingency which mark disruptions of the ongoing process of constructing meaningful local orders together, which is otherwise largely unproblematic. Meaningful practices require a great deal of coordinated order at all points (Garfinkel 2002; Sacks 1992; Jefferson 1988; Schegloff 1992; Sacks, Schegloff and Jefferson 1974). Therefore, when disruptions do occur, interaction cannot move forward until order has been restored and either some account has been produced, or the trouble repaired. This confers a prominence on troubles, while leaving the "normal" ordinary looks of things unexamined.

It is important to realize that disruptions provide no more than clues to those points *where* practices seem to be consistently failing. They do not in themselves reveal *why* the production of order failed, or what a "normal order" at that point would have looked like. Furthermore, narratives about those failures, a widely accepted source of data about practices, are inherently misleading. They are the construction of persons after the fact, who have no idea of what the taken-for-granted practices for ordering are, because they *are* taken-for-granted. In fact, accounts, as C. Wright Mills (1940), pointed out, are vocabularies of motive that are held to standards of what is an acceptable justification in a particular institutional situation. Therefore, accounts, having the purpose of justifying and excusing in specific institutional contexts, play no role in ordering ongoing action except in so far as they occupy turn spaces and project next turns.

This focus on troubles has also shaped the development of sociology, which can be seen largely as the study of disruptions: deviance, social problems, anomie, alienation, crime, poverty, bureaucratization, class, race and gender conflict, suicide, disability, etc. This is in some sense inevitable, as breaches in ongoing interaction provide natural points where the problematic nature of order comes momentarily into view. However, the discipline has generally proceeded as though these points were directly representative of order per se, rather than symptomatic of failures in the mutual local production of order. This assumes that what was learned studying disruptions could be directly applied to orders that occur unproblematically and therefore without being noticed. It does not follow that this is the case.

Thus, statistical and interpretive sociologies render the essential detail of practices invisible and focus on topics that, while they have some potential to indicate problems in underlying orders, when taken as orders in their own right, suggest that contingency is the natural state of social order. As if this were not bad enough, there is a further problem. Although very good studies of practice in detail have been produced since the 1960s, they are generally read from a perspective that assumes social order is conceptually based. The reader replaces "doing" words with "belief" words, eliminating the detail which is the essence of the study, not even realizing that they have done so (see Rawls 1985 for an elaboration of this problem).

Reducing studies of detailed practice to conceptual and interpretive terms, the accepted practice in most disciplines, makes the research worse than useless, both theoretically and in actual settings. The arguments of both Durkheim and Garfinkel have been badly obscured in this way, as has the best research by their students and followers. The simple fact is that practices are not reducible to concepts. Nor are they generalizable, although insights drawn from studies of practice often are. The idea that everything must be reduced to concepts is itself a fallacy. Therefore, all attempts to formulate "practices" by reducing them to "recipes" that can be "applied" across multiple settings, neutralize the value of the studies, and can damage the sites where they are applied. This is not a methodological shortcoming that could be overcome by a "generalizable" method either. It is the nature of the practices themselves and must be respected if research is to be at all informative.

The details of situated practice, which are rendered invisible by traditional conceptual and quantitative approaches, are indispensable to understanding contemporary social processes. The failure of sociology as a discipline to embrace this idea has led to the ironic result that sociologists find themselves left behind, as the sociological object becomes indispensable across disciplines as Durkheim predicted. Meanwhile, engineers and computing scientists lead the way, in business schools and technical centres, studying social processes with a theoretical and research orientation that is, ironically, inspired directly by sociological studies of practice, but unacknowledged by the discipline (Rawls 2008b).

As a consequence, sociology appears to have become obsolete at the very historical moment when it has begun to drive the most innovative research across many disciplines in both the public and private sectors. This would be easier to understand if classical social theory had failed to consider the importance of situated practice and the consequences of globalization for the study of "society" in the traditional sense. Or, if Garfinkel had not initiated the study of social practice in detail starting in the 1940s. It would then simply be the case that a sociology originally focused on traditional social structures had outlived its usefulness. But, in fact, these changes were predicted by Durkheim and others in the 19th century. Durkheim's most famous work elaborated the process in some detail and urged a sociological focus on practice and forms of social connectedness, and interactionists have continued to insist on the importance of practice throughout the 20th Century.

Ironically, the discipline now being left behind was founded on Durkheim's idea that situated practice would become the principle form of social solidarity in a modern context and his elaboration of rules for the study of such practices (Durkheim 1895). A sociology based on this insight would offer solutions to problems now being faced by many academic disciplines. But, without an overhaul of theoretical assumptions and research practices dating from 1930–1950 that subsume practices to values and beliefs, the best research on practices will continue to be assimilated by theoretical perspectives that render it in conceptual terms: an intellectual castration of the first order.

Durkheim and Practices

What concerned Durkheim was that in the face of the increasing complexity, growing anomie and manifest inequality of modern life, scholars often advocated returning to a form of collective consciousness in which everything is explained by a single unifying set of beliefs and values that constrain action (Durkheim 1933 [1893], and 1928 [1962]). He feared that the form of social order advocated by such reformers, i.e. strong belief based communities, and the constraints it placed on knowledge and freedom, would destroy modern life. What philosophers and social theorists need to understand, Durkheim argued (1933 [1893], Book III, Chapter 1), is that the essence of modern life, modern science, and the potential for freedom, equality and justice, *lies in the details of practice* and their functional prerequisites (Rawls 2003).

The mistaken assumption that solidarity in modern society requires a minimum of shared belief gets in the way of setting practices free from conceptual constraint. Because people believe that beliefs are necessary for solidarity they often try to fix contemporary troubles by strengthening communities of belief. However, since solidarity in modern societies is based on shared practices, not shared beliefs, this no longer works. Old forms of generalized belief system are only disruptive in a context of modern practices. Communities of belief produce differences between people which interfere with full reciprocity and spontaneity of practice. For Durkheim (1928 [1962]) this meant that August Comte and other social thinkers, and he included socialism in this category, who believed that solidarity required allegiance to general principles, were actually impeding progress toward more egalitarian solidarities based on practice.

Another negative consequence of Comte's emphasis on general theory, according to Durkheim (1933 [1893]: 360), is that "it is said there is no need for going into detail". The detailed studies that are necessary for a sociology of practice, Durkheim argued (1933 [1893]: 361), stand in fundamental conflict with the requirements of general theorizing: "Since detailed studies make us lose sight of the whole vista of human knowledge, we must institute a particular system of researches to retrieve it and set it off." In contrast to conventional sociology, however, in the contest between general and situated details of practice, Durkheim came down on the side of details. Society is not disorganized, he argued, just because practices are now comprised of more detail and, therefore, we do not need to resort to belief based communities to strengthen solidarity. Neither should the study of social order abstract from the details of practice to construct general theories. In a differentiated socio-economic system each practice must develop its own independent, self-regulated and detailed organization as well as corresponding "trust" relations between participants. It is those details that sociology must come to know.

In describing those modern practices that cannot be reduced to general theory, Durkheim focused on science. His point was that scientific practices have become more important than the theoretical side of science. According to Durkheim (1933 [1893]: 362) "It is certain, however, that to gain an exact idea of a science one must practice it, and, so to speak, live with it. That is because it does not entirely consist of some propositions that have been definitively proved." The more active and creative side of science, can only be known through practice. According to Durkheim (1933 [1893]: 362), "Along side of this actual, realized science, there is another, concrete and living, which is in part ignorant of itself, and yet seeks itself; besides acquired results, there are hopes, habits, instincts, needs, presentiments so obscure that they cannot be expressed in words, yet so powerful that they sometimes dominate the whole life of the scholar." This taken-for-granted "habitual" element of practice is the heart of science. "All this" Durkheim says (1933 [1893]: 362) "*is still science; it is even its best and largest part*, for the discovered truths are a little thing in comparison with those which remain to be discovered." Beliefs only discover themselves. Science based on belief is circular. Practices, on the other hand, when freed from beliefs, have the potential to generate new beliefs and "discover" new "truths". It is Durkheim's position (1914 [1983]) that what is most important about modern science is that practices are allowed to self-regulate and "fly before beliefs". Unlike traditional religious cosmologies, which Durkheim also identified with science, modern science consists largely of its practices, in the form of "bench science", not its beliefs.

Attempts to organize this wealth of detail through general theory are problematic, Durkheim says (1933 [1893]: 363), because "the dissonances of detail disappear in the total harmony". As each science has come to consist in this detail, modern science itself would be lost through a focus on generalization. The procedure Durkheim adopted in 1912 for his own penultimate study of religious practice, *The Elementary Forms of the Religious Life*, was what he referred to as a "single case method" (Durkheim 1912 [1915, 1995]: 463; Rawls 2004: 136, 267–9). Focusing on a single case allowed Durkheim to preserve detail without coding, or reducing descriptions of ritual "movements and cries" to general classifications. Unfortunately, the detail proved overwhelming for readers who were searching for generalizeable categories, the point was missed and the argument generally neglected (Rawls 1996, 2004).

Durkheim's own arguments were, as a consequence, incorporated into just the sort of general theoretical perspective that he felt was so damaging. He has largely been interpreted as a proponent of studying "society" and social institutions in the abstract, and identified with Talcott Parsons's version of functionalism. Ironically, Durkheim's later efforts to include the details of practices in the sociological equation have been misinterpreted as an idealistic reduction of details to conceptual indicators, while his earlier insistence on empirical aspects of detail, and his emphasis on the natural sciences, are taken as a recommendation that sociology adopt a positivist scientific methodology.[1] As a consequence, the discipline of sociology that Durkheim was so instrumental in founding now proceeds on the basis of just the sort of conventional, value based, conceptual, theoretical and methodological hegemony he argued so forcefully against.

This misreading of Durkheim, while making his work more popular than it might otherwise have been to conservative ways of viewing social relations in the mid-Twentieth Century, renders his arguments impotent with regard to the large and important questions raised by globalization today. Yet, these questions define sociology's original territory – then and now.

Situated Practice and the Sociological Object in Classical Social Theory

While there are important differences between their positions, the major classical social theorists held several fundamental arguments with regard to practice/meaning and the social construction of self, in common with Durkheim. They all, in various ways, argued that not only concepts, but reason itself resulted from participation in social processes. They were not positivists who took the natural world and human perceptions of it as a concrete reality which could be objectively "known". But, neither did they treat concepts, whether individual or social in origin, as a primary reality. They did not begin with the individual, but rather treated as primary various sorts of relationship between persons: subject/object relations, relations of production, forms of association, Gemeinschaft vs. Gessellschaft, the enactment of ritual, and taking the attitude of the other toward the self. Different

---

1 The conflicting interpretations of Durkheim resulted in the belief that there were two different Durkheims, an earlier and a later thinker, whose positions contradict one another. This view remains popular and in my view is a great handicap to the understanding of Durkheim's overall argument. See Rawls 1996 and 2004 for an extended analysis of the continuity between Durkheim's early and later work.

forms of social relation, they held, would produce sets of concepts and forms of consciousness corresponding them.

Karl Marx, Emile Durkheim, Max Weber, George Herbert Mead and Georg Simmel all argued that the prevalent assumption that the individual is a primary reality and that the individual, or groups of individuals, are the primary fabricator of concepts is at the root of the epistemological dilemma in philosophy.[2] Marx centered his argument at several key points on a critique of individualism, echoing Jean Jacques Rousseau's (1761 [1923]) argument in his *On the Origins of Inequality* that it is capitalist "civil" society which has rendered man an individual in the philosophical sense, and therefore, the individual cannot be the starting point of analysis. Also referencing Rousseau, Durkheim (1933 [1893]) argued that the individual only comes into being under conditions of an advanced economic division of labour. Similarly, Weber (1968 [1921]), Simmel (1978 [1918]) and Mead (1924) argued that self-consciousness is the result of social relations, and that the individual, as we know it in modern society, is the result of specific industrial capitalist economic and social relations.

In an advanced division of labour context, situated practices, shared locally between persons at specific sites of exchange, would necessarily replace traditional belief based communities, which, because they are eroded by cultural contact, are not adaptable to conditions of global exchange to the same degree. Thus, as Durkheim argued, social solidarity based on shared practice would inevitably replace solidarity based on shared belief when differentiated labour and global economic exchange reached a certain dynamic density. Durkheim called this new form of solidarity based on practice "organic solidarity", a distinction he shared with Weber and Simmel, and designated what he referred to as the "social facts" of organic solidarity as the special object of sociology. This required a theory and methodology focused on practices, an argument Durkheim outlined in Book III of *The Division of Labor in Society* (1933 [1893]) reiterated in *The Rules of the Sociological Method* (1895), and illustrated with his own study of practice in *The Elementary Forms of The Religious Life* (1912 [1915, 1995]).

While Durkheim and Marx both emphasized the importance of practice, or praxis in a division of labour context, Durkheim was more or less alone in specifying practice based solidarities as a defining feature of organic solidarity in an advanced division of labour context. Since organic solidarities are held together by situated practices, the job of sociology hence-forward would be to focus on situated practices, or "communities of practice" as they are now coming to be called. This involved a focus on what Durkheim called "sounds and movements" and a recognition of their priority over concepts and beliefs (Rawls 1996, 2001, 2003, 2004).

---

2 I have included Simmel primarily for his arguments in *The Philosophy of Money* (1978 [1918]), even though there is a strong individualist aspect to some of Simmel's work. For a further discussion see my reply to Levine (Rawls 1988).

Trust, Justice and Practice

Because a transition to situated practice forced people to give up beliefs, and made "trust" relations with regard to practices necessary, it was Durkheim's position that the advancement of the division of labour created a new form of morality based on the need for justice, reciprocity and freedom for individuals in a context of situated, practice based, exchange relations. Durkheim distinguished between morality in traditional societies, which, he argued, corresponded to traditional beliefs and values, and what he called "justice" in a modern division of labour context, which, like practices, would transcend the boundaries of group beliefs and values. Justice, he said, was made necessary in a division of labour context by several functional requirements of practice based social orders that were not requirements in more traditional societies. Practices themselves demand a high degree of equality and reciprocity not needed by traditional social forms.

The arguments of Garfinkel and Goffman with regard to the need for "trust" and mutual commitment to a "working consensus" as a foundation for what Garfinkel called "stable concerted action" are consistent with this position. But, the trust and equality required by practices cannot be taken as a given. Trust and reciprocity are ongoing accomplishments, and interference with their production and display can come from either institutional or interactional levels of social order. Garfinkel and Goffman distinguished between the demands of practices, or interaction orders, and what Garfinkel referred to as "contexts of accountability" (Rawls 1987).

The important thing, as Durkheim argued, is to focus empirically on elaborating the "social facts" of social orders, to figure out *how* new social forms are produced and how they work, what is necessary to promote greater freedom and equality, allowing empirical research to precede and influence theory. A focus on theory, norms, beliefs and concepts would, he maintained, only get in the way of this endeavor, obscuring the basis of modern forms of justice and reason, in particular. Unfortunately, Durkheim himself was interpreted as advocating a theoretical and conceptual sociology of exactly the type that he was arguing against and his arguments about morality were deeply misunderstood. Thus, for much of the last century sociology has continued to be more Comtian and conceptual than Durkheimian, all the while claiming to be cast in a Durkheimian mold.

The Fallacy of Misplaced Abstraction

The Pragmatist philosopher Alfred North Whitehead (1978 [1929]: 7–13) coined the phrase "the fallacy of misplaced concreteness" in reference to the prevalence early in the 20th century for treating concepts and abstractions as though they accurately represented a concreteness of things in themselves. Current practice tends to avoid the positivist fallacy of misplaced concreteness by treating concrete reality as a mediated creation through symbols or texts. As a result there is a tendency in modern sociology and philosophy to treat experience as equivalent to conceptual systems and corresponding beliefs. Attempts to treat practices as concrete and witnessable are generally dismissed as positivist. Popular works which feature the word "practice" in their titles, such as Bourdieu's (1971 [1977]) *A Theory of Practice*, or Steven Turner's (1994) *The Social Theory of Practices*, tend to focus on the conceptual limits of meaning, not on the concrete details of practices. The fact that knowledge is ultimately shaped by the human perceiver is interpreted to mean that concepts, beliefs, and attitudes alone define the limits of human knowledge.

While Whitehead (1978 [1929]) was quite right to point out the fallacy of misplaced concreteness in the positivism and realism of his own day, it is equally problematic to argue that reality exists wholly and entirely as systems of concepts and interpretive frames. With regard to the domain of social practice, this is a fallacy in the opposite direction. I call this "the fallacy of misplaced abstraction". Social practices which are, unlike natural events, essentially concrete witnessable events produced by, for, and in the presence of others, to be "seen" and "heard" by those others as having the recognizable "gestalt" properties of interactional "moves" of very particular sorts, have been reduced to conceptual abstractions, as if those abstractions were not only an inherent characteristic of the social event, but defined its publicly recognizable character: As if an abstraction *could* make a concrete event recognizable to anyone.

The currently popular "fallacy of misplaced abstraction" needs to be distinguished from simple idealism because it doesn't treat the world itself as ideal, but only human knowledge as limited by ideas. Persons are thought to live in a demonstrably empirical world. But, it is believed they can know nothing valid or useful about that world on an empirical level. Wittgenstein's arguments not withstanding, the so-called "linguistic turn" has tended toward an examination of concepts and their relation to one another within conceptual universes, not toward conversation as concrete practice, or language as conventions of "use".[3]

A Practice View versus Pragmatism

It is currently popular to treat pragmatism and a practice view of social order and mutual intelligibility as interchangeable. However, the differences between the two positions are profound. Ironically, Durkheim and later Garfinkel were both actively engaged in debates with pragmatism, and intended sociology (as a practice oriented discipline) as a solution to the dilemmas inherent in the pragmatist position.[4] Their focus on empirical details of social practice is quite

---

3 In fact, Wittgenstein's argument about the problem of family resemblance is often used to support the view that concepts are necessarily contingent, rather than to point toward the necessity of conventions of use to overcome those contingencies.

4 Garfinkel's (2004 [1948]) engagement with pragmatism was less direct, involving an extended consideration of Schutz's (1945) debate with James in "Multiple Realities".

different from the pragmatist idea that individuals pursuing goals together develop a sufficient consensus and understanding to achieve their goals. In the modern context of globalization this difference is critical. The practice view requires a focus on enacted practices as concrete witnessable events in detail and a rejection of individualism. Pragmatism, in focusing on plans and goals, encourages a focus on a narrative context of accountability and an individual and conceptualist view, rather than on the details of practices. Such narratives also take a retrospective rather than a prospective view.

In challenging pragmatism, Durkheim argued that in addition to the origin of concepts in general in social practices, there are also certain fundamental ideas without which social cooperation and hence social solidarity are simply not possible (Rawls 1996). These basic and essential ideas (cause and classification among them), and the practices that produce them, fulfil an indispensable social function.[5] These ideas are less relative than other ideas, universal in a broad sense, because they correspond to specific and transcendent social/emotional aspects of experiencing practices. Both sorts of ideas are more intersubjectively grounded in Durkheim's schema than in pragmatism. Furthermore, because of the role played by practices in creating meaning, Durkheim argues that it is possible for a focus on practice to get to some more or less ultimate "truth" about things, as long as practices are allowed to operate free from beliefs and researchers approach the study of practice as such.

Garfinkel's approach to practice, also often conflated with pragmatism, is more focused than Durkheim's on the argument that the details of practices, in empirically specifiable ways, give meaning to words and symbols, rather than the reverse. Garfinkel points out that in spite of the indexicality of most words and actions, they are not experienced as ambiguous. In the concrete circumstances of their use, in ordered sequences, their meaning is given by the developing phenomenal field contours of the practices of which their "saying" or "seeing" is a part. Garfinkel also sharpens the distinction between contexts of accountability and the ongoing production of taken-for-granted orders, that pragmatism conflates.

Turn by turn, sequence by sequence, interaction orders are built up in which developing conversational moves can be seen as moves of very particular sorts (Rawls 1989, 1990). Persons are not left trying to decode "words", or sorting through "noise", for relevant sounds. The gestalt properties of the developing boundaries of interactional forms are either clear or not – and when they are not – things do not just continue. Under such conditions turns exhibit problems, "hitches" as Schegloff refers to them, and repairwork is implicated (Schegloff 1992).

Practices stand in a constitutive relationship to the meaning of words, which is a different relationship from representation, in which words are supposed to refer to things. The developing contours of practices create the meanings that

---

5 This is Durkheim's functionalism, a much more radical idea that later interpretations give him credit for.

words are in particular situated occasions of use. Thus, Durkheim's theory of meaning is a precursor to Wittgenstein's argument that meaning is a function of use. Garfinkel elaborates what meaning as "use" looks like in practice. Neither treats meaning as a referential relationship. For Durkheim, the association of the sign with the emotion felt when engaged in the practice *recalls* the essentially social and collective *feelings* created by the practice, feelings that were shared by all participants, not individual thoughts or concepts. Thus, in Durkheim's view, it is the experience of collective emotion and for Garfinkel the production and recognition of phenomenal fields, that form the boundaries of concepts, not concepts that form the boundaries of thought and experience.

Because of these differences, reading Durkheim, and more recently Garfinkel, from a pragmatist perspective has been damaging to sociology as a discipline. Although pragmatism was a distinct improvement over enlightenment individualism, the practice position as articulated by Durkheim and fully elaborated by Garfinkel, established a distinctive sociological perspective that went much farther toward grounding the essential philosophical questions in the social and not in individualism.

Conclusion

There is a significant difference between science, the humanities, and sociology, which the tendency to render social practices in conceptual terms obscures. Sociology stands in a very different relationship to its object. Whereas the humanities must try to reconstruct the context in which a text was originally constructed (by a single author working alone), the sociologist stands in the midst of the ongoing construction of texts (by persons working cooperatively together). Society is produced and reproduced all around us all the time. As persons sociologists constantly take part in the social scenes they study and they do have access to the original scenes as they unfold. Sociology as a discipline is interested in all forms of social life. Therefore, the data are everywhere. The job is not to interpret already existing texts, but to see how it is that persons recognizably construct for and with one another, out of the infinite detail of lived experience, the mutually understood sounds and movements that are the prerequisite for the eventual construction of texts, narratives, accounts, statistics, and so on.[6]

---

6 Ignoring the importance of mutual engagement leads to the adoption of an "objective" scientific standpoint from which to perform the conceptual reduction. The problem is that an unengaged standpoint loses for the observer the character of recognizability, which is achieved moment by moment, sequence by sequence without which practices have no ongoing meaning. Sociologists working with "records" and "record work", even though faced with texts, have the task of situating those texts in the mundane practices involved in their production.

In spite of these differences between sociology and the humanities and sciences, sociologists generally treat the problems confronted by science and the humanities as though they are also our problems. Sociologists who study enacted social practice do not confront a reality that is already coded into conceptual typifications. But, they generally believe that they do. They may code it as fast as they experience it. But, it is nevertheless there in front of them in all of its infinite detail. This "infinite" detail is often considered to be the problem. But, it was not a problem for the people we study. Social practice does not need to be coded into sounds and movements out of a meaningless flux of experience. The movements that constitute practices are constructed as recognizable phenomenal fields of movement in the first place. "Words" are not fluxes of sound on which conceptual boundaries need to be imposed, although many scholars believe otherwise. They are sounds constructed by speakers in specifiable situations to be identifiable as words, and not only as words, but as specific words. The work of hearing the "words" may require a careful and selective monitoring of sound. But, the words are not built up out of pieces of sound heard, or interpreted. They are either recognizable, or not recognizable, as having the gestalt properties of a "word".

The detail of such constructions is difficult to "see" when, as Garfinkel (1967) points out, the process of producing and recognizing such detail is "taken for granted". The researcher must figure out how to make work that is ordinarily unseen visible. The research process can be aided by modern methods of data recording which allow for multiple viewings. However, even traditional field methods, depending on nothing more than observational skills, frequently preserve interaction in enough detail for the witnessable sounds and movements that constituted the social order and meaning of the original scenes to be recognizably reconstructed. The critical thing is to recognize the practices themselves as the sociological object and stop reducing them to concepts.

In fact, sociology has gone much farther than the sciences in holding itself to a false model of abstraction. Social science generally assumes that the underlying narrative of beliefs and norms, and the behavioural tendencies generated by those beliefs, are more important than the concrete witnessable details of social practice. Actions are analysed in relation to norms and values, or concepts (most often via secondary data sets), and not in their own right. Only in aggregate tendencies toward norms and values, or in shared beliefs and interpretations, are patterns of order expected to appear, a set of assumptions Garfinkel (1988, 2002) refers to as "Parson's Plenum". The emphasis on aggregation and institutional "macro" structures in contemporary sociology is ironically the result of an inherent individualism that crept into the discipline in the mid-twentieth century, largely under the influence of Parsons.

The advantage of the classical sociological position over pragmatism, postmodern, structural, interpretive and philosophical positions, is that classical social theory did not begin with individual experience. Nor did it begin with the idea of a pre-existing or pre-defining conceptual universe. Classical social theorists did not reduce everything to concepts. Rather, they argued that attention to the empirical details of social relations was necessary in order to establish the forms of association which were behind any particular conceptual reality. But, neither were they positivist. Classical social theorists treated empirical details as socially constructed social objects and society itself as an inherently social construction, in which social identities, not individuals, participated.

Durkheim argued that society, the social being, and shared meaning were simultaneous achievements by and through enacted practice (Rawls 1996, 1997). For Durkheim this is possible only if ritualized movements and sounds come to be associated with feelings that are actually simultaneously produced in an assembled group by the mutual enactment of those movements and sounds (Rawls 1996, 2004). From a point where individuals enact practices together, and in unison, recognizable movements and sounds come to have a shared public meaning. It is the public nature of the ritual, or "language game" which sets limits on meaning and tells participants which feelings or beliefs to associate with the event, not their individual perceptions and feelings.

A focus on practices changes the type of information relevant to sociology. Demographic information about populations, for instance, is not relevant in a context in which the only thing that matters about people is their competence to engage in a particular situated practice. If people are prevented from participating in practices, by conditions such as blindness, for instance, that information may be relevant. But, even then, demographic information does not reveal *how* practices are organized and *why* it is that certain categories of people find themselves excluded (Coates 2003; Coates and Rawls 2004). Any understanding of *what* is going wrong requires an analysis of practice in detail. In spite of these very serious limitations, demographic information is still considered one of the most reliable foundations on which to model social orders. Similarly, narrative accounts based on interviewing are, for all the reasons reviewed here, misleading in the absence of detailed data on practices.

What persons need to know about one another in orders constituted through practice is whether they have the competence to produce and recognize practices and whether they can be trusted to do so. It is not necessary to know about beliefs and values except in so far as they affirm or deny a general commitment to orders of practice. What sociology needs to know is what those practices are and to know them in their sequential details.

References

Bourdieu, P. (1971 [1977]), *Outline of a Theory of Practice* (Cambridge: Cambridge University Press).

Brown, J.S. and Duguid, P. (2000), *The Social Life of Information* (Boston, MA: Harvard Business School Press).

Button, G. (1993), 'The Curious Case of the Disappearing Technology', in Button (ed.), 10–28.

Button, G. (ed.) (1993), *Technology in Working Order* (London: Routledge).
Button, G. and Sharrock, W. (1994), 'Occasioned Practices in the Work of Software Engineers', in Jirotka and Goguen (eds).
Coates, D.C. (2003), 'Sir! Do You Want Your Change!', Annual meeting of the American Sociological Association, Atlanta, GA.
Coates, D.C. and Rawls, A.W. (2004), 'The Local Work of Visual Impairment and Blindness', Annual meeting of the American Sociological Association, San Francisco, CA.
Drew, P. and Heritage. J. (1992), *Talk at Work: Interaction in Institutional Settings* (Cambridge: Cambridge University Press).
Durkheim, E. (1895), *The Rules of the Sociological Method* (Chicago: Free Press).
Durkheim, E. (1912 [1915, 1995]), *The Elementary Forms of the Religious Life* (Chicago: Free Press).
Durkheim, E. (1914 [1983]), *Pragmatism and Sociology*, trans. J.C. Whitehouse, edited and introduced by J.A. Alcock (Cambridge: Cambridge University Press).
Durkheim, E. (1928 [1962]), *Socialism*, trans. C. Sattler (New York: Collier Books).
Durkheim, E. (1933 [1893]), *The Division of Labor in Society* (Chicago: Free Press).
Garfinkel, H. (1952), 'The Perception of the Other: A Study in Social Order' (unpublished PhD dissertation, Harvard University).
Garfinkel, H. (1956), 'Some Sociological Concepts and Methods for Psychiatrists', *Psychiatric Research Reports* 6, 181–195.
Garfinkel, H. (1963), 'A Conception of and Experiments with "Trust" as a Condition of Stable Concerted Actions', in Harvey (ed.).
Garfinkel, H. (1964), 'Studies of the Routine Grounds of Everyday Activities', *Social Problems* 11, 225–250.
Garfinkel, H. (1967), *Studies in Ethnomethodology* (Englewood Cliffs, New Jersey: Prentice-Hall).
Garfinkel, H. (1988), 'Evidence for Locally Produced Naturally Accountable Phenomena of Order, Logic, Reason, Meaning, Method, etc. in and as of the Essential Haecceity of Immortal Ordinary Society', *Sociological Theory* 6:1, 103–109.
Garfinkel, H. (2002), *Ethnomethodology's Program: Working Out Durkheim's Aphorism* (Boulder, CO: Rowman & Littlefield).
Garfinkel, H. (2006 [1948]), *Seeing Sociologically* (Paradigm Publishers: Boulder Colorado).
Garfinkel, H. (2008 [1952]), *Toward a Sociological Theory of Information* (Paradigm Publishers: Boulder Colorado).
Garfinkel, H. and Sacks, H. (1970), 'On Formal Structures of Practical Action', in McKinney and Tiryakian (eds).
Goffman, E. (1959), *The Presentation of Self in Everyday Life* (Chicago: Free Press).

Goffman, E. (1962), *Asylums: Essays on the Social Situation of Mental Patients and Other Inmates* (New York: Doubleday Anchor).
Goffman, E. (1963) *Behavior in Public Places: Notes on the Social Organization of Gatherings* (New York: Free Press).
Harper, R. (1998) *Inside the IMF: An Ethnography of Documents, Technology and Organizational Action* (London: Academic Press).
Harvey, O.J. (ed.) (1994), *Motivation and Social Interaction* (New York: Ronald Press).
Heath, C. and Luff. P. (2000), *Technology in Action* (Cambridge: Cambridge University Press).
Hughes, J., Martin, D. and Rouncefield, M. et al. (2003), 'Dependable Red Hot Action', in Kuutti, Karsten and Fitzpatrick et al. (eds).
Jefferson, G. (1988), 'On the Sequential Organization of Troubles Talk in Ordinary Conversation', *Social Problems* 35, 418–441.
Jirotka, M. and Goguen, J. (eds) (1994), *Requirements Engineering: Social and Technical Issues* (London: Academic Press).
Kuutti, K., Karsten, E. and Fitzpatrick, G. et al. (eds) (2003) *Proceedings of ECSCW '03* (Helsinki, Finland: Kluwer Academic Publishers).
Latour, B. and Weibel, P. (eds) (2005), *Making Things Public: Atmospheres of Democracy* (Cambridge, MA: The MIT Press).
Livingston, E. (1987), *Making Sense of Ethnomethodology* (New York: Routledge and Kegan Paul).
Manning, P.K. (1979), 'Metaphors of the Field: Varieties of Organizational Discourse', *Administrative Science Quarterly* 24, 660–671.
McKinney, J.C. and Tiryakian, E.A. (eds) (1970), *Theoretical Sociology* (New York: Appleton-Century Crofts).
Mead, G.H. (1924), *Mind Self and Society* (Free Press: Chicago).
Mills, C.W. (1940), 'Situated Action and the Vocabulary of Motives', *American Journal of Sociology* 5, 904–13.
Mondada, L. (2005), 'BEcomING COLLECTIVE: The Constitution of Audience as an Interactional Process', in Latour and Weibel (eds).
Orr, J. (1996), *Talking About Machines: An Ethnography of a Modern Job* (Ithaca: Cornell University Press).
Rawls, A.W. (1985), 'Reply to Gallant and Kleinman On Symbolic Interaction versus Ethnomethodology', *Symbolic Interaction* 8:1, 121–140.
Rawls, A.W. (1987), 'The Interaction Order Sui Generis: Goffman's Contribution to Social Theory', *Sociological Theory* 5:2, 136–149.
Rawls, A.W. (1989), 'Language, Self, and Social Order: A Re-evaluation of Goffman and Sacks', *Human Studies* 12:1, 147–172.
Rawls, A.W. (1990), 'Emergent Sociality: A Dialectic of Commitment and Order', *Symbolic Interaction* 13:1, 63–82.
Rawls, A.W. (1996), 'Durkheim's Epistemology: The Neglected Argument', *American Journal of Sociology* 102:2, 430–482.

Rawls, A.W. (1997), 'Durkheim and Pragmatism: A Old Twist on a New Problem', *Sociological Theory* 15:1, 5–29.

Rawls, A.W. (1998), 'Durkheim's Challenge to Philosophy: Human Reason as a Product of Enacted Social Practice', *American Journal of Sociology* 104:3, 887–901.

Rawls, A.W. (2001), 'Durkheim's Treatment of Practice: Concrete Practice vs Representations as the Foundation for Reason', *The Journal of Classical Sociology* 1:1, 33–68.

Rawls, A.W. (2002a), Editor's introduction to *Ethnomethodology's Program: Working Out Durkheim's Aphorism*, by Harold Garfinkel (Boulder, CO: Rowman & Littlefield).

Rawls, A.W. (2002b), French translation of Rawls (1996), *The Mauss Review* 19.

Rawls, A.W. (2003), 'Conflict as a Foundation for Consensus: Contradictions of Industrial Capitalism in Book III of Durkheim's Division of Labor', *Critical Sociology* 29:3, 295–335.

Rawls, A.W. (2004), *Epistemology and Practice: Durkheim's The Elementary Forms of Religious Life* (Cambridge University Press: Cambridge).

Rawls, A.W. (2006) Editor's introduction to *Seeing Sociologically*, by Harold Garfinkel (Boulder, CO: Paradigm Publishers).

Rawls, A.W. (2008a), Editor's Introduction to *Toward a Sociological Theory of Information*, by Harold Garfinkel (Boulder, CO: Paradigm Publishers).

Rawls, A.W. (2008b), 'Harold Garfinkel, Ethnomethodology and Workplace Studies', *Organization Studies* 29:5, 701–732.

Reisman, D. (1950), *The Lonely Crowd* (New Haven, CT: Yale University Press).

Rousseau, J.J. (1761 [1923]), 'A Discourse upon the Origin and Foundation of the Inequality among Mankind', in *The Social Contract and Discourses*, translated by G.D.H. Cole (London and Toronto: J.M. Dent and Sons).

Sacks, H. (1992), *Lectures in Conversation* (Oxford: Blackwell Press).

Sacks, H., Schegloff, E. and Jefferson, J. (1974), 'The Simplest Systematics for the Organization of Turntaking in Conversation', *Language* 50, 696–735.

Sellen, A.J. and Harper, R. (2001), *The Myth of the Paperless Office* (Cambridge, MA: The MIT Press).

Schegloff, E.A. (1992), 'Repair after Next Turn: The Last Structurally Provided Defense of Intersubjectivity in Conversation', *American Journal of Sociology* 97:5, 1295–1345.

Simmel, G. (1978 [1918]), *The Philosophy of Money* (New York: Routledge).

Suchman, L. (1999 [1987]) *Plans and Situated Action: The Problem of Human Machine Communication* (New York: Cambridge University Press).

Turner, S. (1994), *The Social Theory of Practices: Tradition, Tacit Knowledge, and Presuppositions* (Oxford: Polity Press).

Weber, M. (1968 [1921]), *Economy and Society*, trans. and edited by Roth and Wittich (New York: Bedminster Press).

Whitehead, A.N. (1978 [1929]), *Process and Reality* (New York: Macmillan).

Chapter 6
Working Out What Garfinkel Could Possibly be Doing with "Durkheim's Aphorism"

Michael Lynch

Introduction

In some of his writings published over the past decade, Harold Garfinkel (1996; 2002) draws strong and explicit linkage between ethnomethodology's program and what he calls *Durkheim's aphorism*: "the objective reality of social facts is sociology's fundamental principle".[1] Since, to many readers, the doctrines and principles in Durkheim's *Rules of Sociological Method* (1982 [1895]) epitomize an extreme program of sociological positivism (a program that Durkheim himself seemed to move away from in his later work on religion and classification), it may seem puzzling that Garfinkel, of all people, would say that ethnomethodology's program is a matter of "working out" Durkheim's aphorism. Of course, he does not simply adopt Durkheim's aphorism, without first translating it into a characteristically long multi-clausal sentence:

> For its investigations, ethnomethodology took this to mean the objective reality of social facts, in that and just how every society's locally, endogenously produced, naturally organized, naturally accountable, ongoing, practical achievement, being everywhere, always, only, exactly and entirely members' work, with no time out, and with no possibility of evasion, hiding out, passing, postponement, or buyouts, is thereby sociology's fundamental phenomenon (Garfinkel 1996: 11).

Garfinkel (1996: 11, n. 17) asserts that his "restatement" of the aphorism, which loads it with a complicated sense that Durkheim could hardly have intended, identifies ethnomethodology's "center". Still, the very idea that there is such a center, let alone one that somehow is related to Durkheim's *Rules*, can be very jarring to read for those of us who have held very different ideas about the origins

---

1   This "aphorism" apparently is Garfinkel's paraphrase. A similar statement appears in the Preface to the Second Edition of Durkheim's *Rules* (1982 [1895]: "... our basic principle, that of the objectivity of social facts", 45). Rawls (2002: 2, n. 2) writes that this is a "condensed version" of the argument in the first chapter of the 1st edition.

and import of ethnomethodology.[2] No less jarring is the apparent endorsement Garfinkel gives to scholarly work that interprets Durkheim's theoretical writings as though they were setting the table for ethnomethodology.[3] It is jarring because Garfinkel has long insisted, and continues to insist that his program makes a radical break with what he calls "the classics" of the social sciences and, more broadly, with virtually all extant literature on social action and organization. Major philosophers and social theorists have been known to change their views over time, sometimes radically, but in this case Garfinkel's apparent reverence for Durkheim coexists with his continued insistence on a radical break with "the classics". At the very least, this presents a puzzle despite, and even because of, the existing scholarship on the subject. In this chapter, I attempt to work out ethnomethodology's relation to Durkheim's aphorism. My aim is not to restore intellectual consistency in the face of an apparent contradiction, as much as it is to make an issue of the challenge that Garfinkel's program offers to any attempt to reconcile it with Durkheim's *Rules*. This is not to deny the possibility of using the amoeboid resources of interpretative theory to achieve such reconciliation; instead, it aims to indicate what such a literary effort is likely to bypass or slither over.

The Turn to Things

This chapter will have much more to say about how Garfinkel and ethnomethodology take up selected lines from Durkheim than about what Durkheim may or may not have originally meant. I leave it to Durkheim scholars to determine if *The Rules of Sociological Method* can be read in light of Durkheim's later writings to express a consistent epistemology or sociology of knowledge (Lukes 1973; Gieryn 1982; Bloor 1982), and to decide if Durkheim could possibly have anticipated anything close to ethnomethodology's treatment of social facts when he wrote *The Rules*. To my reading, the program laid out in *The Rules* seems consistent with the

---

2 A similar point is made by Martin Hammersley (2005: 143) in a review of Garfinkel (2002). My own, anti-foundationalist, or better a-foundationalist, conception of ethnomethodology is presented in Lynch (1993). Also see many of the contributions in Button (1991).

3 Garfinkel (1996: 11, n. 19) strongly and explicitly endorses a "startling article" by Anne Rawls (1996) on Durkheim's epistemology, though he leaves to the reader's imagination just how ethnomethodology stands toward Rawls' reconstruction of Durkheim's "neglected argument". As the adjective "startling" perhaps indicates, Garfinkel's endorsements can express ironic and contradictory nuances. I am unaware of whether Garfinkel has endorsed Hilbert's (1992) similar effort to trace ethnomethodology to the classical sociological theories of Weber and Durkheim. Both Rawls and Hilbert argue that Talcott Parsons was responsible for establishing interpretations of classical social theory that suppressed, bypassed or ignored a program for sociology presented in the original works that ethnomethodology subsequently developed.

methodology exemplified in Durkheim's *Suicide* (1959 [1897]),[4] and expresses a scientific ambition that is less rather than more nuanced than the epistemology laid out, for example, in Parsons' first volume of *Structure of Social Action* (1937).

Turning Away from Parsons

Parsons claimed to derive his theory of social action from an analysis of the writings of Durkheim and three other major European social and economic theorists (the others were Weber, Pareto and Marshall). While Parsons also trades in scientific idioms,[5] he also expresses an understanding of philosophy of science that owes a strong debt to the neo-Kantian intellectual milieu at Harvard in which Thomas S. Kuhn later cultivated his historical and philosophical conceptions of science under the tutelage of James B. Conant (Hickey 2005: Book VI). Particularly striking in the context of the present discussion is Parsons' (1937: 41–2) "Note on the Concept of 'Fact'" in which he endorses a definition from Harvard economist Lance J. Henderson that stresses that a fact is not simply a thing in the world, but is a *statement* or proposition that frames worldly phenomena in terms of a "conceptual scheme"; a scheme that, in turn, incorporates normative elements specific to a given historical culture. That picture of conceptually and normatively framed reality strongly captivated sociologists in the following decades, but Garfinkel turned away from it and instead took up Husserl's injunction to turn toward "the things [phenomena] themselves".

While it is fair to say that Garfinkel is not, or is no longer, a Parsonian, when he turns away from Parsons' neo-Kantian edifice of functional categories and institutional norms, roles, and actions, this does not mean that he reverts to Durkheim's things. Nor does he simply adopt Husserl's transcendental phenomenology. Garfinkel and other ethnomethodologists rarely explicate "the things themselves" from a first-person, phenomenological standpoint, but they also do not treat those things as objects to be explained through causal statements. Like the phenomenologists, ethnomethodologists delve into the constitutive organization of those things. They elaborate on the practical, embodied and concerted production of ordinary and unordinary phenomena as various as traffic jams, mathematical

---

    4   For example: "… certain currents of opinion, whose intensity varies according to the time and country in which they occur, impel us, for example, towards marriage or suicide, towards higher or lower birth-rates, etc. Such currents are plainly social facts. At first sight they seem inseparable from the forms they assume in individual cases. But statistics afford us a means of isolating them" (Durkheim 1982: 55).

    5   In the first two chapters and appended notes of his first volume, Parsons (1937) introduces his exegesis of the four European theorists by invoking experimental idioms, suggesting that he derived a core of common thematic elements from a careful comparison of theoretical writings by authors from distinct disciplinary and national backgrounds. Note B, an appendix to Chapter 2 of the first volume of *The Structure of Social Action* (1937: 77 ff.), exhibits Parsons' penchant for couching his conceptual arguments in the guise of mathematical equations.

proofs, and optical pulsars (Livingston 1987; Garfinkel et al. 1981). The aim of such explications is not to come up with formal laws that describe or statistically characterize social facts, but come to terms with the concerted actions (with all of their contingencies, tacit organizations, improvisations, and detours) that achieve "facts on the ground".

Durkheim's Science

I'm inclined to agree with Stephen Lukes (1982: 8) that Durkheim's model of social causation seems to draw upon analogies from 19th century physics and chemistry, which have little currency in latter-day philosophy of science. To my reading, many of Durkheim's assertions in *The Rules* seem plain on the face of them. There is little subtlety to them, and I don't believe that sociologists misread *The Rules*, either when they criticize Durkheim for promoting a positivistic view of science (one that preceded the Vienna Circle's more subtle program of logical positivism), or when they credit him with being a predecessor (if not the originator) for the program of multivariate analysis that dominated American sociology departments in the postwar era. Take, for example, a sample of statements from the first two chapters of *The Rules* (Durkheim 1982):

> ... there are ways of acting, thinking and feeling which possess the remarkable property of existing outside the consciousness of the individual (51).

> ... the public conscience restricts any act which infringes them by the surveillance it exercises over the conduct of citizens and by the special punishments it has at its disposal (51).

> ... we are the victims of an illusion which leads us to believe we have ourselves produced what has been imposed upon us externally (53).

> Indeed the notions just discussed are those *notions vulgares*, or *praenotiones*, which he [Francis Bacon] points out as being at the basis of all the sciences, in which they take the place of facts. It is these *idola* which, resembling ghost-like creatures, distort the true appearance of things, but which we nevertheless mistake for the things themselves (62).

> Social phenomena must therefore be considered in themselves, detached from the conscious beings who form their own mental representations of them. They must be studied from the outside, as external things, because it is in this guise that they present themselves to us (70).

> ... we will relapse into past errors unless we submit ourselves to a rigorous discipline. ... *One must systematically discard all preconceptions* (72).

[On Descartes' skepticism and Bacon's doctrine of idols – 'to question all ideas ... previously accepted [and] ... to use only concepts that had been scientifically worked out ... all those of another origin had therefore to be rejected, at least for the time being']: The two great doctrines, so often placed in contradiction to each other, agree on this essential point (72).

He [the sociologist] must free himself from those fallacious notions which hold sway over the mind of the ordinary person, shaking off, once and for all, the yoke of those empirical categories that long habit often makes tyrannical (73).

The mere fact of subjecting them, as well as the phenomena they express, to cold, dry analysis is repugnant to certain minds. The sociologist who undertakes to study morality objectively as an external reality seems to such sensitive souls bereft of moral sense, just as the vivisectionist seems to the ordinary person devoid of normal feelings (73).

One cannot protest too strongly against this mystical doctrine which – like all mysticism, moreover – is in essence only a disguised empiricism (74).

... the condition for any objectivity is the existence of a fixed vantage point to which the representation may be related and which allows all that is variable, hence subjective, to be eliminated (82).

Thus when the sociologist undertakes to investigate any order of social facts he must strive to consider them from a viewpoint where they present themselves in isolation from their individual manifestations (82–83, emphasis in original).

The picture I get from such statements is of a program for a scientific discipline with a distinctive subject matter: social facts. Such facts are *objective*, in the sense of being observable, and external to and independent of the observer. As *social* facts they involve collectivities of persons, and they must be discerned at the collective level (for example, through the use of statistical surveys), because individual persons caught up in particular circumstances of their lives are not equipped to observe them. Ordinary folk may have vulgar prenotions, characterized by partial, distorted, "subjective" conceptions of the facts, but it is necessary to test and correct these notions with rigorously disciplined empirical methods. The "fixed vantage point" provided by such methods enables professional sociologists to expose the variable, circumstantially relative, and vulgar prejudices, mystical doctrines, and Baconian idols that circulate at large. Durkheim revels in the severity of this (imagined) discipline: a presuppositionless mentality that takes the sociologist far from the crowd, requiring a kind of stoic detachment from common belief and morality, which ordinary folk might liken to the repugnant craft of the vivisectionist. He also strives for generality, advising the sociologist analytically to isolate social facts from the particularities of time and place in which they occur in any given instance.

The Documentary Method of Theorizing

I do not intend to suggest that there is no possibility of (mis)reading *The Rules* in light of Durkheim's later work (especially Durkheim 1995), or in light of the much-later development of ethnomethodology. One can, for example, pick out some of Durkheim's (1982) expressions which seem akin to the Husserlian effort to secure a presuppositionless vantage point detached from the natural attitude, from which it is possible to grasp the "things themselves". And, since Garfinkel is explicit about his debt to Husserl and phenomenology, one could thereby link ethnomethodology to Durkheim's *Rules*. Seizing upon such verbal homologies would conflate Durkheim's facts with Husserl's things,[6] but more importantly it would miss the point of what Garfinkel *does* with Durkheim, Parsons, Husserl, and others in the pantheon of theorists and philosophers.

To appreciate that point, it is necessary to accomplish a kind of gestalt switch: instead of taking literary connections as evidence of stable theoretical influences, view them as local documentary accomplishments. Viewed in this way, it is entirely compatible with ethnomethodology's program to claim or even demonstrate that Durkheim's texts can be read retrospectively, in light of later theoretical developments. However, one also can selectively translate passages from Marx, Weber, Parsons, or virtually any other classic theorist into statements that seem roughly compatible with familiar programmatic themes and statements from Garfinkel and other ethnomethodologists.[7] Garfinkel's (1967: Ch. 3) remarkable essay on "the documentary method of interpretation" suggests as much.[8] The

---

6   Hammersley (2005: 143) makes a similar point that "the social facts in which Durkheim is interested contrast sharply in character with those of Garfinkel; unlike Durkheim, Garfinkel is not interested in causality".

7   One can develop such translations for other programmes as well. See, for example, Robert K. Merton's (1949: Ch. 1) translations of passages from Marx into the idioms of functional analysis. Also see C. Wright Mills' (1959: Ch. 2) translations of passages from Parsons into "plain language". In those cases the translations are evidently tendentious, and of course the fact that they can be done does not mean they are convincing.

8   Garfinkel (1996: 18) observes that the documentary method is "a convenient gloss" which is "too powerful" in its coverage – "undiscriminating". While this may be so, Garfinkel's *demonstrations* of the documentary method have unmistakable implications for sociological theory and methodology. The proximal source of the documentary method of interpretation is an essay in which Karl Mannheim (1952) recommends a way of reading historical materials to find an underlying pattern. While one might figure that Mannheim's interpretive method would be a difficult undertaking, Garfinkel shows that it is far too easy and the difficulty is to keep it from running amok. Although "the documentary method" may be too undiscriminating for use as a research method, Garfinkel's treatment of Mannheim's historical method not only gives us insight into a ubiquitous sense-making practice, it also

question is, what does such a reading demonstrate about ethnomethodology's relation to classical sociology? Does such a reading of Durkheim expose the "classic roots" of ethnomethodology (Hilbert 1992; cf. Coulter 1993), or is something else going on?

I suggest that something else must be going on. I do not think that a theoretical genealogy is the appropriate way to characterize Garfinkel's relation to Durkheim. This does not mean that it is incorrect, but that it misses the point. By a theoretical genealogy, I mean an intellectual history that articulates a set of thematic, ideological, or methodological lines of influence from earlier to later writers or thinkers. If one were to conduct such a genealogy in Garfinkel's case, it would be possible to trace a line back through Parsons, and then to Weber and Durkheim, allowing for Garfinkel's recovery of "neglected" aspects of Durkheim's and Weber's theorizing.

The problem with such a constructed lineage is that Garfinkel treats the line of sociology from Weber and Durkheim through Parsons as a subject of "respecification", and his main philosophical resource for initiating such respecification is found in the phenomenological writings and teachings of Gurwitsch, Schutz, Husserl, Heidegger, and Merleau-Ponty. Even with the phenomenologists, Garfinkel stresses that his relation to their writings is disrespectful; that is, he advises that we should "misread" them without embarrassment. Moreover, this misreading is not a matter of synthesizing their work with classic sociological writings, or any other body of theoretical literature. Instead, it is a matter of (re)reading classical social theory, phenomenology, and other writings as though they spoke directly to the conceptual distinctions, practical requirements, and procedures made perspicuous through an engagement with specific constitutive practices. Accordingly, ethnomethodological *investigations* furnish the motives and insights for re-examining familiar sociological and phenomenological topics, distinctions, and maxims. These investigations involve situated *tutorials* conducted within the phenomenal fields under investigation.

Social Facts

My characterizations of Garfinkel's and ethnomethodology's treatment of Durkheim are informed, not only by study of the relevant writings, but from having attended seminars and tutorials with him at UCLA and UC, Irvine in the period from 1972–82 (I have had sporadic contact with Garfinkel in the years after 1982). There are strong connections between his lectures and unpublished writings in the '70s and early '80s and his later publications (particularly, Garfinkel 1996 and 2002). One fairly striking difference between them, however, is the apparent degree to which Garfinkel seems to have come around to the position that ethnomethodology's

---

can lead us to deeply question the sense that is constructed through professional research in fields ranging from historical sociology to artificial intelligence (see Suchman 1990).

program is rooted in, or somehow beholden to, Rawls' (1996) explication of a neglected understanding of Durkheim's writings (Garfinkel 1996: 11, n. 19; 2002: 93, n. 5).

Durkheim's Aphorism

There is no question that Garfinkel treats Durkheim seriously, and has done so for decades. However, he is highly selective in what he takes from Durkheim, and he repeatedly goes back to the same set of points in Durkheim's *Rules of Sociological Method*. "Durkheim's aphorism", which Garfinkel (1996; 2002) writes as "The objective reality of social facts is sociology's fundamental principle," is one of his recurrent "coathangers": a term Garfinkel uses in a different context (Garfinkel et al. 1989) to describe a theme or slogan that functions much like a proverb or proverbial phrase.[9] The idea is that one can hang an open-ended array of anecdotes, observations and insights on the "coathanger". However, at different times he hangs different coats (and tales) on it. In a paper with Harvey Sacks, he quotes the aphorism in a particularly interesting way to introduce the topic of indexical expressions:

> Indexical features are not particular to laymen's accounts. They are familiar in the accounts of professionals as well. For example, the natural language formula, 'The objective reality of social facts is sociology's fundamental principle', is heard by professionals according to occasions as a definition of association members' activities, as their slogan, their task, aim, achievement, brag, sales pitch, justification, discovery, social phenomenon, or research constraint (Garfinkel and Sacks 1970: 338–9).

Durkheim's aphorism in this instance becomes an example of an indexical expression, whose sense, meaning, and pragmatic utility is adaptable to open-ended occasions of use. With this quotation Garfinkel and Sacks produce what literary theorists would later celebrate as a surprising and rather ironic displacement through citation and re-citation. Far from hanging their own theoretical interpretations on Durkheim's aphorism, Garfinkel and Sacks treat it with conspicuous irreverence. Their vernacular formulations ("slogan, ... brag, sales pitch") flatten Durkheim's meta-principle into just another linguistic resource, and they tarnish its professional luster by association with vulgar activities. This irreverence – this indifference to theoretical meaning and significance – violates the sacredness and

---

9 For an extremely insightful account of the logic and "truth" of proverbial expressions, see Sacks (1992). Shapin (2001) documents the strong place that proverbial wisdom holds in the sciences, and Brannigan (2004) explains the resilience and resistance to disproof of classic social psychology experiments by pointing to their use as scientifically authorized parables.

suspends the utility of the aphorism, making an example of it as a literary tool with open-ended uses.

During the time that I studied with him, Garfinkel would occasionally mention Durkheim's aphorism in a more serious vein, but *just how* seriously he was using it was open to question. More often, he would cite another aphoristic line: "The first and most basic rule is *to consider social facts as things*" (Durkheim 1982: 60, emphasis in original). He would recite this rule along with a list of what he called the "canonical properties of social facts": that they are regular, repeating, external, standardized, and particular cohort independent. Garfinkel would then list further properties, which would become increasingly knotted with reflexive implications. He never went very deeply into Durkheim's arguments and examples, as he quickly moved to an elaboration of properties of the phenomena that he and his students had been investigating, such as automobile traffic or pedestrian queues. In short, Durkheim's textual fragments provided pretexts for turning to particular phenomena. Garfinkel used the Durkheimian starting point for investigations of some phenomena, but when explicating others, he sometimes started with themes or lines from Heidegger, Merleau-Ponty, and other philosophers and social theorists. So, for example, Garfinkel et al. (1981) take up Heidegger's "thing" when they explicate the constitutive work of observing an astronomical object.[10] While he expressed reverence for the brilliance of some of the philosophers and theorists (particularly the phenomenologists) whose themes he took up, he was conspicuously indifferent to the project of developing abstract theoretical connections with *any* particular theorist or school of thought. Citations and quotations were starting points, but not for a textual exegesis aiming to identify propositions that would guide, or be tested by, empirical research. Instead, Garfinkel would use the theoretical lines to initiate empirical investigations of a different kind, the upshot of which would frustrate any ambition to validate abstract principles and prove or disprove theoretical propositions.

---

10   Bruno Latour (2004: 233) also plays off of Heidegger's (1967) genealogy of *thing*, in his case emphasizing the etymological connection between *ding* and a quasi-judiciary assembly or "gathering" for settling "matters of concern" (also see Latour and Weibel, 2005 for a conception of *dingpolitic*). The connection with natural science is that the thing becomes the nodal point at which the gathering invests its hopes for settling disputes objectively. In an introductory text (for advanced students), Latour (2005) also takes up a number of themes and methodological initiatives from Garfinkel and ethnomethodology, though without concern for fidelity to the program. Later in this chapter, I discuss the example of the end of a service line (queue) as an ethnomethodological thing. Though far from momentous for politics, the end-of-the-line is a "matter of concern" that constitutes the very gathering of which it is a part.

Social Facts as Things

When he invoked Durkheim's basic rule to consider social facts as things, Garfinkel would often map accountable features of a "thing" of interest on to the list of general properties that Durkheim ascribed to social facts. So, for example, when speaking of queues – service lines such as those that can be witnessed, photographed, and joined at a bank, ticket booth, or supermarket – Garfinkel would refer to properties that satisfied Durkheim's canonical list. A property such as "end-of-the-line" – along with other observable properties such as the point of service, evident order, overall length, and rate of movement of a line – can be identified as being in the world "over and against the analyst"; present not only for the observing sociologist but also for the shopper searching for the end of the line. The *social thing* – end-of-the-line – exhibits the further property of being "independent of the local production cohort": it remains obstinately *there*, in the grocery store, as one after another shopper passes through the line, pays for her groceries, gathers them, and exits. In addition to being independent, the end-of-the-line has the property of being anonymous, visibly and normatively available for "anyone" who would join the "production cohort" by going to the end-of-the-line, positioning her body accordingly, and moving through it. And, while finding the end of a particular line can involve situated investigation and occasional confusion, service lines and their ends are ubiquitous and recurrent things in all sorts of everyday setting. Moreover, as worldly *things* they transcend the sociologist's methods for observing, describing, and analysing their properties, and they seem to comply with a correspondence theory of knowledge: you can find them, describe them, worry about whether you have described them correctly, find after further inquiry that you have been mistaken about their general features, and so forth. And, in the idealized style of a positive science, a sociological analyst can defer to the object's independent, transcendental properties as the objective basis for any (true) statement made about them – if someone questions your account, you can defend it by pointing to the thing and inviting the critic to look for herself.[11]

If Garfinkel had stopped at this point, it would be fair to say that he was using the queue as an illustration of a "social fact" in a positivistic version of sociology (positivistic in the plain sense of being an account that posits the existence of the things described in a world independent of their description). But he would not stop there. Instead, he would go on to observe that the service line and its observable properties are *achieved* (i.e., constitutive). Reciting the aphorism, "The objective reality of social facts is sociology's fundamental principle", he would add that "principle" should be replaced by "phenomenon", and that the objectivity in question is a *produced* objective phenomenon, and the facticity in question is a "social production". While specifying these curious properties of social facts,

---

11   This account is roughly based on notes taken while attending Garfinkel's seminars on 1.16.1980 and 1.25.1982. For a published version of his remarks on queues, see Garfinkel, 2002: Ch. 8, "Autocthonous order properties of formatted queues".

Garfinkel assigned the insight about them to Durkheim. It sometimes seemed as though he was explicating Durkheim's conception of social fact, while beginning to develop a strange account that Durkheim never would have imagined, and may even have found incomprehensible. As Garfinkel proceeded through his explication of "Durkheimian" properties of queues, his account would seem to become increasingly estranged from the textual starting point in *The Rules*. Nevertheless, while it *seemed* that he was leaving Durkheim behind, he would continue to insist that what he was saying (in his characteristic way) *might as well have been* what Durkheim had said.[12] As I understood such remarks, they were not suggesting that we should search Durkheim's texts for evidence of how his theorizing anticipated Garfinkel's uptake. Though he didn't say so in so many words, Garfinkel seemed to be using Durkheim's first rule of method less as a theoretical platform and more as a textual starting line for a very different kind of investigation of social things.[13]

Contrary to Durkheim, who rigorously distinguishes the sociologist's objective *facts* from the member's vulgar *prenotions*, Garfinkel treats social facts such as end-of-the-line as constitutive phenomena. End-of-the-line is a constitutive thing. The sociologist does not discover the end of a line by administering a specialized instrument; instead, the line is composed as one after another shopper discovers the end of the line and positions her body accordingly. Though the end of a particular line can be ambiguous, there is nothing mysterious about the thing in question: end-of-the-line. It does not take a rocket scientist – or even a professional sociologist – to "discover" the end of a line. The discovery requires a normal competence, both in the sense that any normal member of the society should be expected to know where to go when instructed "go to the end of the line", and in the sense that a person risks getting negatively sanctioned when failing to recognize the end of the line.

The emphasis in Garfinkel's account of social facts on the *produced* or *achieved* facticity of the phenomena in question contrasts with Durkheim's emphasis on the coercive and causal force that social facts exert upon the members who are swept up in them unawares. Without implying an extreme individualism, Garfinkel's picture is less reified, allowing for greater flexibility and contingency in the

---

12   Garfinkel (2002: 246, n. 2) suggests that there is a way to credit Durkheim on the origins of "Ethnomethodological radical analytic studies of social order". He invites readers to compare his own account of "autocthonous properties" of queues with Durkheim's characterization of social facts, but what he does not say is that the vulgar, endogenous origins of such properties radically differ from the professional analysis that Durkheim (1982) explicitly requires for the disciplined observation and elucidation of social facts.

13   Aside from expressing a speculation, years later, about what Garfinkel might have meant, my reference to what Garfinkel did not say in so many words alludes to a property of communicative actions discussed by Garfinkel and Sacks (1970) that, in any case, we mean more than we can say in so many words. Garfinkel turned that property into a pedagogical practice, challenging his students to work out what he meant, and disdaining requests for explicit definitions and "just-so" explanations.

composition and maintenance of social facts. The famous exercises in *Studies in Ethnomethodology* (Garfinkel 1967: Chs. 1–3) demonstrate such flexibility and contingency, even while illustrating the familiar sociological lesson that compliance to a normative order is the means through which the "force" of social structure is exerted and achieved.

The replacement of "fundamental principle" [of method] with "fundamental phenomenon" [of ordinary activities], and the emphasis on *produced* objectivity (as opposed to objectivity determined through professional analysis) seems to initiate a move away from Durkheim. If the aphorism and the list of rules and properties of social facts are foundational for Durkheim, they are not for Garfinkel, at least not in the same way. Durkheim explicitly aimed to found a discipline of sociology, which would be scientific and objective, with subject matter distinct from those of biology and psychology. Professional members of the discipline would have privileged access to the facts through the use of methods for collecting and analysing them. Durkheim recognized that social facts are produced through social actions, but he stressed their collective existence and transcendence from the subjective pre-notions that obscure the vision of everyday actors. *Method* was the disciplinary means for getting access and correctly elucidating this transcendent order of facts. This view of sociology and of social facts is, of course, anathema to the non-positivistic and anti-positivistic sociologies that shadowed the development of scientistic sociology throughout the 20th century. Garfinkel is often linked to the anti-positivistic counter-sociologies, and he sometimes acts the part. However, while his treatment of social facts is neither dismissive nor ironic, it is far from a "straight" uptake of Durkheim's rules and principles. If there is a line that runs from Garfinkel to Durkheim, it is interestingly twisted. During his lectures, Garfinkel evinced little concern with remaining faithful to Durkheim's or any other theorist's or philosopher's original writings – indeed, as noted earlier, he explicitly recommended a procedure for "misreading" them. The procedure consisted of locating everyday (or occupationally-specific) phenomena that can be investigated as tutorial resources for opening up familiar theoretical topics for a fresh and critical insight.

Situated Tutorials and Perspicuous Phenomena

Consider, for example, a standard qualitative method: a series of open-ended interviews in which the interviewee instructs the interviewer about relevant activities. So, for example, when Samuel Edgerton and I interviewed astronomers at Harvard-Smithsonian Astrophysical Observatory in the late 1980s (Lynch and Edgerton 1988), we asked them to instruct us on whether "aesthetic" issues were relevant to the work of digital image processing. We didn't define "aesthetics" – we simply used the term as a "coat hanger" (Garfinkel et al. 1989) to collect whatever the astronomers told us. It turned out to be a theme that provoked commentary, as the astronomers found it strange to talk about their work as involving "aesthetics" but were able, and even eager, to talk to that theme and to show us their equipment and demonstrate their practices. We were given tours, demonstrations, and to a limited extent we were given ad hoc lessons. Though "aesthetics" was little more than a conversation starter, the tutorials we received did instruct us about what that word could mean, and how this case could be used as a basis for critically reflecting upon discussions of the relation between art and science in art history, and history and philosophy of science.

Members' Tutorials

In such a case, the interview is not primarily significant as a data-gathering method that enables a social scientist to compare and contrast results from one interview with similarly framed data from other interviews. Instead, the exchange of questions and answers is more like a session in which a novice requests information and gets instructions from an old hand. In cases such as Edgerton's and my research, the interview is not an attempt to master a practice, but it is not separable from the interactional and demonstrative devices through which such mastery can be gained.[14] Even in the case of analysing tape-recorded "naturally occurring" interactions, a kind of tutorial is involved. In the early 1980s, when Garfinkel, Livingston, and I were working on a study of a tape-recording of the voices of two astronomers and a night assistant as they found themselves making what later was credited as the first observation in the optical spectrum of a pulsar (Garfinkel et al. 1981), I attempted to transcribe the tape using the system developed by Gail Jefferson for conversation analysis. I ran into occasional difficulty with hearing and writing down what the parties were saying, but not because their voices were indistinct. Repeated playback of the tape helped clarify some of the islets of ambiguity, but equally important was supplementary reading about pulsars and astrophysical theories of them. We also played the tape to one of the participants, and got some points of clarification as well as the recollections it touched off. Such investigations of the setting allowed for recognition of *how* the parties were talking, which implicated the very transcribable details of what they might have been saying.

Such members' tutorials are continuous with the constitutive organization of the "social facts" under investigation, because those "facts" are themselves composed through instructed actions and interactions. They differ from the tutorials a social analyst undertakes when studying the concepts, distinctions, and debates in an academic literature. However, a fieldwork tutorial can alert the student to identify gaps in the literature, and to gain fresh and critical insight into that literature. This kind of circulation from literature to tutorial and back differs fundamentally from the more common way in which the relationship between social science theory and

---

14 In some ethnomethodological studies, guided by Garfinkel's unique adequacy requirement, such mastery is pursued as a condition for further investigations – Edgerton and I did not aspire to such a degree of mastery in our study. See Garfinkel (2002: 175–6).

empirical social facts tends to be presented. Instead of treating the facts as evidence for or against theoretical propositions and predictions, ethnomethodologists use their tutorials to respecify the fundamental terms in which theories are cast. Perspicuous phenomena are "things" (and settings of activity) that re-tune our sensibilities, so that when we turn back to the familiar distinctions, concepts, and debates of a social science we can read them differently.

Respecifying What a Fact Is

As I read Garfinkel's citations of Durkheim's *Rules*, he uses his studies of queues and traffic as tutorial resources for taking up Durkheim's notions of "social fact" and "social thing". He does so, not in order to illustrate Durkheim's theorizing, but to respecify social facts and social things in a way that virtually destroys Durkheim's ambition to treat them as the exclusive intellectual property of a professional cadre of sociological analysts. The end of a service line, a recurrent traffic jam, and a routine greeting sequence can each be considered as a social fact in Durkheim's terms. But professional sociologists have no privileged access to them as phenomena or as facts. Indeed, they are available for anybody who would join the line, get through the traffic jam, or engage in the greeting. A sociologist who would present descriptions of them under the guise of professional social science findings faces a daunting "So what?" question. I suppose that it would be possible to use ethnomethodological investigations as a basis for becoming a queue-engineer, an expert on traffic jams, or a greeting therapist, but another payoff may be in the offing. As instructions for developing a theoretical account of what in the world a "social thing" might be, the queue, traffic jam, and greeting offer themselves as tutorial resources that offer detailed understandings that greatly surpass Durkheim's seminal writings: the *thing* is singular, vivid, concrete, and yet observably and intelligibly organized. Such a thing also surpasses *any* stable set of instructions. This gets us to the crux of the matter. The connection between Garfinkel and Durkheim's aphorism is bridged by the peculiar, albeit familiar, expression *working out*. It would be a mistake to suppose that this is a matter of interpreting what Durkheim meant through a hermeneutic exercise of reading his published and unpublished writings, reflecting on his biographical situation, and linking him to intellectual ancestors and contemporaries. All of these are, of course, difficult and highly respectable modes of academic work, but what Garfinkel proposed was another way of working; one that can be characterized as "empirical", but not in the sense of collecting facts or testing theories *against* observations. Instead, it is a matter of *investigating* what a fact *is*. Durkheim was preoccupied with social facts, and his theorizing took up the burden of showing that such facts required a distinctive sociological methodology. Garfinkel's preoccupation extends to facts of the natural sciences, as well as to social facts construed as "natural" in an everyday sense of the word. His methodology is indifferent to natural/social distinction, except when that distinction is locally and constitutively relevant.

Working out what a social fact *is*, is not a matter of coming up with a definition that covers all cases. It is a matter of investigating what a fact or thing is in *any* particular case, whether it is a case of finding the end of a queue or of discovering an optical pulsar. Even if we treat Durkheim's aphoristic guidelines as useful starting points, we need to work out what they mean, just as we need to work out how to follow mundane instructions in the midst of the things and scenes at hand. The aim, however, is not to show that Durkheim's ideas, however remarkable and visionary, are correct; instead, the *working-out* is the phenomenon of interest – it is not simply a means to corroborate a theory or demonstrate a principle.

Conclusion

Garfinkel treated queues as a way to make perspicuous (rather than to illustrate) the things – routine, recurrent, organized activities – Durkheim had glossed as "social facts". The reference to Durkheim was explicit, but the properties of the things that Garfinkel elaborated had a jarring relation to the Cartesian and Baconian distinctions Durkheim used to frame his account of social facts. I don't mean to suggest that Garfinkel promoted a view of "society in the mind" or of the "subjective" constitution of social reality; instead, he would tread a fine line between notions of internal meaning and subjective understanding and the Durkheimian picture of external social facts coercively impinging upon individuals who are, at best, dimly aware of them. I find it difficult to imagine how one could pass from Durkheim's *Rules* to Garfinkel's program without thoroughly disrupting the Durkheimian picture. This, I think, is where Garfinkel achievement lies. It is not that he eschews theory in favor of a technical account of the phenomena. Although he does develop an original and strange account of queues and traffic, I seriously doubt that his writings are destined to make serious contributions to the technical literatures on those subjects; instead, he develops a radical account of "social facts as things" that sets sociology back 100 years.

At least some of us view that negative achievement as the chance for a new start rather than an opportunity to restore a lost or neglected program. While exemplary studies are only available in fits and starts, Garfinkel's ethnomethodology sets out a very different way to understand and investigate social *things*. The idea is to take them for the manifest things they are and to work out *how* they are achieved, without reifying their properties or dissolving them into phantasms.

Two puzzles remain about Garfinkel's treatment of Durkheim's *Rules*. One has to do with the question, why Durkheim? From what I have argued, it might seem that Durkheim's aphorism, or any other fragment taken from his or any other theorist's writings, is no more than an arbitrary starting point for ethnomethodological investigations. Is there something distinctive or compelling in Durkheim's writings, or is it simply the case that tagging an investigation to Durkheim's canonical writings serves a legitimating function and also caters to the expectations of students enrolled in a sociology curriculum? Without denying either of these alternatives, I suggest that the particular attraction of Durkheim's pithy and guileless formulations in the *Rules* is their striking contrast to the convoluted prose we so often find in contemporary social theory (including, of course, Garfinkel's notorious prose). The movement from Durkheim's aphorism to Garfinkel's formulations is not a contrapuntal one; instead, it is more akin to a catalytic movement. When Garfinkel takes hold of them, and reintroduces them into the saturated verbiage of social theory, the simple crystalline aphorisms can precipitate a novel understanding. Even more attractive is Durkheim's forthright emphasis on *facts* and *things*, terms that have become so difficult to accept at face value in contemporary social theory. Garfinkel neither accepts nor ironicizes face-value "facts" and "things" – he keeps them active as facts and things, but with a stress on *active*, while delving into their constitutive properties.

The second puzzle has to do with Garfinkel's recommendation to "misread" canonical writings. If Garfinkel can misread Durkheim, why object to the way anyone else reads Garfinkel? The question is, what does the (mis)reading *do*? This question may seem to invite the mind-deadening instrumentalism of the sort of textbook account that recommends theories as tools for empirical research, or "paradigms" as lenses through which to view the world, but I intend it to mean something quite different from that. Garfinkel (mis)reads Durkheim not in order to legitimate ethnomethodology by tagging it to a classic theoretical foundation. Nor, in my view, does he engage in the competitive game of claiming a correct hermeneutical relation to the ancestral tradition for his sect instead of the dominant congregation. He uses Durkheim's summary aphorism as a take-off point for a heretical program that nevertheless is intelligible *as* sociology. As soon as the program starts to lay down tracks, further inquiry about its relationship to Durkheim is likely to become irrelevant, and even regressive. Just where else the tracks may be headed is another story: "Having just come out of a jungle, I can't promise you that in leading you in to show you what I've found that I won't lose the way for all of us" (Garfinkel 1952: 1).

Acknowledgements

Earlier versions of this chapter were presented at meetings on Sociology after Durkheim at the University of Surrey (21 June 2006) and Mind and Society at the University of Manchester (23 June 2006). I'm grateful to Geoff Cooper and Ruth Rettie for the invitation to the Surrey meeting and for their editorial advice, and to Wes Sharrock and Christian Grieffenhagen for the opportunity to present the chapter at Manchester. I also would like to thank the other participants at both conferences and the reviewers who gave me helpful criticisms and comments.

References

Bloor, D. (1982), 'Durkheim and Mauss Revisited: Classification and the Sociology of Knowledge', *Studies in History and Philosophy of Science* 13:4, 267–97.

Brannigan, A. (2004), *The Rise and Fall of Social Psychology: The Use and Misuse of Experimentation* (New York: Aldine de Gruyter).

Button, G. (ed.) (1991), *Ethnomethodology and the Human Sciences* (Cambridge: Cambridge University Press).

Coulter, J. (1993), 'Ethnomethodology and the Contemporary Condition of Inquiry', *Contemporary Sociology* 22:2, 261–63.

Durkheim, E. (1959 [1897]), *Suicide* (New York: Free Press).

Durkheim, E. (1982 [1895]), *The Rules of Sociological Method* (New York: Free Press).

Durkheim, E. (1995 [1912]), *The Elementary Forms of Religious Life* (New York: Free Press).

Fyfe, G. and Law, J. (eds) (1988), *Picturing Power: Visual Depiction and Social Relations* (London: Routledge and Kegan Paul).

Garfinkel, H. (1952), 'Notes Toward a Sociological Theory of Information', Memo No. 3 (17 April), Organizational Behavior Project (unpublished paper, Department of Sociology, UCLA).

Garfinkel, H. (1967), *Studies in Ethnomethodology* (Englewood Cliffs, NJ: Prentice Hall).

Garfinkel, H. (1996), 'Ethnomethodology's Program', *Social Psychology Quarterly* 59, 5–21.

Garfinkel, H. (2002), *Ethnomethodology's Program: Working out Durkheim's Aphorism* (Lanham, MD: Rowman & Littlefield).

Garfinkel, H., Livingston, E. and Lynch, M. et al. (1989), 'Respecifying the Natural Sciences as Discovering Sciences of Practical Action (I and II): Doing so Ethnographically by Administering a Schedule of Contingencies in Discussions with Laboratory Scientists and by Hanging Around their Laboratories' (unpublished paper, Department of Sociology, UCLA).

Garfinkel, H., Lynch, M. and Livingston, E. (1981), 'The Work of a Discovering Science Construed with Materials from the Optically Discovered Pulsar', *Philosophy of the Social Sciences* 11:1, 131–58.

Garfinkel, H. and Sacks, H. (1970), 'On Formal Structures of Practical Actions', in McKinney and Tiryakian (eds).

Gieryn, T. (1982), 'Durkheim's Sociology of Scientific Knowledge', *Journal of the History of Behavioral Sciences* 18:2, 102–29.

Hammersley, M. (2005), 'Book Review: *Ethnomethodology's Program: Working Out Durkheim's Aphorism*', *Qualitative Research* 5:1, 141–44 <http://qrj.sagepub.com>.

Heidegger, M. (1967), *What is a Thing?* trans. W.B. Barton, Jr. and V. Deutsch (Chicago: H. Regnery).

Hickey, T.J. (2005 [1995]), *History of Twentieth-Century Philosophy of Science* (Forest Park, IL: Thomas J. Hickey) <http://www.philsci.com>.

Hilbert, R. (1992), *The Classical Roots of Ethnomethodology: Durkheim, Weber, and Garfinkel* (Chapel Hill: University of North Carolina Press).

Latour, B. (2004), 'Why Has Critique Run out of Steam? From Matters of Fact to Matters of Concern', *Critical Inquiry* 30:2, 225–48.

Latour, B. (2005), *Reassembling the Social: An Introduction to Actor-Network Theory* (Oxford: Oxford University Press).

Latour, B. and Weibel, P. (2005), *Making Things Public: Atmospheres of Democracy* (Cambridge, MA: MIT Press).

Livingston, E. (1987), *Making Sense of Ethnomethodology* (London: Routlege and Kegan Paul).

Lukes, S. (1973), *Emile Durkheim, His Life and Work: A Historical and Critical Study* (London: Allen Lane/Penguin).

Lukes, S. (1982), 'Introduction', to E. Durkheim, *The Rules of Sociological Method* (New York: Free Press), 1–27.

Lynch, M. (1993), *Scientific Practice and Ordinary Action: Ethnomethodology and Social Studies of Science* (Cambridge: Cambridge University Press).

Lynch, M. and Edgerton, S.Y. (1988), 'Aesthetics and Digital Image Processing: Representational Craft in Contemporary Astronomy', in Fyfe and Law (eds).

Lynch M. and Woolgar, S. (eds) (1990), *Representation in Scientific Practice* (Cambridge, MA: MIT Press).

Mannheim, K. (1952), 'On the Interpretation of Weltanschauung', in Mannheim (ed.).

Mannheim, K. (ed.) (1952), *Essays on the Sociology of Knowledge* (London: Routledge and Kegan Paul).

McKinney, J.C. and Tiryakian, E.A. (eds) (1970) *Theoretical Sociology: Perspectives and Development* (New York: Appleton-Century-Crofts).

Merton, R.K. (1949), *Social Theory and Social Structure* (New York: Free Press).

Mills, C.W. (1959), *The Sociological Imagination* (New York: Oxford University Press).

Parsons, T. (1937), *The Structure of Social Action*, Vol. 1 (New York: Free Press).

Rawls, A. (1996), 'Durkheim's Epistemology: The Neglected Argument', *American Journal of Sociology* 102:2, 430–82.

Sacks, H. (1992), 'On Proverbs', in *Lectures on Conversation*, Vol. 1 (Oxford: Blackwell), 104–12.

Shapin, S. (2001), 'Proverbial Economies: How an Understanding of Some Linguistic and Social Features of Common Sense Can Throw Light on More Prestigious Bodies of Knowledge, Science for Example', *Social Studies of Science* 31:5, 731–69.

Suchman, L. (1990), 'Representing Practice in Cognitive Science', in Lynch and Woolgar (eds).

Chapter 7
Mathematical Equations as Durkheimian Social Facts?

Christian Greiffenhagen and Wes Sharrock

Introduction

It is widely assumed that one of the main fracture lines within social thought is between those who affirm and those who deny the reality of 'social facts' or their equivalent, between those who insist that action is constrained by objective social structures and those who deny that there are such constraints and adopt what is variously called 'subjectivism' or 'voluntarism' instead. Emile Durkheim's definition of the expression 'social facts' is widely viewed as a key precursor of the former view and thus remains relevant to contemporary sociological discussions about whether society is essentially an 'objective' or a 'subjective' reality (or a Janus-faced combination of the two).

Responses to Durkheim's (1982 [1895]) recommendation that we should 'consider social facts as things' (60) are often taken as critical for assigning those who accept the existence of social facts to the objective side of the argument and those who deny this to the subjective side.[1] We are sceptical of the suitability of social facts as the primary demarcation for the articulation of diverse sociological positions, because we do not think that questions about the existence of social facts are as clear cut as might seem.[2]

Durkheim uses the model of natural facts to derive what he sees as the fundamental characteristics of social facts (that they are external to and independent of individual will). This extension from natural to social facts may make it seem that social facts must be strange things indeed, but if we consider the sort of social phenomena Durkheim includes under his definition we might see the notion rather differently. Consequently, we will treat Durkheim's idea of social facts as allowing two different estimates of significance. The first one, based on what Durkheim

---

1 Since ethnomethodology is typically placed on the denial side, it might seem bewildering that Garfinkel would subtitle his *Ethnomethodology's Program* (2002) as 'Working out Durkheim's Aphorism' and would endorse Anne Rawls' re-reading of Durkheim (1996, 2004). See the chapters by Lynch and Rawls (this volume) for further discussion of Garfinkel's relation to 'Durkheim's aphorism' (to treat social facts as things).

2 And we should note that the objective – subjective dichotomy does not even strictly apply to Durkheim himself (cf. Rawls 2004).

has to say about the general nature of social facts, suggests that the identification of social facts and relations between them provides the basis for an ambitious new science that deals with a new kind of entity and whose results will overturn our existing understandings of life in society. As Garfinkel and Sacks (1970) put it many years ago, this 'inflationary' reading takes Durkheim's statement as sociology's 'slogan, [...] task, aim, achievement, brag, sales pitch, justification, discovery, [...] or research constraint' (339).

The other reading relates to the examples of social facts that Durkheim gives and suggests that the idea of social facts does no more than trace the outline of existing understandings that inform the life of the society, pointing to features that are integral to anyone's conduct of their daily affairs. This 'deflationary' reading is not sceptical of the existence of social facts (since on this reading there is nothing to be sceptical about), but is cautious about the use of the notion of social facts as a platform for sociology's self-promotion.

We will review these issues in relation to the argument that mathematical equations (such as '$2 + 2 = 4$') are social facts, developed by one of the most resolute of contemporary Durkheimians, David Bloor (e.g. Bloor 1982). Our disagreement with Bloor is not so much about whether mathematical equations are social facts, but more about what saying that they are might amount to. For Bloor, it is the start of the project of a professional sociology, which will yield a new understanding of the real nature of mathematics and which is at odds with the understandings that – allegedly – underpin practical dependence on mathematical calculations. In contrast, we question whether Bloor has pinned down the understandings involved in mastery and use of mathematical equations, and whether, therefore, showing that and how mathematical equations *are* social facts involves any more than clarificatory reference to an assortment of familiar mathematical considerations.

Two Readings of 'Social Facts'

Durkheim (1982 [1895], 50–51) answers his question 'What is a Social Fact?' (Chapter 1) thus:

> When I perform my duties as a brother, a husband or a citizen and carry out the commitments I have entered into, I fulfil obligations which are defined in law and custom and which are external to myself and my actions. Even when they conform to my own sentiments and when I feel their reality within me, that reality does not cease to be objective, for it is not I who have prescribed these duties; I have received them through education. Moreover, how often does it happen that we are ignorant of the details of the obligations that we must assume, and that, to know them, we must consult the legal code and its authorised interpreters!

Further:

> Not only are these types of behaviour and thinking external to the individual, but they are endued with a compelling and coercive power by virtue of which, whether he wishes it or not, they impose themselves upon him. [...] If I attempt to violate the rules of law they react against me so as to forestall my action, if there is still time. Alternatively, they annul it or make my action conform to the norm if it is already accomplished but capable of being reversed; or they cause me to pay the penalty for it if it is irreparable. [...] In other cases, although it may be indirect, constraint is no less effective. I am not forced to speak French with my compatriots, nor to use the legal currency, but it is impossible for me to do otherwise. If I tried to escape the necessity, my attempt would fail miserably. As an industrialist nothing prevents me from working with the processes and methods of the previous century, but if I do I will most certainly ruin myself.

The important elements in Durkheim's account of social facts are:

- That they are *external* to individuals;
- that they are endowed with *coercive power* (they causally compel individuals to do things); and
- that individuals are often *ignorant* of them (and therefore must consult 'authorised interpreters').

The more common 'inflationary' reading takes the identification of social facts as the basis for a new kind of science that is modelled after the natural sciences (which deal with natural facts):

> Social phenomena must therefore be considered in themselves, detached from the conscious beings who form their own mental representations of them. They must be studied from the outside, as external things, because it is in this guise that they present themselves to us (70).

It is further assumed that members of society have only limited understanding of social facts and it is up to social scientists to discover the hidden realities of society. On this inflationary reading, sociology will yield, for the first time, a true understanding of the nature of social facts and the ways they affect human lives.

Note that the challenging part of Durkheim's proposal 'to consider social facts as things' (60) is not the suggestion that there *are* social facts, but the claim that social facts are *things*. The argument for social facts itself is almost indisputable, since it is an argument from truisms: that I speak the native tongue to communicate with native speakers; that I employ economically viable technologies in perpetuating a competitive economic enterprise; or that I founded my household, but not the institution of the family. This opens the possibility for a different reading, one that does not dispute the existence of the substantive social facts (such as the currency or the family), but sees the injunction to treat them as things as unnecessary and misleading. This reading takes Durkheim's innovation as one in nomenclature, not ontology. Rather than denying the reality of social facts, this reading follows up on the idea that they 'present themselves to us'. Rather than pointing *away* from the 'mental representations' 'conscious beings' make of social facts, Durkheim's own account of social facts is seen as pointing attention *toward* them – toward understandings available to anyone.

Durkheim takes the externality and coercive power of social facts as the basis for an argument that a new kind of understanding of our actions is being introduced, in which our actions are occasioned not by our individual thoughts but by the demand and compulsion of social facts. Hence the label 'inflationary', since on this reading members of society are being told something *new* (in particular: that many things that they consider as 'natural' are in truth 'social', i.e., conventional). However, both externality and coercive power could equally be seen as expressions of incontestable truisms that members of society *are* aware of. The constraint involved in Durkheim's own examples is more conditional than causal: *if* I want to speak to someone else and be understood by them, then I should speak the language they understand; *if* I want to engage in valid economic exchanges, I should employ a valid currency; *if* I want to prosper economically, I should take measures to avoid operating permanently at a loss (and therefore adopt up-to-date business practices). Alternatively, the constraint is constitutive in nature (cf. Garfinkel 1963), i.e., defines what counts as valid actions: whilst individuals decide to found a family, individuals do not invent the idea of 'the family'. Finally, the constraint of social facts may involve a variety of practical and ethical considerations.

Just as Freud liked to flatter himself that psychoanalysis achieved a triumph over the most profound resistance, though it could equally well be understood as having pandered to a ready audience, so sociology admires itself for having to overthrow pervasive resistance to the truth that human reality is social. Durkheim certainly thought in that way, but we have tried to show that there are only two things about his case that could possibly be objected to: firstly, the terminological innovation 'social facts' (though in truth there is little enough to be objected to here); secondly, the association of the innovation with superfluous realist ontology. The substantive basis for this ontology is something that anyone could agree with – indeed, something that everybody acknowledges in practice. It is only if social facts are treated as in a certain sense beyond the comprehension of ordinary members of society that Durkheim has opened an entire realm accessible *only* to the sociologist. On the deflationary reading of social facts, sociologists are more akin to Monsieur Jourdain's teacher who explains how a familiar practice – speaking – is identified as 'speaking prose' in the discourse of grammarians (cf. Molière's *The Bourgeois Gentleman* [1670], Act 2, Scene 4). It is only in the inflationary reading that there is a suggestion that social science has a more general and complete perspective on social life that it aims to share with ordinary members – possibly against their resistance.

The point can be reinforced by a juxtaposition of Durkheim's statements with some remarks of Alfred Schutz. These two are commonly seen as embodying fundamental oppositions, representing objectivism/realism and subjectivism/constructivism respectively. However, there is a striking similarity in their remarks about the social world:

> [...] in the natural attitude of everyday life the following is taken for granted without question: [...] that a stratified social and cultural world is historically pregiven as a frame of reference for me and my fellow-men, indeed in a manner as taken for granted as the 'natural world'; [...] that therefore the situation in which I find myself at any moment is only to a small extent purely created by me. [...] The life-world is thus a reality which we modify through our acts and which, on the other hand, modifies our actions (Schutz and Luckmann 1973, 5–6).

Both Durkheim and Schutz argue that the social world is – for the most part – not created by individuals and that individuals are often constrained by it. The main difference between them is the intended status of their respective remarks. Schutz is not stating his own sociological doctrines, but is engaged in a descriptive enterprise, delineating the quality of commonplace experience under the natural attitude, the matter-of-course, taken-for-granted orientation of individuals to their practical circumstances. We are not suggesting that there is no difference in their treatments of social facts, but that their projects differ less in respect of the substantive content than might first appear. Durkheim's arguments are substantively in harmony with Schutz's, i.e., there seems to be little or no disagreement in their statements about happens in the world (e.g., about the legal code, about our interactions with others, about our social institutions, etc.). Thus while there are considerable differences in philosophical convictions between realists and phenomenologists, there is no need to introduce the notion of social facts to give rise to those differences. Whatever the intellectual gulfs between Durkheim and Schutz, it is not because one is asserting and the other rejecting the existence of social facts.

We thus want to suggest that much of the recent debates (e.g., objectivism-subjectivism, structure-agency) are misplaced. These debates treat the disagreements between the respective positions as a matter of affirming or denying the existence of social facts (or the constraining character of them). Resistance to Durkheim's sociological programme is thus commonly understood as also entailing doubt about whether there are any social facts (i.e., that there are subjective states only). This is the reason why ethnomethodology and phenomenology are typically taken to be on the subjective (or agency) side of the traditional dualisms. In contrast, we have been arguing that many of the disagreements with Durkheim's project are not about whether there *are* social facts, but about the character of social facts – and its implications for the project of social science.

Mathematical Facts

Durkheim's influence is very directly felt in one of the central contributions to the sociology of mathematics, that of David Bloor (cf. 1973, 1976, 1983, 1994). To Bloor, mathematical statements (such as '2 + 2 = 4') invite a neo-Durkheimian approach, since they are experienced as Durkheimian facts, being external to individuals and endowed with a coercive power. If mathematical expressions can be treated as facts, what species of facts are they? Philosophers have tried to establish that they are natural facts (empiricism) or that they are logical facts (logicism). A neo-Durkheimian perspective insists that they are, rather, social facts. As White (1947) put it very early on:

> Mathematics does have objective reality. And this reality, as Hardy insists, is *not* the reality of the physical world. But there is no mystery about it. Its reality is cultural: the sort of reality possessed by a code of etiquette, traffic regulations, the rules of baseball, the English language or rules of grammar (302–303).

There is a relatively straightforward way in which everyone could acknowledge White's point. The mathematical symbols that we use today are conventional in the sense that other symbols could (and have) been used. Rather than using the symbol '5' to signify the number five, we could use other symbols – and most of us are aware of other symbols to signify this number, e.g., the Roman numeral 'V' or five strokes '|||||'. Similarly, rather than using a decimal system (base 10), we could use a duodecimal system (base 12), i.e., be counting in dozens. In that sense, the rules of arithmetic are as conventional as the rules of traffic.

In this context, sociologists often draw on Wittgenstein's (1976, 1978) reflections on mathematics, which are seen as demonstrations of the conventional character of mathematics. For example, Wittgenstein's discussion of a pupil continuing a number series taught by his teacher (1953, §§185–242) or the visual proof that 2 + 2 + 2 = 4 (1978, I, §38) are often taken as 'proof' that mathematics is social in character. However, just as there were two different ways of reacting to Durkheim's 'discovery' of social facts, so there are in the case of Wittgenstein's reflections on mathematics. We will compare Bloor's understanding with our own, which is intended to be more in accord with Wittgenstein's aims in philosophy.

Bloor sees Wittgenstein as enabling an extension of Mannheim's (1936) sociology of knowledge to mathematics. Mannheim famously excluded mathematics (and the natural sciences) from his sociology of knowledge, since the truths of mathematics seem to be eternal, true in all times and places, and do not seem to vary with socio-cultural formations. For Bloor, Wittgenstein's demonstrations of the conventional character of mathematics open the way for a sociological treatment of mathematics. However, for Bloor, Wittgenstein does not go far enough, since he did not develop a theory to explain causally the social character of mathematics.

In our reading of Wittgenstein, Bloor's sociology of mathematics does not actually add anything to the initial claim that mathematics is social. Bloor is thus an example of an inflationary treatment, since he puts the sociologist in a position to see something about mathematics that ordinary members of society are supposedly unaware of. In contrast, we see Wittgenstein as being engaged in a deflationary project, where reminding people of what they already know (e.g., that other arithmetics could, and have, been used) is enough to answer – or dissolve – any questions that one might have, eliminating the impression that the 'problem' of mathematical objectivity calls for the creation of an explanatory theory.

Bloor's Sociology of Mathematics

If mathematical statements are facts, then what endows them with factual status? For Bloor, this entails asking what *causes* mathematical statements to obtain. He recognizes three possible causes: natural-empirical, logical, or social. Like Durkheim, Bloor's argument is eliminatory: if it can be shown that the objectivity of mathematical facts is neither a natural-empirical nor a logical necessity, then mathematical statements must be social facts.

Bloor (1994)[3] takes the equation $2 + 2 = 4$ as an example of a mathematical fact, since it is typically taken to be an eternal truth ($2 + 2$ cannot equal 0, 3, or 5, but *must* equal 4). Bloor also thinks that most people when asked to explain why $2 + 2 = 4$ would argue that it expresses an empirical fact (i.e., a statement about reality) or a logical fact (i.e., a fundamental logical principle). Therefore Bloor aims to establish that $2 + 2 = 4$ is neither an empirical nor a logical but a social fact. He does so by showing that there are alternatives, i.e., by giving examples in which $2 + 2$ does not equal to 4:

> Sociologists are professionally concerned with the conventional aspects of knowledge. So I will try to identify the conventional components of the concepts '2' and '4' and 'addition'. Conventions are shared ways of acting that could in principle be otherwise. They are contingent arrangements, not necessary ones. Thus it is conventional that we drive on the side of the road that we do, and (if proof were needed) we could point to others who drive on the other side. Even if everybody, as a matter of fact, drove on the same side, we could easily imagine the alternative. Demonstrating conventionality therefore involves demonstrating alternative possibilities. Although this necessary condition is easy to state it isn't always easy to satisfy in practice. For one thing, our imaginations are limited. Another reason is that candidate alternatives often meet objections. Reasons are found to sideline, trivialize or re-interpret them so that their character as alternatives is disguised (Bloor 1994, 21).

---

3 See Greiffenhagen and Sharrock (2006) for a discussion of Bloor's (1976) earlier arguments about alternative mathematics.

Bloor thinks that there will be strong objections to the idea that mathematical equations are conventional, which sociologists have to overcome. One of the most common objections to the idea that mathematics is (only) a convention is that mathematics seems to apply to reality. If it is just a convention that 2 + 2 = 4, then why do two sheep added to two sheep always make four sheep?

Bloor is not denying that two sheep added to two sheep results in four sheep, but wants to undermine the idea that this could contribute to an empiricist *justification* of mathematics (i.e., that mathematical equations are true *because* they correspond to reality). Consequently, he gives another purportedly empirical example, in which 2 + 2 does not equal 4. He asks us to imagine a number wheel with four segments, labelled '0', '1', '2', and '3', where turning the wheel in one direction 'we think of ourselves as adding' (25):

> Just as we felt a naturalness about carrying out our counting technique from one empirical circumstance to another in the past, so we feel a naturalness about this. [...] Then, of course, we make the inevitable discovery: we set the wheel at 2, and then turn it so as to add a further 2, and we get back to zero. 2 + 2 = 0 (26).

Turning the number wheel is as 'empirical' as adding sheep. So Bloor has given us two examples, one in which 2 + 2 = 4 and one in which 2 + 2 = 0. For Bloor, this does not show that mathematical equations aren't applicable to reality, but that their applicability cannot be used to justify them.[4] Having demonstrated that empiricism cannot be used to justify mathematical facts, Bloor dismantles logicism (justifying mathematical equations as derivative consequences of fundamental logical principles) by showing that logicist justifications will be circular, i.e., will have to presuppose the principles they aim to deduce. Having eliminated the possibilities that mathematical equations are natural or logical facts, Bloor sees himself as having successfully demonstrated that they are social facts.

---

4 We might notice that in the attempt to make the number wheel out as one that does not fit the '2 + 2 = 4' case, Bloor conflates *cumulatively adding up* the total number of points passed through on the number wheel with using the points on the number wheel to *track the location* of the pointer. That is, if we ask how many points on the number wheel we have moved through as we rotate it, then we will correctly pronounce that – having moved through initially two points and then two further points – we have moved through four points. It is a different question to ask what numbered point on the wheel will be reached – if we make two moves and then two more – the answer is, of course, the fourth point in the rotation, the one identified as '0'. The number wheel is thus not counter-evidence to an empiricist view.

The Conventional Character of Mathematics

In order to clarify our differences with Bloor, let us reflect on what Bloor is trying to do. Bloor is asking whether 2 + 2 must equal 4, but he is not really asking about this one equation, but rather using that single (iconic) equation as a proxy for a whole *system* of arithmetic. This system of arithmetic is one that has no ready name to identify it, but we will refer to it as the 'default' system (which is briefer than other correct designations, e.g., 'arithmetic with base ten and Arabic numerals'). It is the default arithmetic in the sense that it is the one taught in schools and employed across a wide diversity of practices.

The question 'Must 2 + 2 = 4?' can be asked as a question *about* the default mathematical system or as a question *within* the default system. If asked *within* the default number system, the answer is 'yes', since any other answer is wrong. That this is so is part of what identifies the system, and, also, what identifies the equation as belonging to the system. If asked *about* the default system, then it is not entirely clear what the question is asking: 'Can you think of mathematical systems in which 2 + 2 is not 4?'; 'Are there empirical situations in which 2 + 2 is not 4?'; or: 'Are there historical reasons why we have this arithmetic system?' Asked *about* a system (rather than within one), '2 + 2' does not *yet* have a definite sense, since it only constitutes a notational form. For example, '+' in the case of adding sheep has the sense of 'accumulating a totality', whereas in the case of the number wheel it has the sense of 'tracking positions in a cycle'. All that Bloor demonstrates is another mathematical triviality: the same symbols can be used differently in different calculi (cf. Ambrose 1955, 208).

The difficulty in specifying what exactly the question 'Must 2 + 2 = 4?' is asking points to a second issue, namely: Of *whom* is this question being asked? Asked of a professional mathematician, understood as asking 'Is there more than one arithmetic system?', it is mathematically trivial that there are. Asked of ordinary users in the street, unprepared for it, the question may well create difficulties, since it is not clear in what sense those using the default system understand that it is a distinctive system, let alone what 'other systems of arithmetic' might be. This is not because they are unaware or unfamiliar with 'other systems of arithmetic' (most people are familiar with twelve-hour clocks in which 11 + 3 = 2), but because the sense of the question is unclear. It is easier to know how to respond to 'Could one drive on an alternative side of the road?' than to 'Are there alternative systems of arithmetic?'.

Of course, Bloor is not so much asking *whether* 2 + 2 = 4, but *why* 2 + 2 = 4, i.e., what kind of justification one might give for this mathematical fact. Bloor wants to argue that it is true *by convention* that 2 + 2 = 4 (which is why he is often taken to be a relativist). In contrast, we want to ask: In which sense does convention make it true that if we add two things and two things, it always comes out as four?

It is certainly the case that the development of a specific arithmetic system is contingent (a different 'default' system could have been institutionalized).

However, this does not entail that the operations within a particular system are contingent. There is a difference between the necessity in adopt*ing* a system and the necessity imposed by an adopt*ed* system. As Wittgenstein (1976, 241) remarks: 'We must distinguish between a necessity in the system and a necessity of the whole system'. The observation that 2 + 2 is 'always' 4 is thus not a false generalization, rebutted by the existence of other arithmetics, but the expression of the necessity imposed by a particular system of arithmetic. Whenever one is operating in *this* number system, then if one is given 2 + 2 one *must* sum it to 4.

The origin of confusing the different kinds of necessity is to take mathematical expressions as propositions, i.e., as descriptions of states of affairs. As Wittgenstein emphasized, equations should not be treated as representations of any kind of realities (natural, logical, or social), but rather as *means* of representation, i.e., as providing a framework within which description of states of affairs may be constructed (Wittgenstein 1978, VII, §2). That is to say, Wittgenstein argued that mathematical statements should (in order to avoid confusion) be considered as rules – and rules although 'conventional' are *in themselves* neither true nor false.

Bloor, in a sense, is asking where the correctness of an arithmetic system resides. He rebuts the two traditional answers (in nature or in logic), which leaves him, through a process of elimination, with the answer: in society. In contrast, Wittgenstein questions whether it makes sense to ask about the correctness of an arithmetic system without specifying a particular context or purpose. For Wittgenstein, 'correct' is not constant across different systems of conventions, but has a different sense, a different application, depending upon the system of conventions. It cannot be that all systems of conventions are equally correct, because there is no general, independent standard of 'correctness'. The puzzle as to how conventions can apply to reality is thereby dissolved, for compliance with the rules of the arithmetic *establishes* what we mean by 'correspondence with reality'.

Why 'the Sociologist'?

Wittgenstein, by characterizing mathematical expressions as rules, is making a 'sociological turn' that reminds us of the roles that arithmetical expressions play in our practices and the kinds of questions that can be sensibly asked of them. Need the sociological turn go further? Bloor thinks so. Our above claim to be more in tune with Wittgenstein does not mean that Bloor misguidedly thinks of himself as following through Wittgenstein's approach. Bloor is aware that Wittgenstein thinks philosophical inquiries require no controversial empirical evidence, but Bloor rejects this idea and reproaches Wittgenstein for chickening out on the necessity to move on from philosophical to empirical (scientific) investigations. It is this claim that is the nub of our disagreement with him.

In our view, pointing out that mathematical equations are rules is sufficient to undermine traditional philosophical positions. Furthermore, the observation that there is no necessary arithmetical system points toward mathematical truisms, not to either sociological findings or the need for an explanatory sociological theory. Wittgenstein argues that rather than making extensive historical and anthropological investigations into the different kinds of mathematics one can find (although such enterprises may be interesting), we should pay more careful attention to the *form* of the mathematical statements that are to be found in the mathematics we are already familiar with. The status of '2 + 2 = 4' as a universal truth is not undermined by showing that there are circumstances in which it is false, but by realizing that the idea of 'universal truth' is misleading, because '2 + 2 = 4' does not function as an empirical proposition but more like a rule and, as such, can be *neither* true *nor* false.[5]

Bloor is insistent that the sociologist plays a part, but the idea that this is necessary arises, we think, from the fact that Bloor has taken an argument addressed to the source of philosophical problems and treated it as a diagnosis of the functional structure of the practical understanding of arithmetic. Bloor construes the 'problem' in the following way:

> Food is a cultural universal, because everybody has to eat to survive. Does this preclude the sociologist having significant things to say about food? Clearly not, because there is still the question of how people eat, who eats what, and when, and with whom. We might say that while 'nutrition' is a biological category, 'the meal' is a sociological category. [...] We must see if analogous ideas and distinctions apply in the case of 2 + 2 = 4. Can numbers be divided into their physical, biological and social aspects in the way that the ingesting of food can? (Bloor 1994, 22).

The term 'sociological' can be applied in two ways: firstly, to identify a certain genre of observations, which note the connection of activities to social groups, cultural traditions, social relations, etc.; secondly, to characterize remarks originating with those who are sociologists by occupational title and theoretical affiliation (thereby implying that it is through specific sociological tools – methods or theories – that these remarks were discovered or are validated). That there are local cuisines and local culinary practices is 'sociological' in the first sense, for

---

5 If there is any difficulty in understanding why '2 + 2 = 4' is said to be a rule, recognize that one is taught it as an injunction, saying what one has to do: 'whenever you see '2 + 2 = ' then write '4'. In other words, arithmetical equations can be seen as rules for the transformation of notations. In applied calculations, they are rules for the transformation of empirical propositions – if you have two sheep and you buy two sheep you can then (correctly) say you have four sheep. There is no opportunity here to venture into the background debates between David Bloor and Michael Lynch over Wittgenstein and rules (Bloor 1992; Lynch 1992a, b), but our views are much closer to Lynch's than Bloor's, and agree with Friedman's (1998, 266) observation that 'Lynch's Wittgenstein is both closer to the actual Wittgenstein and more sophisticated philosophically than Bloor's'.

such observations did not and need not originate as deliverances of sociological professionals. Although travellers would not necessarily label these observations as 'sociological', observations about cultural diversity can and are made by non-sociologists. In contrast, a comparison of the birth rates among the lower, middle, and upper classes more clearly belongs to the sociologist as a professional.

Now remember that Bloor sees his project as establishing 'the conventional aspects of knowledge', i.e., 'to identify the conventional components of the concepts '2' and '4' and 'addition' (21). We have argued that Bloor's observations about the 'conventional components' of arithmetic are 'sociological' in our first sense. It is not that people are always aware that there are a multitude of arithmetic systems, but rather that 'demonstrating' the conventional aspects of knowledge resembles the neighbour coming back from a trip to China and telling everyone: 'They eat rice rather than potatoes over there, and they use chopsticks rather than forks and knives' – thereby 'demonstrating' the cultural diversity of the meal and cutlery.

Bloor believes that such observations may be acceptable to non-sociologists in the case of traffic rules or meals, but not in the case of mathematics. In other words, the attempt to show that there are alternative mathematics will meet with resistance: 'candidate alternatives often meet objections. Reasons are found to sideline, trivialize or re-interpret them so that their character as alternatives is disguised' (21). This is why Bloor thinks that demonstrating the conventional aspects of knowledge is the task of the professional sociologist, since it is presumably only the sociologist who is able to see the implications of the availability of alternatives and who is able to prevent those implications being sidelined, trivialized, or re-interpreted. Our disagreement with Bloor is thus not on whether there are alternatives, but whether there are those reactions to those alternatives.

In our view, Bloor does not adequately clarify the implications of the availability of alternatives for the default system. In other words, once we have read his paper on 2 + 2 = 0, what has *changed*? That there are alternative arithmetics does not make any difference to everyday practical computations using the default system. In particular, the number wheel system does not have an impact on most practical calculations: buying two pairs of apples is still four apples – and not '0' apples (since this is not a situation to which the number wheel system is applicable). For many everyday calculations, it simply does not matter that the default arithmetic system is not a unique system. Nor do we think that it is appropriate to conceive everyday users of the default arithmetic as though they are in denial about the conventionality of mathematics. Just as we did with Durkheim, we would argue for a deflationary reading of Bloor, which puts members of society in M. Jourdain's situation: his difficulty is not that he does not know how to speak prose (for that is what he does before and after being taught by the philosopher), but that he simply isn't familiar with the name that grammarians give to the activity of which he is a practical master. Equally, there are grounds to suppose that many members of the society are *practically* familiar with more than a single arithmetic system and that they can and do, in practice, comfortably switch from using one form to using another when it is appropriate (e.g., when using a twelve-hour clock or counting in dozens). In that sense, Bloor does not demonstrate something new to members of society, but simply reminds them of something that they are already familiar with (but perhaps incapable of recognizing as the intended referent of 'conventional').

None of this really matters to Bloor, since his target is not the computational validity of calculations that people perform, but the 'justificatory underpinnings' of those calculations. We say this, because we are trying to make sense of the fact that the availability of alternative arithmetics for us is more like a triviality, whereas for Bloor it has epistemological implications. Bloor seems to be engaged in a therapy of ideology, which supposedly accompanies, even underpins, the practical mastery of arithmetic. Bloor seems to suppose that children being drilled in arithmetic are *additionally* supplied with justifications for using this practice as a means of binding them into it (i.e., they will act in accord with it, because they are under the delusion that they could not do otherwise). In line with critique of ideology more generally, Bloor supposes that in the case of arithmetic ideology takes the form of naturalizing a practice, i.e., as treating arithmetic as though it originates in the natural order of things and *therefore* is immutable. For Bloor, the typical reaction to $2 + 2 = 4$ (that it is impossible to do otherwise) is evidence for this ideology.

The rather standard sociological assumption that practices are sustained by virtue of associated justifications is perhaps too easily made, and only serves to ensure a sociological surplus above what is required to understand the problem at issue. The idea is that the naturalization of a practice *prevents* its participants from calling it into question (since they cannot doubt what must inevitably be the case). If the practice is de-naturalized, then it will be apparent that they *could* do otherwise, enabling them to withdraw support from this practice. However, even if people with practical mastery of arithmetic did labour under such a naturalizing illusion, it does not follow that they could simply resign from the default arithmetic and make up their own, since many practices that they engage in have the default arithmetic installed in their organizational and technological infrastructures. More importantly, we have been arguing that mastery of arithmetic does not depend upon any such naturalizing justification. Practical mastery of calculation in our society involves a fundamental familiarity with the default arithmetic, but the practical familiarity with it as the default one does not exclude practical participation with other, non-default, arithmetic practices. In other words, the conventions of the default system are not destabilized by the fact that its users 'could do otherwise' when, in fact, they cannot, because, in fact, people have no difficulty in already 'doing otherwise' in the sense that they frequently operate according to conventions other than those of the default system.

Conclusion

We have tried to suggest that buying into the idea of 'social facts' does not involve any very momentous decision, since it can be seen as simply a nomenclatural matter, i.e., as only naming a range of unremarkable, entirely familiar, and in a practical way very well understood affairs. It is not the recognition that one lives amongst collectively accumulated institutions and practices that causes the trouble, but that Durkheim moves from this observation to ontological doctrines about social facts.

Rafanell (this volume) quotes Durkheim arguing that we are under 'an illusion [if] we believe that we ourselves have produced what has been imposed upon us externally'. On what we have termed the inflationary reading, ordinary members of society commonly believe that they have freely created what is in reality imposed upon them. However, Durkheim's documentations of the existence of social facts allow for a deflationary interpretation, where 'having to' use the local language and local currency is a practical rather than causal necessity: living in society does consist in acting within its local institutions and customs, but this does not entail believing that these are the only institutions and customs there could possibly be.

Using David Bloor's campaign for a Durkheimian sociology of mathematics as an illustration, we argued that the notion that people are subject to illusions about the objectivity of the practices they engage in becomes an *a priori* assumption that is projected onto the workings of practices with the effect of distorting the sense that attaches to the ways of these practices.[6] Bloor's whole argument on mathematical equations assumes that their users are under such an illusion, believing that when asked '2 + 2 = ?' they have no choice but to answer '4'. Bloor seeks to demonstrate users' delusional state by establishing that they 'could do otherwise', i.e., that alternative mathematical systems might accommodate different answers to '2 + 2 = ?'. However, it is not so much the idea that equations are conventions that propels Bloor's argument as ambiguity about 'could do otherwise'. One certainly could do otherwise then write 4, since one could refuse to complete the question or reinterpret the question. However, giving a different answer to a different question (e.g., interpreting the equation as part of a different arithmetic system), says nothing about what one 'has' to do to if one wants to complete *this* equation correctly. Bloor's attempt to invoke alternate mathematical systems itself depends upon the very thing that it purports to explain, namely that if one understands (for example) the number wheel system properly, then one understands that if asked '2 + 2 = ?' *one has no choice* but to say '0'. The compulsion does not result from any causal force, but from the identifying requirements of that system delimiting what are valid actions within it. Bloor has not shown that there is space for a

---

6 Sociologists are apt, at crucial moments, to think of individual consciousness as solipsist, which is perhaps why they have had such a hard time recognizing that positions which they (critically) designate as 'subjective' actually emphasize intersubjectivity (cf. Greiffenhagen and Sharrock, 2008).

sociological explanation as to why the users of arithmetic need to operate under a socially necessary illusion, since there is no such illusion.

Bloor sees the sociologist's job as therapeutic, i.e., as convincing members of society of the conventional aspects of knowledge in the face of their reluctance to accept this. However, this therapeutic strategy only works by assuming that members' practical doings (their use of the default system) are underpinned by a naturalized ideology of that practice (universalistic beliefs). In contrast, Wittgenstein's therapeutic method (cf. Anderson et al. 1986, Chapter 6) cures us of the idea that practices are founded in theoretical presuppositions. With respect to mathematics, Wittgenstein does not replace empiricism or universalism with social constructivism or relativism, since he argues that the understanding of philosophical problems does not come from any theory, but from careful reflection on our mastery of the relevant practice, e.g., of elementary arithmetic. While Bloor's therapy is a therapy *from* one (ideological) theory *to* another (correct) theory, Wittgenstein's therapy is a therapy *away from theory.*

Acknowledgements

We would like to thank the editors (Geoff Cooper, Andrew King, and Ruth Rettie) and one anonymous reviewer for helpful comments on an earlier draft. Christian Greiffenhagen acknowledges support from the British Academy (a Postdoctoral Fellowship and a Small Research Grant) and Wes Sharrock support from the Arts and Humanities Research Board (award number B/IA/AN10985/APN17690).

References

Ambrose, A. (1955), 'Wittgenstein on Some Questions in Foundations of Mathematics', *Journal of Philosophy* 52:8, 197–214.
Anderson, R.J., Hughes, J.A. and Sharrock W.W. (1986), *Philosophy and the Human Sciences* (London: Croom Helm).
Bloor, D. (1973), 'Wittgenstein and Mannheim on the Sociology of Mathematics', *Studies in History and Philosophy of Science* 4:2, 173–191.
Bloor, D. (1976), *Knowledge and Social Imagery* (London: Routledge and Kegan Paul).
Bloor, D. (1982), 'Durkheim and Mauss Revisited: Classification and the Sociology of Knowledge', *Studies in History and Philosophy of Science* 13:4, 267–297.
Bloor, D. (1983), *Wittgenstein: A Social Theory of Knowledge* (London: Macmillan).
Bloor, D. (1992), 'Left and Right Wittgensteinians', in A. Pickering (ed.).
Bloor, D. (1994), 'What Can the Sociologist of Knowledge Say about $2 + 2 = 4$?', in Ernest (ed.).
Durkheim, E. (1982 [1895]), *The Rules of Sociological Method*, edited by S. Lukes, translated by W.D. Halls (London: Macmillan).

Ernest, P. (ed.) (1994), *Mathematics, Education and Philosophy: An International Perspective* (London: Falmer).

Friedman, M. (1998), 'On the Sociology of Scientific Knowledge and its Philosophical Agenda', *Studies in the History and Philosophy of Science* 29:2, 239–271.

Garfinkel, H. (1963), 'A Conception of, and Experiments with, "Trust" as a Condition of Stable Concerted Actions', in Harvey (ed.).

Garfinkel, H. (2002), *Ethnomethodology's Program: Working Out Durkheim's Aphorism* (Lanham, MD: Rowman & Littlefield).

Garfinkel, H. and Sacks H. (1970), 'On Formal Structures of Practical Action', in McKinney and Tiryakian (eds).

Greiffenhagen, C. and Sharrock W. (2006), 'Mathematical Relativism: Logic, Grammar, and Arithmetic in Cultural Comparison', *Journal for the Theory of Social Behaviour* 36:2, 97–117.

Greiffenhagen, C. and Sharrock, W. (2008), 'Where Do the Limits of Experience Lie? Abandoning the Dualism of Objectivity and Subjectivity', *History of the Human Sciences* 21:3, 70–93.

Harvey, O.J. (ed.) (1963), *Motivation and Social Interaction* (New York, NY: Ronald Press).

McKinney, J.C. and Tiryakian E.A. (eds) (1970), *Theoretical Sociology: Perspectives and Developments* (New York: Appleton-Century-Crofts).

Lynch, M. (1992a), 'Extending Wittgenstein: The Pivotal Move from Epistemology to the Sociology of Science', in Pickering (ed.).

Lynch, M. (1992b), 'From the "Will to Theory" to the Discursive Collage: A Reply to Bloor's "Left and Right Wittgensteinians"', in Pickering (ed.).

Mannheim, K. (1936), *Ideology and Utopia: An Introduction to the Sociology of Knowledge* (London: Routledge and Kegan Paul).

Pickering, A. (ed.) (1992), *Science as Practice and Culture* (Chicago: University of Chicago Press).

Rawls, A.W. (1996), 'Durkheim's Epistemology: The Neglected Argument', *American Journal of Sociology* 102:2, 430–482.

Rawls, A.W. (2004), *Epistemology and Practice: Durkheim's 'The Elementary Forms of Religious Life'* (Cambridge: Cambridge University Press).

Schutz, A. and T. Luckmann (1973), *The Structures of the Life-world*, translated by R.M. Zaner and H.T. Engelhardt (Evanston, IL: Northwestern University Press).

White, L. (1947), 'The Locus of Mathematical Reality: An Anthropological Footnote', *Philosophy of Science* 14:4, 289–303.

Wittgenstein, L. (1953), *Philosophical Investigations*, translated by G.E.M. Anscombe (Oxford: Blackwell).

Wittgenstein, L. (1976), *Wittgenstein's Lectures on the Foundations of Mathematics, Cambridge, 1939*, edited by C. Diamond (Chicago: University of Chicago Press).

Wittgenstein, L. (1978), *Remarks on the Foundations of Mathematics*, 3rd edition, edited by G.H. von Wright, R. Rhees and G.E.M. Anscombe, translated by G.E.M. Anscombe (Oxford: Blackwell).

PART 3
Social Theories

Having considered some theoretical formulations of sociological objects, and conceptions of practice that, amongst other things, raise important questions about how theory is used in sociological analysis, we now focus directly on the practice of theory today and some of the reconfigurations to which it may be subject. Each chapter pays particular attention to some aspects of the current contexts in which theory is used, in order to consider the relation of general arguments – about theory's role, boundaries and limits – to more specific historical moments.

Mik-Mayer confronts widespread concerns about the tendency for theory to prefigure and form its object. Ethnomethodologists (see Part 2) see the use of theory as a potentially problematic example of the documentary method of interpretation at work, while Latour makes a related recommendation that we (simply) follow the actors; in both cases we see a caution about, or even an injunction to avoid, the use of theoretical constructs, since the latter's relation to the lived word of social actors is uncertain at best. This issue reverberates throughout methodological discussions in social science, for example in the arenas of discourse analysis and conversation analysis. Mik-Mayer argues that the formulation of this opposition – between theorizing, and receptivity to empirical phenomena in their own terms – misses the fact that there is no clear separation between everyday and theoretical discourses, and that theoretical categories can themselves often become constitutive features of social practice. She uses a study of welfare policies and interventions in relation to obesity to substantiate her argument, and shows in the first place that what Hacking, following Goffman, calls a looping effect is at work: that is, in this case, that categories such as risk and citizenship that have their roots in social scientific discourse have a significant presence and influence in the therapeutic and welfare context. Moreover, in the second place, she argues that sociological theories – notably, of governmentality – are indispensable to understand the movements of these categories.

Tsatsaroni and Cooper begin their discussion of theory from a historically specific domain and context: a set of arrangements that can be glossed in terms of 'audit culture' and the ways in which researchers in the sociology of education have responded to them. Noting, and to some extent sympathizing with, the perception that this set of arrangements can easily be characterized as hostile to theory, they also point to the problematic way in which, in such a context, theory can be reified: historical developments of this kind are taken to represent threat, corruption or contamination of theory, and theory, in turn, can then be taken as a given form of resistance. Rather, they suggest, since theory is by its very nature *always* subject to and constituted by processes of transformation and translation, as this book demonstrates, the challenge is to reformulate our understanding of theory in ways that can do justice to its dynamic character. They consider the value of work – in particular that of Bernstein, Latour and Derrida – which, in different ways, places the idea of translation at its very centre. The different ways in question represent different models of theory, and as such provide resources for understanding some fundamental differences of approach (which might be described, respectively, as modernist, minimalist or performative) to the role, purpose and value of theory. We would add that consideration of the relative value of such fundamental differences of approach is highly pertinent to any assessment of the continuing value of classical sociological theory.

Similarly, du Gay firmly locates his discussion of theory in the contemporary intellectual context and, in common with some of the work in the sociology of education discussed in the previous chapter, understands this as a turning away from theory: however, he sees this change in less unequivocally negative terms. Rather, he reflects back upon the 'moment of theory' that appears to have passed, and subjects it to a more sceptical and reflexive analysis. If identity was one of the key thematic areas in which this moment – understood in terms of the influence of certain forms of critical, philosophical and continental theory – was visible, it is also (now) possible to use understandings of identity to analyse this phenomenon. Du Gay suggests that at least part of the apparent success of particular modes of theoretical practice can be attributed to the particular kinds of identity and status that are conferred upon the theorist. Moreover, viewed from the perspective of a subsequent moment in which theory is not, of itself, a self-evident good, questions about the (practical) value of theorizing can now be raised. Again, this opens up questions about the limits of theory, and the problematic relation between theory (in this case certain forms of critical theory) and everyday understandings.

While there are some marked differences of emphasis and substance in the three chapters, in each case there is an attempt to address, or an orientation towards, certain recurrent questions, many of which have considerable resonance with points that have already been raised. What is the role of theory today? What sorts of reconfigurations is it undergoing? What kinds of theories, if any, do we need to provide analytical purchase on the objects of interest? And, if there is such a need, can it be reconciled with what we might regard as an ethical requirement for a degree of modesty in relation to other forms of explanation, including 'lay' understandings?

Chapter 8
Social Theory in Situated Practice: Theoretical Categories in Everyday Discourse

Nanna Mik-Meyer

Introduction

There is a long tradition of keeping data free of theory in sociological analyses that focus on people's actions. We see this tradition in ethnomethodology's (EM) focus on common sense knowledge (Garfinkel 1974: vii); likewise conversation analysis (CA) sets theoretical generalities aside by focusing on how actors create social order in specific situations. Indeed, as Boden (1994) has pointed out, CA has thus turned the problem of social order upside down. Rather than inquiring into how people respond to a given social order, CA instead examines how people construct this order at a particular time and in a particular place. In this sense, CA eschews abstraction and theoretically loaded categories, arguing that the researcher should turn to the detailed, sequential organization of conversation in its specificity.

There is no doubt that this "bottom-up" (Hacking 2004) approach in sociology has contributed enormously to the development of sociology in general (Rawls 2002), and that much sociology could benefit from being "filled out" with "bottom-up" analysis, as Hacking (2004: 278) suggests. However, the narrow focus of both CA and EM on how a local social order is created "on the spot, out of the materials at hand" (Rawls 2002: 18) may also impose limitations on the analysis of local practices.

Within the research area of the sociology of the body (which this chapter uses as the focus for the discussion), there exists a very close-knit relationship between "scientific consciousness" and "everyday consciousness" (Bourdieu 1993: 54). Not only do sociologists speak of "bodies at risk" and connect concepts like "control" and "responsibility" to neo-liberal values in Western societies, but lay persons also use these concepts in, for example, certain institutional settings, particularly where the institution in question has a health, welfare or therapeutic remit. Even though we are not necessarily dealing with what Bourdieu (1993: 21) conceptualizes as "an artificial language" – that is, theoretically loaded expressions that only people in a particular field understand – we are still dealing with theoretically loaded categories that are reproduced *both* in sociology *and* among the people we study. The following questions of Bourdieu's therefore become critical:

> Is the act of construction the work of the scientist or the native? Does the native have categories of perception and where does he get them from, and what is the relationship between the categories constructed by science and the categories that ordinary agents implement in their practice? (Bourdieu 1993: 54).

Sociologists need to examine "the relationship between the categories constructed by science and the categories that ordinary agents implement in their practice" (ibid.). Whilst this formulation would be congenial to ethnomethodologists, who have been assiduous in highlighting the conceptual confusions that can and do result from neglecting the significance of this relationship, I would argue that since theoretical categories can be shown to have a presence in everyday talk, their exclusion from sociological analysis can be problematic. To fully comprehend and analyse everyday practices, sociologists can therefore benefit from allowing theoretically loaded research questions and categories into the analysis of everyday practice.

I argue that the accomplishment of a local social order (in a specific time at a specific place) has to take into account the flow of categories from the field of professional discourse, which includes sociological discourse, to the discourse used by the actors we study. (The existence of the same sociological categories in both sociology and practice is not solely – as sometimes implied in CA and EM – the result of a flow of categories in the opposite direction.) If the categories used by these actors stem in part from social science, then researchers need to free themselves from the long tradition in CA and EM that wants to keep data free of theory. Our research questions should therefore not merely be framed by sociological categories such as turn-taking (CA) or membership (EM), that is, categories that relate exclusively to the local social order; they can also benefit from the use of categories and concepts relating to broader societal phenomena. Theoretically informed research questions make assumptions about the nature of the social order, but these very assumptions can be productive for a thorough understanding of the creation of a local social order.

This chapter pays particular attention to the process whereby broader theoretical categories become incorporated into everyday discourse. Sociological researchers not only study practices and more general societal processes but also, as a by-product of the discourse they use, help to produce social practices. One of the consequences is that lay people focus on and use only parts of the theories or some of the language of sociology – not all. Thus, for example, when governmentality-inspired researchers talk about "risk", their discourse also includes discussions of underlying or attendant value systems, such as neo-liberal ideas of self-control, responsibility, and self-motivation. But if a lay person focuses on and uses the term "risk" by itself, then researchers have to realize that the neo-liberal values that accompany the concept of "risk" need the researcher's attention. Empirically the researcher has to analyse whether these values frame the conversation even though they are absent from the conversation itself.

We all – lay persons and sociologists alike – live in the society that sociology describes and analyses and, to a greater or lesser extent, we all play a part in the constitution and maintenance specific dominant discourses. Garfinkel (1967: 34) writes that "indexical [i.e., contextual] expressions and indexical actions [are] an ongoing achievement of the organized activities of everyday life". To supplement Garfinkel here, I argue that we also need to deploy sociological understandings of the wider contexts within which everyday life practices take place. In other words, these contexts frame processes that are not necessarily made visible by the actors we study, but can be made visible by the inclusion of sociological categories stemming from sociological analyses of Western societies.

For example, Hacking (2004) – positioning Foucault's approach as "top-down" and Goffman's approach as "bottom-up" – argues that researchers can benefit by viewing these approaches as complementary instead of mutually exclusive. Similarly, the goal of this chapter is to point towards the benefits that researchers can gain from including theoretically loaded sociological categories in the analysis of everyday talk. Given that our goal as sociologists is to analyse classification processes among different actors – as much of CA and EM does – we also need to understand, for example, how particular institutions came into being if we are to understand their classification process (Hacking 2004: 278).

Hacking (2004: 279) uses the concept "dynamic nominalism" to stress that "naming has real effects on people and changing people have real effects on subsequent classifications" (ibid. 280). The effects he focuses upon, however, do not necessarily have to be direct effects that researchers can observe in the actual interaction where the classification processes occur. When Hacking (2004: 297) writes that classification can be "incorporated into the rules of the institutions … related to the interaction with institutions", he is pointing towards classifications that while "inaccessible to the person classified" nevertheless relate to scientific knowledge about that specific type of person.

Symbolic interactionists such as Gubrium and Holstein (2001) are attentive to the institutional aspect of identity work among different actors, and they incorporate in their analysis theory and sociological categories produced in research focusing on processes outside the actual interactions. This chapter, however, argues for an even stronger use of broader sociological categories in analyses of social interaction. Instead of viewing sociological theories as "a great danger", as EM researchers do (Rawls 2002: 29), I want to invite into the analysis sociological categories coming from sociologists who theorize about the nature of Western societies.

The argument for using these kinds of theories emerges from a number of reflexive considerations that all – in slightly different ways – touch upon the relationship between theory and praxis. From the standpoint of a more general theory of science, a well-known argument is that a particular theoretical approach leads to a certain analytical focus. Because the sociologist constructs the object of sociological research, theory must never be separated from data (Bourdieu 1993: 51). Since a researcher cannot approach an empirical field without a theoretical understanding of it, the only alternative to an analysis that is theoretically informed in an explicit manner is an analysis that merely reproduces the researcher's (unconscious) understanding of the field. This argument parallels some of the objections made by Wetherell (1998) and Billig (1999a, 1999b) to Schegloff's suggestion (1997, 1998, 1999a, 1999b) that discourse needs analysing in its "own terms" (i.e., those of the participants) and that the analyst should not "fuse" it with theory.

While this general discussion of how theoretical approaches lead to a certain analytical focus is important, this chapter also focuses on the following two methodological considerations: (a) that sociological categories (often) are embedded in the praxis sociologists focus upon, and (b) that a theoretically informed analysis is therefore required to make this intelligible.

Law and Urry's (2004) stimulating piece (about the "performative" character of sociological methods and theories) touches upon precisely this issue. Their argument is that theory, method and practice are mutually dependent, and that research therefore needs to bring the "two-way traffic" connecting society and science into focus (Law and Urry 2004: 392). Sociology is "relational" or "interactive" because sociologists "*participate in, reflect upon,* and *enact* the social in a wide range of locations including the state" (ibid.). Consequently, research methodologies and sociological theories become "performative"; that is, methods and theories have effects, make differences, and enact realities (ibid. 392–393).

All research objects reflect their wider context, in part because of the implication of research practices in broader social practices. But the mutual dependency of theoretically loaded categories such as risk and social practice is especially clear when we turn to the human body. To show how this dependency operates, this chapter uses an analysis of contemporary Danish welfare practices related to excess weight and obesity.[1] Using the familiar understanding of the West as a neo-liberal society regulated by risk assessments and moral reasoning (Ericson and Doyle 2003; Douglas 1992), we can investigate how sociological categories that have developed from this understanding affect praxis, and vice versa.

This investigation can be highly productive in analysing the "fat body" from a sociological perspective primarily inspired by symbolic interactionism. In other words, the act of doing a sociological analysis of Danish practices reveals the simultaneous existence of theory and praxis operating within this particular understanding. Here theory becomes both constitutive *of* and constitutive *for* practice. We must therefore take a pragmatic approach to sociological theory, treating it not as an overarching explanatory model of the world but as a set of

---

[1] The terms used in these settings are far from neutral; however given that their frequent usage is unavoidable in what follows, I have, for stylistic reasons, omitted to use scare quotes or similar qualifying devices when referring to such words as fat, overweight, obese, and obesity.

relevant sociological categories that are productive in an analysis of an object under investigation. Categories such as risk are not merely the tools of sociologists wishing to understand local practices; rather, actors themselves already use these categories in making sense of their world.

The "Two-Way Traffic" Connecting Society and Science

The Theoretical Approach Leads to a Certain Analytical Focus

Constructivist-inspired studies concerning the body conceptualize it as a social and cultural – rather than a biological – phenomenon (for example, Orbach 1978; Bordo 1993; LeBesco 2004). This choice – to focus on the body as either a social or a biological phenomenon – illustrates the standpoint that the separation of theory (*how* we look at something) from the object under investigation (*what* we are looking at) is impossible.

Within this perspective, 'being overweight' or 'obese', for example, are part of what Greco (2004) terms "the politics of indeterminacy": the concepts are regulated not only by medical science but also by social and moral norms (Greco 2004: 4–9). While health politics in medical research is often discussed as if health were a determinate value (i.e., "a value that can be identified with a set of objective evidence" (ibid. 6), the constructivist perspective rejects the idea of "objective evidence" altogether. Within the constructivist perspective the body is construed as an "unfinished entity" (Shilling 1993), that is, an entity constantly in the process of being classified. Research into the social dimensions of obesity therefore needs to consider how the body is made "finished" in different social environments.

Since its classification is influenced by dominant social and cultural discourses, the body is a locus of power: specific bodies are always defined as "normal" or "abnormal" at specific times (Blaikie et al. 2004). Thus, power is implicated in the constructions 'overweight' or 'fat', and needs to be brought to the forefront of the analysis of, for example, interactions between health consultants and ostensibly overweight persons. To engage in such an analysis is to make a theoretically informed choice; as, arguably, would be the decision to eschew the use of power as an organizing concept. The researcher's categories – for example, whether the overweight persons are presented as either "clients" or "participants/members" – may reflect the choice made, and will lead to a particular analytical focus (Bourdieu 1993). Three points stemming from a constructionist approach are particularly important here.

Firstly, it is central to a constructionist approach to view the fat body as an unfinished entity that is being negotiated in a range of different situations. This relational approach will consequently accept and focus on such discourses as, for example, the medical one that dominates the field today. Viewing the body as part of a politics of indeterminacy, thereby placing moral issues at the center of the work, also directs the gaze of the researcher to specific parts of the empirical material – parts that will contain morally based arguments and so forth.

Secondly, viewing the fat body as strongly influenced by dominant discourses automatically directs the research interest towards areas such as politics, the media, and other powerful institutions. Examining how political instruments (for example, laws that demand health policies in public and private organizations) are being integrated into the actual work becomes central, thereby demanding specific actions from both health consultants and overweight persons. National health plans become material that the researcher has to consider and incorporate, along with other material such as media coverage of nationwide health initiatives. In short, viewing the body as a locus of power that is subordinated to changing political trends makes specific empirical material necessary for the research.

Thirdly, theoretical categories such as "somatic individual", "risk", and "indirect techniques of government" (for example, Lemke 2001; Novas and Rose 2000; O'Mally 2000) inform the research in a particular way. "Somatic individual" and the theory immanent in this category produce an interest in programs and concrete technologies, such as conversations (between an overweight person and a health consultant) aimed at making the overweight person view his or her situation as one of risking illness. Theories of risk define overweight and fat people as being "at risk"; this group then becomes one that provokes policy and welfare actions informed by neo-liberal values (for example, the valuation of self-restraint, self-governance, will power, responsibility and self-control). The risk discourse thus produces overweight and fat people as persons who should want to change their (problematic) situation. The extensive literature on a dominant neo-liberal discourse with its focus on indirect governing techniques also produces a certain gaze from the researcher: the presumption of the existence of "indirect techniques" for governing individual subjects influences the research plan, chosen method, empirical focus, and so forth.

Sociological Categories in Everyday Discourse

Theoretical and methodological choices "enact" reality in a certain way, to use Law and Urry's (2004) term – and are to some extent, as we shall see, already integrated in the practices sociologists study. Approaching the issue of being overweight within the constructivist approach outlined here, sociologists enact a reality that places power issues at the forefront of the analysis. Letting theories such as sociology of risk and governmentality inform the researcher's perspective establishes a focus that presumes that a government of risk exists and that this government produces specific strategies "that try to identify, treat, manage or administer those individuals, groups or localities where risk is seen to be high" (Rose 2001: 7).

This particular perspective (Ericson and Doyle 2003; O'Mally 2000; Rose 2001) has in recent years become more and more influential in sociological analysis, not least in analyses that focus on health and the body. Within this literature on governmentality, subjects are presumed to have a self-restraining and self-governing capacity. Therefore the researcher will pay extra attention to categories such as control, responsibility, and, self-motivation. Because neo-liberalism is a political strategy that underscores responsibility and self-motivation among subjects (see for example Rose 1996; Dean 1999) an analysis which does not attend to the significance of this strategy runs the risk of unreflectively reproducing aspects of the neo-liberal view that differences in health are a matter of choice, thereby making inequalities inevitable (Ericson et al. 2000: 532–533).

An important research focus in the analysis of neo-liberalism is the new governing techniques that the state uses. The theory of governmentality assumes that these techniques work "indirectly ... controlling individuals without at the same time being responsible for them" (Lemke 2001: 201). In this case, indirect governing techniques might include how (new) laws within the health area set a range of different initiatives aimed at reducing the number of overweight and fat people.

One new mechanism for "empowering" the citizen is a "citizens' contract" (Andersen 2007), which can be viewed as an indirect technique of government by which citizens accept and sign a contract stating they will improve, for example, their health. The introduction of the contract in meetings between clients and social workers both constitutes a new tool in the interaction (that will be visible in the actual dialogue) and links to a specific form of government (i.e., a specific set of values).

The literature on governmentality makes us as researchers even more attentive to the many technologies applied by state representatives: for example, health consultants aiming at turning "social risks" such as poor health and unemployment into a matter for the individual, rather than the state, to deal with. In other words, a social risk problem becomes individualized into a problem of "self-care" (Lemke 2001). Again we see the potential relevance and importance of sociological work on risk and governmentality for the understanding of everyday action in health and welfare settings.

The extensive literature on the body, risk, and neo-liberal society has provided my research with a range of interesting approaches to the study of excess weight and obesity in present Danish society. These approaches have directed my attention to how theoretically loaded categories are applied by actors in praxis and how, even when not used explicitly, these categories still guide the actor's understanding of the other's utterances.

In contrast to EM and CA, this perspective then focuses on how actors reproduce theoretically loaded categories. The use of these categories – for example, risk, control, responsibility, and self-motivation – in a conversation between a health consultant and an overweight person might have their origins in various different discourses, for example, those deriving from politics, the media, and healthcare research practices, although they are sociological in character. Through the professional language of (social) science, the categories are translated into, for example, the sociology of governmentality and risk. This translation process has consequences for the future classification process (cf. "looping effect" [Goffman 1990/1960]; Hacking 2004). My argument is therefore that theories of risk and governmentality are important because on the one hand they provide analytic purchase on the phenomena of interest, and on the other because they cannot be separated from these phenomena but have played a part in their construction.

Now, before offering some cases that show the mutual dependency between theory and practice, I will briefly present some background information on the subject.

Being Overweight in Danish Society Today

Over the last ten to twenty years, people's individual health situations have become not only personal and welfare issues but also issues upon which many private organizations focus. In 2001 the English National Audit Office estimated that the indirect cost of being overweight or fat in the UK, for example, amounted to £2 billion a year, including 18 million days lost through illness and 40,000 working years due to the high mortality rate among this category of persons (National Audit Office 2001). In Denmark we see the same development, leading Danish politicians to propose a variety of programs for reducing the number of overweight and fat persons. One popular instrument is the "personal health conversation" between an employee and a health consultant. In these conversations the employee explains his or her lifestyle (for example, eating, smoking, and drinking habits) so that the health consultant can advise him or her how to improve his or her health. A signed contract between the two parties documents that the individual employee will try to work towards a healthier lifestyle. The tools in these conversations (the focus on the individual's own responsibility, the signing of a contract, etc.) thus correspond with the findings within governmentality-inspired research into neo-liberal societies.

We also see the explosion in Denmark of projects under such titles as "summer, healthy and slim", "fit for work", "body and work: do you want to lose weight? Are you prepared for an active working life?", and "lifestyle clubs" in a number of Danish cities. The purpose of these projects is to help overweight people support each other while changing their lifestyle. The number of examples of actions targeted at this group is presumably related to the belief that being overweight is a problem not only for each individual but also for society (in that, for example, health complications can lead to being unfit for work). Many programs take an explicit stance towards the imagined psychological situation of overweight people. A look at the popular media gives a reasonably clear image of what that situation involves. The overweight persons live with an awareness of a number of (often horrible) scenarios of what might happen if they do not lose weight. Moreover, the contents of popular science magazines indicate that the overweight face a good deal of psychological profiling, meaning that psychology-identified factors are causally related to being overweight.

The analysis in this chapter draws from a two-year research project on weight and obesity in Denmark, beginning in 2005. In the main study, I have taken a qualitative, ethnographic approach, consisting of: participant observations; recorded conversations between health consultants and overweight employees (at which I was not present); interviews with health consultants, managers, and overweight employees; and studies of documents from the participating institutions and the wider political realm. A general focus on identity constructions in this line of work situates the analysis within an anti-essentialist approach that naturally also affects the status of the empirical material. All the texts that enter the analysis are *social* texts; they should not be understood as "pure data" in a more naturalistic sense (Holstein and Gubrium 1997).

This chapter draws on (a) 26 recorded personal health conversations between health consultants and overweight persons in two institutions that offer health programs to overweight and fat employees, and (b) six interviews with health consultants and overweight persons in one of these institutions. The personal health conversations were recorded in one large and one medium-sized municipality in Denmark. Both municipalities offer health initiatives to their overweight employees or to other overweight persons who are on short-term leave from their jobs or who have recently left the labor market.

Both groups of persons received a letter about my research several days before the conversation, stressing that participation would be very welcome, with their consent. I explained that participation would be anonymous and that they could decide not to allow me to have the recording after the conversation if they changed their mind (none did). The recorded conversations lasted about one hour each. I have listened to the recordings twice; the first time, I noted down the themes under discussion as the tape played; the second time, I marked specifically which themes I wanted to have transcribed. For example, I typically skipped long monologues from the health consultant on nutritional matters, while transcribing passages that favored dialogue between the two parties. In general, 20 to 40 minutes of each conversation has been transcribed. Of the 26 recordings, 22 are women and four are men. Most are in their 40s and 50s (except two in their 60s), and all are ethnic Danes. The health conversations were conducted in Danish, and I have translated all extracts for this chapter.

The interviews took their point of departure from an interview guide focused on the content of the projects (why the overweight persons had signed up for the project and why the institutions had decided to work with weight problems) and on how the overweight persons and the health consultants viewed being overweight and fatness in broader terms. The interviews, carried out in an open-ended way, lasted between 20 minutes and one and a half hours and all interviews were transcribed in full.

The following cases illustrate issues both overweight people and health consultants bring up in interviews and in conversations with each other. Case 1 uses three interview extracts from two interviews: one with an overweight woman and one with a health consultant. Case 2 uses three interview extracts from a recorded health conversation. The two cases are revealing in two ways. First, they show how the sociological categories of the risk society are immanent in the person's discussion about overweight and fatness (both visibly and invisibly in the conversations). Second, they show how a specific theoretical and methodological approach has a "performative" effect on the actual analysis. This effect occurs both on a general level, where the selection of actors for the study takes place, and on a specific level, where the selection of materials to extract from the interviews and health conversations occurs. The account that emerges from these choices obviously depends heavily on the categories that suggested them.

Case 1: "If you have a BMI over 30/35, then you are fat in risk group one": Sociological categories in everyday discourse[2]

In interviews, observation notes, and a variety of documents the different actors in the projects used many of the categories that are central to sociological theories of risk, morality and neo-liberalism. The overweight and the health consultants talked about "risk", "illness", "being active", "laziness", "(ir)responsibility", "initiative" and related terms. (These categories also appeared on many homepages about being overweight and fat.)

The first two interview extracts derive from an interview with a self-described "fat woman," who is part of a program aimed at helping overweight and fat persons to lose weight.

> Interviewer: Your experiences with the job market are mixed …?
>
> Respondent: On my first job I didn't go to a job interview … if I had gone, I would probably never have gotten the job.
>
> Interviewer: No …?
>
> Respondent: And I wouldn't have dared to [go to an interview].
>
> Interviewer: How big do you think one can be without being a problem?
>
> Respondent: I don't know – but I do think one can be a little overweight, because most people are, but once you are fat, because I am fat and I know that when people say 'but you are only large or overweight …', but you are fat when you weigh 60 kilos too much. Then you are fat!
>
> Interviewer: Then you are fat …?

---

2 Body Mass Index (BMI) is a relationship between weight and height that is associated with body fat and health risk. A BMI over 25 is considered overweight and a BMI over 30 is considered obese.

Social Theory in Situated Practice 149

> Respondent: There is this table: If you have a BMI over 30/35 then you are fat in risk group one and so forth ... if you have a BMI over 40 you are in risk group three.
>
> Interviewer: What does risk group three imply?
>
> Respondent: It implies that you are even more exposed to health complications [than fat persons in risk group one].
>
> Interviewer: Like what?
>
> Respondent: Bad heart, diabetes, and all those things.

This woman has clearly learned to relate her body weight to a risk profile. Her "at risk" identity "finishes" her as a person with a problem identity; she is not only more exposed to health complications, but she might also have difficulties finding a job. She reproduces medically based knowledge about the connection between BMI, risk group, and health complications as presented to her on the first day of the program. Such knowledge is reproduced and reinforced in a range of different settings: in the media, the Danish Ministry of Health homepage, and so forth. This small extract thus exemplifies what Latour (1987) has called "action-at-a-distance": present actions connect to events that have taken place earlier, thereby involving new actors in the analysis. While the linkage of weight, risk, complications, and job capability probably also reveals something about our society and its governing techniques, only by bringing in theory aimed at diagnosing contemporary Western society through a focus on techniques of government can we properly contextualize and make intelligible the nature of this linkage.

Later in the interview the woman talks about how difficult it is to be fat, both because of a range of physical limitations and because of the way people look at her. Thus my next question is a follow-up to her thoughts about these issues:

> Interviewer: How do you think people look at overweight people?
>
> Respondent: I think as lazy and indolent, because one keeps getting told 'but why don't you do anything about it [the weight problem]?' But it's not as easy as they make it sound, they make it sound like you should just do this and that, it is just because you are lazy ... They think you just lie around on the sofa all day long and eat all the time. They think you can't help yourself because you don't have any self-control – and that is a big conflict for overweight people – because what you need is just to have some control, so you can control yourself.

Giving her fellow citizens a voice in this passage, she reproduces a common conviction that fatness is primarily a problem of lack of self-control combined with laziness and indolence. Relating her answer to values characteristic of neo-liberal societies, she diagnoses why she – being fat – naturally belongs to a group of persons whose lifestyle is viewed as problematic. Her body demonstrates the ultimate lack of self-control, a highly valued personal competence in neo-liberal societies.

The next account derives from an interview with a health consultant working on the same program. In the middle of the interview, another overweight woman enters the room to pick up her clothes. This woman is still present while the health consultant says:

> Oh, I am so glad that you [addressing the woman] remembered to get water, and it's so good that you have started to exercise. It is wonderful. Look [addressing me, the interviewer] how she has taken the initiative and has taken responsibility for herself; this is what we give priority to here. Because it's wonderful, isn't it?

Again we are presented with central categories of neo-liberal discourse, namely, the capacity to show initiative and be responsible. In this case the health consultant is discussing a person who is actually in the same room. Talking in the third person about a person who is present is degrading to that person, and it is a social act most often – when it happens – committed towards children. So besides pointing to the seemingly natural discourse of initiative and responsibility (two personality traits that overweight people seriously lack, according to health consultants) the consultant's manner of presenting the information also points towards power issues.[3]

It is difficult – if not impossible – for the researcher to answer Bourdieu's (1993: 54) questions (as raised at the start of the chapter) on precisely how everyday categories of perception relate to categories that science constructs. Nevertheless, we as researchers must pay special attention to this obviously overlapping use of categories in science and in local practices. Even though the use of categories such as risk, self-motivation and control in this case may carry different meanings for professional sociologists and lay members, we cannot – and should not – look away from the "two-way-traffic" that connects science and society (Law and Urry 2004).

The more knowledge we have about dominant (scientific) social discourses, the more informed will our choices be of which parts of the conversations we should focus upon in our analysis. I am not arguing for a sociology in which local actors becomes puppets of the social order – we need to research the actual accomplishment of the social order by the actors – but I am arguing for a sociology in which conducting theoretically informed analysis is accepted, perhaps even valued.

---

3   To further discuss how a focus on power issues can be related to the inequality that defines the overweight person's (client's) relationship to the health consultant (expert) is beyond the scope of this chapter.

*Case 2: "I punish myself every time I stuff a piece of bread in my mouth":
Teaching the fat identity*

In the following dialogue we see how a health consultant and an overweight woman jointly transform the woman's lifestyle into a problem that is her responsibility. Separating the health consultant's opinions from the overweight woman's opinions is nearly impossible; both show acceptance of – and hence reproduce – health (in this case, not being overweight) as a meta-value (Greco 2004). The woman has arrived for her third health conversation. She is going to be weighed, to have her fat percent measured, and to talk about her weight loss. At the end of the conversation with the Health Consultant (HC), she needs to sign a new contract listing the issues she needs to work on. Her first statement comes right after she learns how much weight she has lost.

Woman: Yes, it is not as many kilos as I would have liked to lose, as I said, but it is fair enough.

HC: And your fat percent has been lowered. I will put that in the file as well.

Woman: Thank you very much. It is actually exciting to view these numbers. They made a big impression on my family, when I showed them how to measure health.

HC: How?

Woman: Well, hmm, just as I was tremendously overwhelmed by realizing how big a fat percentage one's body actually has and the effect on you, and my blood numbers and all that stuff, it affected them tremendously when we talked about it. They might start taking me seriously now.

HC: Compared to when you started here, what you thought was possible then, a lot of things have happened, that is a major jump [you have made] …

Woman: I am aware that I have not lost the 3 kilos per month that I wanted. I am ashamed by that fact, because – and somehow it is a question about that I am not being good to myself, because – every time I put something in my mouth that I shouldn't have, then I am not being good to myself. Then I punish myself. That's what I am doing even though I am a compulsive eater. I actually perceive it as a punishment. I am not capable of being good to myself [last sentence is said in a voice stifled with sobs]. It is unbelievable that one wants to be so bad to oneself, because – when one is fat as I am – I am damaging myself every time I put something in my mouth that I should not have. And I need to work on that, it is something you need to work with, like when you want to quit smoking, you have to start by asking yourself: 'Do you really want to stop smoking?' ... The worst part is that sometimes I have thought: 'You were not even hungry.'

HC: But it's obviously something else it is about ...?

Woman: That's the problem! And I punish myself every time I stuff a piece of shit bread in my mouth. That's what I mean: I need to *work* more with myself and my head. [The conversation ends by the woman's signing a new contract stating all the things she must do before her next meeting with the consultant].

An immediately relevant context for analysing this extract is that the specific program aimed at "helping" overweight people to lose weight was initiated by the Danish State. The program states that being overweight is a societal problem that has to be solved or at least mitigated. Although this extract does not explicitly mention the categories developed within the governmentality perspective as in Case 1, we can nevertheless extrapolate them for analysis.

From a general perspective I believe we can see the interview extract as exemplifying a person who freely participates in upholding a stigmatizing social order. The overweight woman finds it "exciting to view these numbers", as she says, numbers that nonetheless demonstrate that her life situation is highly problematic. The numbers have made a "big impression" on her family, which is also learning that her lifestyle is a problem that needs dealing with. These few phrases alone show that the woman and her family are beginning to learn all the "wisdom" about health that simultaneously – and essentially – produces her lifestyle as a problem. The woman is ashamed about her small weight loss, thereby demonstrating that she is learning (and struggling) to become a responsible individual, even though her body weight does not yet show her success.

She then engages in a quite extensive process of submission, in which she talks about how "bad" her actions are, while simultaneously assuring the health consultant that she will be working on that problem (i.e., she will develop into a fully responsible person who will be in control of her food habits and will subsequently become a person she need not be ashamed of). From the theoretical perspective that this chapter outlines, we see the creation – whether by the health consultant or by the media exposure of people to neo-liberal values – of a person who has no control over her food intake (the irresponsible, weak-willed, out-of-control subject), a person who needs therapy via the project so that she can become responsible, strong-willed and self-controlled.

In the woman's last sentence, we see how she has accepted that her problematic "at risk" identity requires her to undertake thorough work on herself: "I need to *work* more with myself and my head." She has not only accepted her new problematic identity, but she has also accepted the challenge that it is her responsibility, and no one else's, to develop into a "normal" person. That she is asked to sign a new contract indicates yet another way of "finishing" her as a problem person with a problematic body, thus reproducing the unequal power balance between her and the health consultant.

If we view the contract as a technique of government, its aim would be to ensure better harmony between a dominant health discourse and the woman's understanding of herself. The form and purpose of the contract is not developed by a person in the woman's situation (even though she presumably will benefit from it); its form, aim, and demands are a direct result of a dominant health discourse that the woman gradually absorbs (Hacking's 2004 "dynamic nominalism"). She actively participates in her own submission by continuously reassessing her situation within the frame of the contract's demand for information. We witness a classification process that is "inaccessible to the person classified" but that nevertheless relates to scientific knowledge about being overweight and fat, and to the particular circumstances connected to the origins of this particular institution (which include an increased focus on health in society, and the development of new laws) (Hacking 2004: 278, 297). The contract thus represents a subtle and hidden technique of government, ensuring the state's control over its citizens in a neo-liberal era, an era that officially claims to want to free its citizens from state constraints.

By allowing sociological categories developed in literature on governmentality and risk into the analysis, as in this short analysis of conversation extracts, I have attempted to show that theoretically informed research questions are essential for highlighting issues of inequality and techniques of governance, both of which are important elements in shaping and structuring the conversations in question.

Conclusion

In contrast to CA and EM studies, this chapter has directed attention toward the possibility that there exists a flow of sociological categories *from* the discourse of science *to* the discourse used by local actors. If so, then theoretically loaded categories might not "render *invisible* the processes of constructing social order that they are attempting to explain" (Rawls 2002: 29); rather, they can help the researcher focus upon processes that perhaps are not visible if they – and their mutual linkage – were to be left out of the analysis. Treating social scenes merely as empirical, and not conceptual (Rawls 2002: 28), and thereby ignoring the presence and significance for practice of dominant scientific discourses, which include sociology, does not necessarily encourage research capable of discovering "the logic of practice" (Bourdieu 1999).

A lot of recent symbolic interactionist inspired work on identities and institutions (such as Gubrium and Holstein 2001) demonstrates a promising development of sociological analyses of social interaction. In this kind of research, the focus is upon the institutional and organizational setting and the way in which this setting produces specific identities. This work is indeed very stimulating, precisely because it focuses on how we can see any institutional setting's social order as immanent in the actual interaction among individuals (much like the work of Goffman, cf. 1990).

In this chapter I have therefore directed attention to two aspects of the relationship between theory and praxis. The first is that different sociological approaches reflect different theories of society and, consequently, form the object of investigation in different ways. In other words, a specific theoretical approach leads to a specific analytical focus. The second is that theoretically loaded categories from dominant discourses are already present in everyday talk.

As to the second process in particular, I argue that researchers who profess to avoid theory already use a series of theoretical categories to inform their analysis: for example, "adjacency pair" (CA) or "accountability" (EM). Likewise, more traditional categories from sociology such as "status" and "gender" inform some CA and EM, but categories such as "self-governance", "responsibility", "control", "knowledge/risk", etc., are conspicuously absent. I have attempted to show that we can gain new insights if we *also* apply sociological categories such as these that more explicitly link to theories of contemporary society in our analysis of local practices. As the first case analysis shows, these concepts – that professional sociologists link to the analysis of contemporary western society as neo-liberal, with an explicit focus on risk – are already also adopted in the local practices we study. Borrowing a term from Law and Urry (2004), these categories "enact realities".

My argument becomes especially relevant when the research area has captured the attention of the political establishment and the media, as the issues of weight and obesity have. So even if we want to investigate fatness from, for example, an EM perspective, we can gain important insight into how people's actions relate to the many contexts in which they are part (for example, the local, situated context; the institutional context; the political context; and a professional sociological context). However, to do so we must allow into the analysis sociological categories that emerge from work on processes outside people's interactions. In analysing the "two-way-traffic" between society and science, we will therefore be able to do more than analyse how scientifically constructed categories relate to the categories used by ordinary people in their everyday life (Bourdieu 1993). We will also be able to make our analysis more open to discussions (and disagreements) from other researchers when we explicitly show how our analysis relates to sociological categories stemming from specific sociological models of society such as the governmentality risk approach.[4] Research is always situated, no matter how often we might tell ourselves that it is not, and reality is always enacted within this situation.

If neo-liberal selfhood in the twenty-first century has become "intrinsically somatic" (for example, Rose suggests making the body the key site for work on

---

4   In this way, CA-, EM-, and SI-inspired researchers could detach themselves from the "narrowness" that these sociological studies have been accused of (see, for example, Maine's 2003 discussion of the critique of narrowness in SI).

the self), then sociological research on the body in contemporary institutional settings would benefit from taking sociological work on the twenty-first century body more seriously than it is taken today. For example, by conducting an EM-inspired analysis of local practices through examining how sociological theory is linked to, is present in, and helps to shape situated practice, we get an analysis that captures the empirical material in a more consistent way within a constructionist perspective than do researchers who believe that theory suppresses the "complex, nonconceptual character of actual, 'real' behavior" (Gusfield 2003: 133). Therefore, as researchers "enact the social" through their theoretical perspective and their choice of method, their responsibility as sociologists is to clarify how our theories and methods have conditioned the specific analysis we present.

References

Andersen, N.Å. (2007), 'Creating the Client Who Can Create Himself and His Own Fate – the Tragedy of the Citizens' Contract', *Qualitative Sociology Review* 3:2, 119–43.
Billig, M. (1999a), 'Whose Terms? Whose Ordinariness? Rhetoric and Ideology in Conversation Analysis', *Discourse and Society* 10:4, 543–58.
Billig, M. (1999b), 'Conversation Analysis and the Claims of Naivety', *Discourse and Society* 10:4, 572–76.
Blaikie, A. et al. (2004), 'General Introduction. The Sociology of the Body: Genesis, Development and Futures', in A. Blaikie et al. (eds) *The Body. Critical Concepts in Sociology*, Vol. 1 (London: Routledge).
Boden, D. (1994), *The Business of Talk. Organization in Action* (Cambridge: Polity Press).
Bordo, S. (1993), *Unbearable Weight: Feminism, Western Culture, and the Body* (Berkeley: University of California Press).
Bourdieu, P. (1993), *Sociology in Question* (London: Sage).
Bourdieu, P. (1999) *The Logic of Practice* (Cambridge: Polity Press).
Dean, M. (1999), *Governmentality. Power and Rule in Modern Society* (London: Sage).
Douglas, M. (1992), *Risk and Blame* (London: Routledge).
Ericson, R.V. and Doyle, A. (eds) (2003), *Risk and Morality* (Toronto: University of Toronto Press).
Ericson, R., Barry, D. and Doyle, A. (2000), 'The Moral Hazards of Neo-Liberalism: Lessons from the Private Insurance Industry', *Economy and Society* 29:4, 532–58.
Garfinkel, H. (1967), *Studies in Ethnomethodology* (New Jersey: Prentice-Hall, Inc.).
Garfinkel, H. (1974), 'The Origins of the Term "Ethnomethodology"', in Turner (ed.).

Goffman, E. (1990/1960), *Asylums: Essays on the Social Situation of Mental Patients and Other Inmates* (New York: Doubleday).
Greco, M. (2004), 'The Politics of Indeterminacy and the Right to Health', *Theory, Culture & Society* 21:6, 1–22.
Gubrium, J.F. and Holstein, J.A. (eds) (2001), *Institutional Selves: Troubled Identities in Organizational Context* (Oxford: Oxford University Press).
Gusfield, J.R. (2003), 'A Journey with Symbolic Interaction', *Symbolic Interactionism* 23:1, 119–39.
Hacking, I. (2004), 'Between Michel Foucault and Erving Goffman: Between Discourse in the Abstract and Face-to-face Interaction, *Economy and Society* 33:3, 277–302.
Holstein, J.A. and Gubrium, J.F. (1997) 'Active Interviewing', in Silverman, D. (ed.).
Latour, B. (1987), *Science in Action: How to Follow Engineers and Scientists through Society* (Buckingham: Open University Press).
Law, J. and Urry, J. (2004), 'Enacting the Social', *Economy and Society* 33:3, 390–410.
LeBesco, K. (2004), *Revolting Bodies? The Struggle to Redefine Fat Identity* (Boston: University of Massachusetts Press).
Lemke, T. (2001), 'The Birth of Bio-Politics: Michel Foucault's Lecture at the Collège de France on Neo-Liberal Governmentality', *Economy and Society* 30:2, 190–207.
Maine, D. (2003), 'Interactionism's Place', *Symbolic Interaction* 26:1, 5–18.
National Audit Office (2001), *Tackling Fatness in England.* Report by the Comptroller and Audit General HC 220 Session (London: The Stationery Office).
Novas, C. and Rose, N. (2000), 'Genetic Risk and the Birth of the Somatic Individual', *Economy and Society* 29:4, 485–513.
O'Mally, P. (2000), 'Introduction: Configurations of Risk', *Economy and Society* 29:4, 460–84.
Orbach, S. (1978), *Fat Is a Feminist Issue* (New York: Berkley Books).
Rawls, A.W. (2002), 'Editor's Introduction', in H. Garfinkel *Ethnomethodology's Program: Working out Durkheim's Aphorism* (edited and introduced by A.W. Rawls) (Lanham, MD: Rowman & Littlefield Publishers, Inc.).
Rose, N. (1996), 'The Death of the Social?', *Economy and Society* 25:3, 327–56.
Rose, N. (2001), 'The Politics of Life Itself', *Theory, Culture & Society* 18:6, 1–30.
Schegloff, E.A. (1997), 'Whose Text? Whose Context?', *Discourse & Society* 8, 165–87.
Schegloff, E.A. (1998), 'Reply to Wetherell', *Discourse & Society* 9, 413–16.
Schegloff, E.A. (1999a), '"Schegloff's Texts" as Billig's Data: A Critical Reply', *Discourse and Society* 10:4, 558–72.
Schegloff, E.A. (1999b), 'Naivete vs. Sophistication or Discipline vs. Self-indulgence: A Rejoinder to Billig', *Discourse and Society* 10:4, 577–82.
Shilling, C. (1993), *The Body and Social Theory* (London: Sage).

Silverman, D. (ed) (1997), *Qualitative Research: Theory, Method and Practice* (London: Sage).
Turner, R. (ed.) (1974) *Ethnomethodology* (Harmondsworth, UK: Penguin).
Wetherell, M. (1998), 'Positioning and Interpretative Repertoires: Conversation Analysis and Post-Structuralism in Dialogue', *Discourse and Society* 9:3, 387–412.

Chapter 9
Appropriation, Translation and the Opening of Theory

Anna Tsatsaroni and Geoff Cooper

Introduction

Consideration of the possible reconfiguration of social theory needs to take into account the latter's reflexive qualities, by which we mean that whilst theory may be affected, perhaps transformed, by the changing socio-political contexts within which it is embedded it also seeks to develop a critical understanding of these changes. This reflexive dimension of social theory is a key point of orientation for this chapter, which considers the issue of theory's possible reconfiguration – conceptualized here as translation – in both of these senses: that is, as subject to change and the interpreter of change.

Our point of departure is the apparent lack of space for sociological theorizing in the current 'audit culture', and the ways in which sociological discourse can become appropriated and perhaps distorted within a given 'governmental' context. However, this kind of formulation seems to imply both that there is an external, insulated place from which these apparently uncongenial discursive contexts can be theorized, and that theory is somehow specifiable in its proper form, regardless of the contingent historical pressures to which it is always subject. If, as many would argue, holding such a view is today more and more problematic, it becomes necessary to explore the complexities of the relations between theory and its contexts. Hence our questions: what is the place of theory in a changing situation? If theory is itself subject to change and transformation, how are we to understand the accounts it gives of the forces to which it is subject? And to what extent are well established models of sociological theorizing suited to understanding these processes of transformation?

Our approach to this cluster of questions is to begin from the specific example of how best to understand audit processes, consideration of which can provide insight into the broader issues of knowledge production and transformation that are our main concern.

We first examine some sociological responses to audit culture within educational research, noting some limitations in the way that the problem has been posed. We then look at an empirical example of how social theoretical terms can themselves be subject to translation within a policy context, and consider ways in which this is theorized. Our reading suggests the value of critically exploring the concept of appropriation. A strong motif of this discourse, appropriation contextualizes the problem of how we can think of knowledge transformations in the 'concrete' historical conjuncture named by 'audit'; but also, because it implies an in some ways problematic distinction between 'proper' and 'improper' uses of theory, the term points towards and opens up the wider issue of translation. We consider, firstly, the possibility that translation is an intrinsic feature of knowledge production and, secondly, how this might be understood in theoretical terms. We do so with reference to Basil Bernstein's important and insightful work on the translation of knowledge, work which can be located within the classical sociological tradition, and conclude by looking at some very different work on translation from outside this tradition. We suggest that Latour and, especially, Derrida provide valuable resources to start developing a different problematic on this specific (but fundamental) issue, and to raise important questions about the place of theory and the process of theorizing.

Theories of Audit in Educational Research

Within academia there is a strong sense that academic work takes place in an increasingly uncongenial socio-political climate. Phenomena such as the widespread use of performance indicators and other audit technologies, the dominance of narrow evaluative criteria of efficacy, and commodification throughout the public sphere have been experienced by many academics as a great threat to research and scholarship, affecting especially social science research practices.

Within the field of educational studies, the notion of audit has been central to the descriptions and understandings of knowledge production practices in the current political conjuncture. Its explication often relies on the work of a number of social and political theorists such as Power (1997), who defines an 'audit society' as a society organized to observe itself through the mechanisms of audit in the service of programmes for control. Rose (1999), also, uses the notion of audit technologies to refer to a rather mundane set of routines that purport to enable judgements to be made about the activities of professionals, now including academics; a process in which the technical requirements of audit displace the internal logics of expertise. The literature on educational research practices that takes up the notion of audit has been steadily growing, and three categories of research writing can be provisionally identified.

Firstly, theoretical forms of writing on audit. For example, Steven Ball focusing on (supra)national policies on education and research, conceptualizes policies as 'disciplinary tactics' which attempt to change not only what academics do, but who they are (Ball 2001). Connecting this notion with concepts such as performativity and governmentality, he draws a line between instrumental political discourse and practice, and critical (sociological-scientific) discourse and practice. The latter is used to critique and argue against the imposition of policy on research practices. For instance, he addresses the restrictive 'steering' of educational research by the state and the development of a hegemony of 'state relevance' (Ball 2006). 'Effectiveness research' is here seen as a prime example of educational research's gradual fragmentation and re-incorporation into the state and its objectives: a process described as the 'taming of academy'.

A second category is empirically orientated research that studies the impact of audit on academics. A representative example is Middleton (2004). She aims to reveal, through detailed interviews, 'powerful stories' showing how current systems of evaluation are 'disciplining the subject'. This, she argues, affects academics' senses of professional identity, the substance and methods of their research priorities, the choice of how and where to disseminate their findings, and their (un)willingness to participate in institutional activities and responsibilities.

A third category can be identified by looking at contributions to recent debates and disputes in the field of educational studies. These texts can be seen as responses to perceived or actual political imposition of the audit 'culture' on research. Examples here include: taking a position for or against the proliferation of competing theoretical discourses; defending expanded notions of 'scientificity' to help sustain education as a field of scholarship and research; and expressing concern about attempts to typify education research, to re-order theoretical traditions and to create new orthodoxies in the field (e.g. Clegg 2005; Yates 2004; Hodkinson 2004; Wellington and Nixon 2005; Lather 2006).

These forms of research writing are significant contributions to the topic of the state and stakes of education research today, yet such approaches entail some limitations. The first is an 'analytic danger' that might result from the way the problem is formulated, where Educational Studies and sub-fields within it are taken in essentialist terms as bounded, internally consistent entities that are under threat from external forces. Paradoxically, attempts to conceptualize the assumed problem (of a hostility to theory) often lead to the *proliferation* of theories, in a competition for the 'proper' interpretation. There, in turn, lies a second danger. This is when theory becomes 'a sacred within a profane world'. Consider the following:

> I wish to argue that the absence of theory leaves the researcher prey to unexamined, unreflexive preconceptions and dangerously naive ontological and epistemological *a prioris*. I shall wail and curse at the absence of theory and argue for theory as a way of *saving* educational studies from itself (Ball 2006: 62; second italics added).[1]

---

1 Our citation of this passage is intended to be merely illustrative and not to indicate a disagreement with what is a very powerful piece of writing on the subject: in this respect, our use of the passage exemplifies some of the very issues of (possibly unfair) translation that form our topic. The clash between definitions of 'relevant' research in policy and critical theories leaves a whole range of alternative practices out of the picture. Critical theories tend to see 'description' as fundamentally lacking, but much policy relevant research also marginalizes such 'positive' and often time-consuming descriptions. Perhaps both regard

Here theory, or certain theoretical traditions, is opposed to the audit culture and invested with critical value as a source of resistance. This in turn can serve to exclude the possibility of the theory being submitted to a critical reflection within the research community itself. We would therefore argue that such an approach, though it may not coincide with powerful policy discourses on research, is not completely foreign to them. Indeed, the overwhelming focus on an all powerful *audit culture* and its effects on researchers or research productions, brought into the field of educational studies from other disciplines and areas of research, does not allow enough space for debate over the object of sociological inquiry. The explicit or implicit assumption that such a research culture has been already fully instituted within the field, often unreflectively shapes researchers' own practices. This again somehow mirrors/duplicates the ways in which policy makers, in conceiving reality in particular ways, go on to act upon it, e.g. by selecting those theories and perspectives that they think (or simply argue) would improve it.

Thus far we have suggested that, in sociological literature within the field of Educational Studies, 'audit culture' has been approached in terms of its effects on institutions, people, knowledge, and theory. The ordinary usage of the phrase in practical fields such as politics and policy has been imported into sociological language to designate a particularly harmful state of affairs and to do the work of critique. Furthermore, 'critique' is accentuated by the linking of this phrase with its assumed equivalent within the language of sociology, namely that of instrumental rationality. But to the extent that 'audit culture' is taken for granted by educational researchers it may reinforce dominant interpretations of social reality which they wish to contest. At the same time, the empirical status of the category is uncertain. We therefore suggest that it is important both to consider how audit might be formulated as an empirical object of study, and to open up the question of its sociological theorization. The difficulties on both fronts can be illustrated by a brief reference to a study done in the context of European education policy formation, which in an important sense exemplifies qualities of an audit culture. Moreover, as will be shown, revisiting this study facilitates a movement within what we perceive to be a closed discourse on audit.

The Appropriation of Theoretical Concepts

The study in question (Tsatsaroni 2006) focused on the micro-processes of European Union (EU) education policy formation and their consequences for knowledge definitions. It involved a close reading of a set of documents and reports produced in the EU 'Education and Training Programme: Diverse Systems, Shared Goals' for the purpose of implementing the Lisbon objectives in the education systems

---

themselves as possessing a degree of importance by dint of their political relevance: one cloaked in radicalism, the other in policy relevance and realism. We are indebted to Paul du Gay for providing us with this formulation.

of its member states.[2] A significant concern raised by the study was over the problematic way in which the term 'practice' had been used in the policy texts examined. Several observations were made in this regard.

Firstly, in the reports analysed, different conceptions of practice were employed, drawing elements from diverse intellectual traditions, and mobilizing resources of various kinds. Thus in the partial stabilization of the meaning of practice prevailing in the current EU education policy discourse, the influence of a number of heterogeneous discourses could be traced.

Secondly, in the apparent discrepancy between a commonsense use of the notion of practice, characteristic of the Commission's Staff Working Paper (see note 2), and a notion of practice especially prevalent in the 'ICT in Education' research field – a highly influential player in European Policy in general, and especially in the programme under consideration through the voice of the respective experts' groups – there was evidence of common ground; a kind of self-evident belief in the power of vision, binding different conceptions of practice and effecting a highly stabilized discourse. Thus, beyond the appropriation of elements from diverse discourses, their apparent neutralization, and their elevation into a version of 'best practice research', characteristic of both the official documents of the Commission and the more scientific reports of the groups of experts, the view dominating the discourse was that practices could be understood (and shared) through showing and by being there to 'see' in person: a particularly strong version of empiricist thinking.

Thirdly, it was apparent that linking the obviously ideological use of 'practice' in the sphere of education policy with its apparently 'scientific' definition, developed within the ICT in Education research field, had helped to ensure both the continuity of the political programme, and the strengthening of the position of ICT in Education researchers within this sphere and in the intellectual field of educational studies. However, in attempting to make sense of the situation the researcher felt that it was not a matter of simply saying that power works best through imposing definitions of social reality. Here, and especially in revisiting the

---

2 Starting from the 'Conclusions of the Lisbon European Council' (March 2000), the documents studied included: (a) 'The Report by the Commission on the "concrete objectives of education and training"' (31 January 2001), COM (200) 59 final, and subsequent related documents; (b) 'Indicators and Benchmarks – 2004 Commission Staff Working Paper 'Progress towards the common objectives in education and training', SEC (2004) 73, 21 January 2004; (c) 'Education and Training 2010: The success of the Lisbon strategy hinges on urgent reforms. Draft interim report on the implementation of the detailed work programme on the follow-up of the objectives of education and training systems in Europe', COM 2003/685 final, 11 November 2003; and (d) the progress reports of the working groups of experts from national governments, as well as various organizations and agencies, responsible for developing and implementing at national level key objectives of this programme. The reports are available from the website of the European Commission's Directorate General for Education and Culture; see <http://ec.europa.eu/education/index_en.html>.

study, the word 'appropriation' functioned like a signpost pointing to a different path of inquiry.

More specifically, in the scientific literature, a number of writers have used the word appropriation to talk about particular uses of social scientific ideas and terms (e.g., culture, equity, social capital) by policy makers. For instance, Jones (2001) observes that neo-liberalism of a pure kind has been tempered by elements of social inclusion, and by an interest in securing legitimacy. Thus he argues that policy makers, to pursue their agenda, risk a degree of dialogue with cultures outside the immediate influence of the dominant policy agenda (see also Hartley 2004; Singh and Taylor 2007). Indeed, social science/sociology is – perhaps, today, more than ever – a major source for direct and indirect borrowing in the construction of the dominant European education (and social) policy discourse. Versions of sociology are constantly adopted, appropriated, incorporated and stripped of their vitality, dynamism and energies. Therefore the appropriation of the term 'practice', and the silencing of discussions about social relations that constitute it, could be linked to on-going struggles for defining and legitimizing meaning within the field of political action. Or appropriation could be taken as another word for audit, exemplifying the tendency to think that terms can be transported from context to context with no alteration of their essential meanings.

The possibilities that a move along the lines of the latter would offer to our inquiry can be best conveyed through a reference to Sobe (2006), whose object of inquiry is accountability in the USA education policy context. Looking at the centrality of accountability in the field of contemporary American educational research, Sobe focuses on the interplay between 'research-based policy' and 'policy effects on research', raising the question of how 'certain objects of reflection, action and intervention are fabricated across the domains of educational research and educational policy' (ibid. 33–34). As he notes, this emphasis, which is not a denial of the actuality of institutional arrangements and networks of actors through which educational agendas are constituted and re-shaped, is a shift to accountability as an analytic strategy for investigating systems of reasoning characteristic of contemporary US educational research conversations. This work shows in particular how an analytic and theoretical concept can be transmuted into an apparent empirical reality and how educational research is drawn into these transformations.

Sobe's analysis is important for our argument in that it not only describes the transformation of theoretical concepts in the process of their circulation and use in different contexts, but also highlights the ways in which the 'problem' of circulation of policies, ideologies, ideas and concepts can be both imposed upon research (for example, through policy discourses on knowledge transfer) and posed by researchers in their own research practices. However, despite Sobe's emphasis on the analytic and strategic use of 'accountability', this term, much like audit and appropriation, remains too close to policy discourse and does not lead to any substantial theorization of the research problem, save to expose and to reveal yet another reality of contemporary American research scene. Nevertheless, his account helps to shift the analytical focus from appropriation to the broader, but investigable, notion of transformation.

A Sociological Theory of Translation

In Basil Bernstein's sociology of education, transformation is discussed with reference to 'recontextualization', a core concept developed to describe initially how educational knowledge and practices are constituted through social processes which involve the selection, simplification, repositioning and refocusing of elements drawn from knowledge producing discourses (1990: 191–193). These processes, entailing transformation of the elements and changes in social relations, constitute the 'pedagogic discourse', the theoretical object of his sociology. As Bernstein notes, pedagogic discourse is a discourse or (a set of) principle(s) for appropriating other discourses, and bringing them together in a special relationship (1990: 183). So, he argues, every discourse is a recontextualized discourse and 'every discourse and its subsequent texts are ideologically repositioned' in the movement 'from the original field of its production or existence to the field of its reproduction' (Bernstein 1990: 200). Therefore the intellectual task is to specify 'formally', in theoretical and empirical terms, the complex process 'between the initial movement (circulation) of a discourse and the effect of that [pedagogic] discourse upon the consciousness and specific positioning of an acquirer' (ibid.).

As Diaz (2001) has argued, pedagogic discourse constitutes the most interesting re-conceptualization by Bernstein of his own work as work devoted to make legible and explicit the logic intrinsic to the reproduction of culture (Diaz 2001). This allows us to argue that Bernstein's work, usually discussed within the frame of theories of reproduction and symbolic control – for Bernstein, the description of the means by which power relations translate into discourse and discourse into power (Bernstein 1990: 205) – constitutes an elaboration of the sociological thesis about the social construction and transformation of all knowledge forms. His theory of (pedagogic) discourse therefore permits us to inscribe the theme of appropriation within the problematics of sociology of knowledge and theories of transformation, notwithstanding the comparative lack of recognition of his important contribution to the latter.

On several occasions Bernstein took the opportunity to distinguish his way of developing theory from the way other theories were produced and used within the sociology of education. This difference is discerned in the repeated statement that 'what is required is less allegiance to an approach but more dedication to a problem' (Bernstein 2001a: 363–364; Bernstein 1977: 171). Thus as a form of discourse, it inserts principles of 'verticality' and strong 'grammaticality' in a field characterized by a 'horizontal knowledge structure, with a weak grammar' (Moore and Muller 2002; Muller 2006; Moore 2006; Bernstein 2000: 155–174): in other words, at the risk of oversimplification, the theory enables cumulative knowledge development instead of adding to a proliferation of approaches.

Bernstein often explains this difference with reference to the paradigmatic case of Bourdieu's 'popular' concept of habitus. This concept, he argues, may serve to solve certain epistemological problems of structure and agency, but there is no necessity between the concept and what counts as its realization. This means that once an illustration is challenged or an alternative interpretation is given there are problems. We might say these are, above all, problems of justifying a research practice that deploys the concept. In contrast, Bernstein's own theory aimed to create languages of description, defined by him as 'a translation device whereby one language is transformed into another' (Bernstein 2000: 132). More concretely, he distinguishes between an internal and an external language of description; the former referring 'to the syntax whereby a conceptual language is created', while the latter refers 'to the syntax whereby the internal language can describe something other than itself' (ibid.).

In the last decade or so the features of the theory briefly indicated above have been subject to considerable elaboration both by Bernstein himself and by Bernstein scholars, explicitly aiming – and/or leading – to a repositioning of the theory within the field of sociology of education and perhaps beyond it, in the sense that there is a growing recognition of its relevance to the study of wider forms of institutional control.[3] This fact raises questions about (changes in) processes of reception: and if reception is but a recontexualization of theory, the reception of Bernstein's theory is more than an ideal case to explore such processes, using recontextualization as an analytical tool. In this respect, it is informative to read the scholarly work produced in the last few years and published in books or special issues dedicated to Bernstein's work, as well as Bernstein's own reflections, in particular those parts of his texts that constitute responses to critics. This is because these are occasions for refining the theory; intervening in the process of positioning the theory in the intellectual field; and demonstrating the power of its conceptual apparatus to describe the (re)production of knowledge as a social process. However, we want to argue here that such texts, rather than simply describing, explicating and explaining the theory, are, in a strong sense, *constitutive* of the theory. In particular, following Bernstein (1990: 200), we want to argue that if the point is not *that* knowledge is transformed in the process of recontextualizations but *how* it is transformed and with what consequences, then paying attention to the mode of reception as translation becomes crucial for understanding and for producing knowledge in a given field. But, secondly, perhaps against Bernstein, and certainly Bernstein scholars, we want to argue that processes of reception cannot be distinguished from knowledge creation; translation is constitutive for theory.

Several Bernstein scholars, especially those positioned within the field as the 'theorists', have focused considerable attention on 'Vertical and Horizontal Discourse: an Essay' (Bernstein 2000: 155–174; see also Bernstein 1996: 169–181). Here, Bernstein analyses the constitution of different forms of discourse,

---

3 See Solomon's comments on the significance of these developments (in Bernstein 2000: 198).

their related knowledge structures, the types of knowledge produced, and their distinctive forms of transmission and reproduction. The basic conceptualization of vertical and horizontal discourse, commentators have argued, echoes, acknowledges and contributes to Durkheim's famous distinction between the sacred and the profane, and constitutes a culmination of the achievements of his form of theorizing (e.g., Muller 2001). In particular, the paper is praised for offering a theoretical language, capable of capturing not only 'relations-between' (e.g., different categories of discourses), but also 'relations-within', the internal structuring of academic discourse, using sociology as a case study. In this sense, it is rightly seen as a distinctive contribution to the social processes of knowledge production which lays the ground for the empirical investigation of fields of research activity, the practices they give rise to, the social relations characterizing them, the modes regulating contact and the conditions for knowledge advancement in a given field.

The scholarly commentary on this essay, in particular, has led to claims that most theories in the sociology of education, the field where Bernstein's theory is located, are 'deficient' in that they represent social relations in education through a process of reinterpretation that does not depart from the empirical level of description. In contrast, in Bernstein, theory as a 'translator' generates a language of a different 'type', i.e. makes possible a 'switch' from empirical description to theoretical conceptualization (Moore 2006: 29–32). Here theories are judged and evaluated by reference to their 'generative power in modeling social relations and integrating empirical data' (Moore 2006: 32).

We shall here only note the function of the word 'translation' in the stabilizing of the theory and its claims, turning instead to instances where Bernstein confronts critics of his work, his recontextualizers within the field (Bernstein 1990: 129) – a dimension not discussed in the literature. Such texts, dedicated to 'clearing misunderstandings', as he argues, are interesting to examine because of the formal readings they produce of an opponent's text. Bernstein (1990) addresses the problems of critical exposition in some detail, and argues that reading a critic's text requires the identification of her/his position within the field, specification of the functional implications of such a position, and attention to the critic's textual strategies. In the appendix to 'Codes and their positioning: a case study of misrecognition' (Bernstein 2000) where he more explicitly takes issue with what he sees as misinterpretations of his theory, he returns to this problem of criticism to formalize further his substantive analysis of the critic's text vis-à-vis his own theory.

Bernstein proceeds by applying his usual three steps approach to research. In the first step he describes the distinguishing features of the critic's account of his theory, such as selective recontextualizing, abstracting some features from the language of the theory and making the original text invisible through repetition of others' representation of the theory.

In the second step, he uncovers the principles organizing the critic's text. A temporal principle applies when a time frame is selected to situate and to represent the theory. Spatial principles, used to position a theory, may be linked to different motivations. These include (Bernstein 2000: 191–193): a 'religious-moral' motivation, which works through simplification and reduction of the theory under critique, as a precondition for revealing 'pollution'; an 'epistemological' one where, on the basis of what counts as legitimate knowledge, a theory is accepted or rejected following a classification of its perceived assumptions; and a 'discourse-based' motivation, as when a theory is tested for evidence of discursive 'violation' incurred by mixing different discourses.

In a third step Bernstein translates this language of values into the language provided by his own theory, one which helps to conceptualize scientific (reading) practices within the field of sociology (of education). Specifically, Bernstein shows that by relating spatial positioning with temporal dimensions, a large set of possibilities for modeling practices becomes available. More formally, the former are subject to classification principles, and the latter to framing rules. Classification and framing, two basic concepts of Bernstein's theory for modeling pedagogical practices (Bernstein 1990; 2000), regulate the recontexualization of scientific theories/texts in peer review practices. Thus we might infer that strong boundaries (classification and framing) are a distinguishing feature of a field that keeps theories separate from one another, therefore inhibiting its development.

This is certainly a concrete demonstration of the power of the conceptual language of the theory to guide inquiry into (changes in) research practices and to produce systematic descriptions of the empirical world. But this writing also constitutes a critique of the use of the values of 'purity' and of the 'proper' in evaluating the worth of a theory; admitting, by implication, that theory development involves violating given norms regulating an intellectual field and that transformation cannot avoid contamination. However Bernstein relies on clear distinctions as when – in the very same text – he distinguishes a 'parasitic circle' of critics that use the values of purity and the proper to avoid 'serious, critical engagement' with a theory or intellectual field. We argue here that it is within the space created by these asymmetrical if not contradictory claims about properties of reading that Bernstein's theory at once gets stabilized as a robust theory and, simultaneously, can be unsettled by the further implications of the term translation.

Questioning the Sociology of Translation

In focusing primarily on the internal relations and structures of scientific discourses and their effects, Bernstein elucidates the sociological dimensions of translation whilst avoiding the kind of social reductionism that some have detected in Bourdieu's work (see for example Dreyfus and Rabinow 1999). Nevertheless it can be argued that like Bourdieu, perhaps because of a shared affiliation to Durkheim, Bernstein continues to take 'the social' as given. We conclude by briefly considering the significance of some recent influential work that not only reformulates the concepts of translation and the social but also has a different orientation to the classical sociological tradition, and is therefore well placed to raise broader questions about the role, status and authority of theory within the essentially modernist framework that informs Bernstein's approach.

Bruno Latour's work is designated by the phrase actor-network theory, but also referred to as 'the sociology of translation' (Callon 1986; Latour 1999), and translation is central to his approach. Indeed, the notion of network was intended, in analogous terms to Deleuze and Guattari's rhizomes, as a way of describing 'a series of transformations – translations, transductions – which could not be captured by any of the traditional terms of social theory' (Latour 1999: 15, original emphasis). Latour's criticism of these traditional terms, not least 'the social' itself, is extensive, but a key aspect of it is that they presuppose given entities and domains and cannot convey the dynamic processes that produce them. For example, Latour sees the (sociologically conventional) attempt to identify the social factors affecting knowledge as inadequate for capturing either the process of translation or the entities that it helps to produce. On the one hand, translation describes movement from one sphere (institutional spaces, organizations for example) to another, where the meaning and value of the knowledge (or technology) in question is subject to change; it is through their embedding in particular networks that meaning and value come to be defined. These networks, it is argued, are not radically disjoint though they have different centres of calculation and centres of value (Latour 1987; Law 1997). On the other hand, the process of translation can itself give rise to these spheres, spaces or domains: Latour's formulation of 'co-production', and related concepts, suggests that both knowledge and social order be seen as arising out of such a process (see Jasanoff 2004).

This, then, is a radical theory of translation that suggests not only that to translate is to transform but that translation produces, rather than simply mediates between, contexts. The social, insofar as it has a place in Latour's work, is something that is produced via associations between heterogeneous actors rather than, as for Bernstein, a key explanatory variable. Whereas Bernstein, following Durkheim, isolates the social as a separate domain and traces its influence, Latour sees this as a form of analytical 'purification' (1993) that cannot do justice to the complexity of a world in which many different phenomena have effectivity and agency. For Latour 'mediation' designates an active process of transformation, and mediators can take many forms – material, technological, textual for example – for which 'social' is a necessarily inadequate descriptor (2005: 40). To return to the example of audit with which we began, this approach, in contrast to some of the critiques already considered, would not look at audit or accountability as a set of social arrangements which have effects on the knowledge produced within them; rather, it would trace their complex interconnection, and the forms of mediation that enable their co-production.

Latour's approach to translation is significant, here, for two reasons. In the first place, it problematizes the idea that the social has analytical coherence. In the second, it does so via an explicit deflation of the role of theory: following the line of argument put forward by ethnomethodologists, the logic of Latour's approach is to follow the actors, trace the development of associations, and avoid the use of *a priori* theoretical constructs or languages which might obscure this purportedly descriptive endeavour. In both respects, he rejects the classical sociological framework that is central to Bernstein.[4]

The objections raised when classical sociological understandings of knowledge transformations are approached from the perspective of Latour's 'minimalist' claims become intensified in Derrida's thinking, a philosophy 'critical' rather than 'dogmatic', in the sense that it is 'aware of the limits of knowing' (Spivak 1996). This thinking crucially includes the theme of 'translation' (Derrida 2004; Johnson 1981), and the place of 'theory' in the apparatus of modern academic institutions. Themes such as these, in fact, always arise in specific contexts of readings and are linked together in a project that in an extremely coded way is often referred to as the deconstruction of metaphysical thinking.

Bennington (2007) explains that metaphysical thinking is, according to Derrida, the attempt to derive complexity from simplicity, especially from an origin which is always a form of presence. This 'archeological' dimension to metaphysics is mirrored by a 'teleological' one in which current complexity can be directed towards some final, perhaps redemptive, state of presence. So Derrida argues that there is complexity at the origin, and one of the many ways in which he has expressed this is through the use of the term 'trace' to deconstruct the core metaphysical opposition of presence/absence and thereby complicate and disrupt the very concept of the origin.

In accordance with this line of thought, translation is not regarded by Derrida as a secondary and derived event in relation to an original text or language. Moreover he suggests that the idea that it is secondary is theological in origin. He argues that the history and problematics of translation in Europe are complex, being established on the very ground or corpus of Holy Scripture; and that, despite subsequent transformations, something of this essential relation to sacred writing seems to remain ineffaceable in the word, with its connotations of a sacred origin (Derrida 2004).

Derrida's approach to the text involves a critical thinking of the movement from the linguistic description of a phenomenon to what that description designates, which in metaphysics and the logocentric tradition leads to 'the hypostasis [ing] of language through the reduction of reality to language' (Derrida 2002: 189). The text cannot be reduced to simple writing on a page and nor can 'reality' be left or assumed to be outside it: rather the play of differance 'compels one to inscribe the reality effect in a general textuality or a differential process that … is not limited to language or writing as they are understood pre-scientifically' (Derrida 2002: 189–190).

---

4 The rejection of classical sociology has itself been subject to some translation however, Latour having recently 'discovered' a line of sociological paternity from Tarde (see Chapter 1).

Derrida's own writing produces translations as 'supplements', which cannot be reduced to some methodological instrumentality; hence they become difficult to describe and impossible to formalize. Deconstruction, one of the many terms used to refer to his approach to the text, is not the establishment of a set of protocols for reading, though it can be seen as a heuristic for interpreting, remobilizing and reconfiguring a text (Derrida 1985). Moreover, reconfiguring is the very 'chance of deconstruction' as when, in a specific reading of a text, a word is transcribed into what in Derrida's own work forms a chain of 'quasi-transcendental' terms such as dissemination, differance, and iterability. This host of related but non-identical terms are intrinsically bound to the texts under deconstruction and never formalized as separate fully-fledged concepts or theories. Indeed there is no general substantive theory of translation or, arguably, of anything else in his work.[5]

Translation or appropriation, according to this view, cannot be understood in terms of the action of social forces or factors upon knowledge. Rather, knowledge itself is understood as inescapably subject to and indeed constituted by processes of transformation. Moreover, as we have seen, Derrida makes this insight an integral part of his writing practice, which he sees as performative rather than constative, as intervening in a text or phenomenon rather than providing a meta-language for its description (Hillis-Miller 2007). There are apparently countervailing currents in his practice and understanding of it. On the one hand, the clear binary opposition of terms such as propriety and appropriation, or fidelity and infidelity are put into question. Similarly, there is an overt openness to alterity that includes welcoming the possibility of radical reinterpretation, transformation through recontextualization, and more generally the continual and inevitable process of differentiation. On the other hand, the recognition that ever wider areas of intellectual work are subject to instrumental uses by, for example, military institutions, media trivialization, and academic institutions, forms part of the motivation to produce texts which, in their singularity and performativity, resist easy re-appropriation (Derrida 2004; Derrida 1994).

But if Derrida's work provides an example of how to problematize the metaphysical dimensions of prevalent ways of approaching, in this case, the question of how knowledge is shaped, transformed, limited or re-appropriated, the lessons sociologists might draw from this are not straightforward: how might deconstruction best be translated into a sociological idiom, and what would be changed in so doing? Like Latour, Derrida problematizes not only humanism but, we have argued, concepts such as 'the social' that are premised on full presence. But – *contra* Latour – Derrida would say that just as the invocation of the social as a conceptualization of an empirical real(ity) cannot provide an exit from metaphysics neither, perhaps, does its avoidance. Appropriation, recontexualization, transformation and translation are then perhaps best thought

---

5 Jameson (1995: 81) suggested that Derrida's work at the limits of metaphysics involves a principled 'avoidance of the affirmative sentence as such, of the philosophical proposition' (see also Bennington 2000: 14; Derrida 1978).

of as spaces or marks where the problematic of 'modern' sociological theorizing, and of post-humanist analysis cross and complicate each other. If the latter point to what remains unthinkable within Bernstein's modernist mode of theorizing, we should resist the temptation to see it as a radical break that renders the deployment of some version of the social redundant (see Lemert 2006, 8–20). Indeed, for sociologists, there may still be advantages in retaining an explicit version of the social rather than having its shadow fall inadvertently across the text, even if engagement with deconstruction would necessarily transform the 'innocence' of such a practice.

It is a difficult task to identify definitive sociological consequences of Derrida's thoughts on knowledge transformation, appropriation and translation, not least because of his performative writing practice. In relation to the translation of theory however, the paradoxical logic that underpins instituting and institutionalizing processes (see Bennington 2007) such as theory itself is pertinent. This logic accounts for both theory's translation into apparently immutable forms, and its character of always remaining fragile, constantly subject to contestation, modification and overthrow. Such a condition, though it might threaten theory, also gives it a chance of being alive, in the sense that life entails an openness to alterity and event. As Bennington (2007) suggests, this analysis opens a kind of responsibility to foster events of thought that cannot fail to unsettle theory and the institutions that attempt to restrain its change; as for example when theory is presented as proper science, as opposed to mere interpretations (e.g. Moore 2006).

Some implications of the position that we have reached include respecting the possible singularity of the phenomenon, and resisting the recourse to a theoretical meta-language to analyse it, whilst being simultaneously wary of taking its singularity (historical singularity for example) as given. More fundamentally, we suggest that it is important to take into account the multiple and inevitable appropriations to which any theory is subject, and the extent to which they register, whether as statements, symptoms or events, the movements and processes – which crucially include 'audit' in its manifold senses – through which they are themselves constituted.

Finally, and instead of a conclusion to this chapter, our itinerary has helped us to articulate the question: what is happening to thought as thought, today, which causes audit, appropriation and transformation to become themes in speaking about knowledge? This, we suggest, is not a question arising out of a pure theoretical discourse but is a theoretico-political issue that should be examined through the problematics of translation. Audit as appropriation 'is' the imperative to translate. It posits a general translatability without 'remainder', the easier to evaluate. It says that translation is always possible, that everything today can be subject to translation, can become transparent. But in the same movement, 'translation' is deconstructing itself, in that it speaks of the impossibility – and even undesirability – of having a general theory about knowledge and its transformations; though, as we have implied, an almost absolute rejection of theoretical statements and a call for pure acts of translation, pure performances, might equally serve to strengthen and stabilize the prevailing ('audit') discourse. The hesitation introduced in embracing the concept of translation, through the consideration of Bernstein, Latour and Derrida, may therefore help to open its questioning.

Throughout the chapter there has been a movement, a kind of opening up of what started as a specifiable question about audit. The examples of audit have given way to broader questions about the social transformation of forms of knowledge, which include key concepts within classical sociological theory. This opening out might be criticized as itself being the translation of sociology into philosophical discourse, leaving the empirical sociologist in a rather uncertain position in relation to the task of analysing the phenomena of interest. We would not dispute this but we would insist that such a theoretical movement has its own value, *contra* those who regard the construction of a reliable, usable and ostensibly scientifically validated model of theory as preferable. For to the extent that it owes something to deconstruction, this movement stands as an effort at opening up theory, rather than attempting to institute a new, distinct discourse (see Derrida 2002; 2004). It thus continues a questioning of the value of statements, of positional or oppositional logic, and shows the limits of the authority and legitimacy of theory and associated practices.

References

Ball, S.J. (2001) 'You've been NERFed!' Dumbing Down the Academy: National Educational Research Forum: "A National Strategy Consultation Paper": A Brief and Bilious Response', *Journal of Education Policy* 16:3, 265–68.
Ball, S.J. (2006), *Education Policy and Social Class: The Selected Works of Stephen J. Ball* (London: Routledge).
Bennington, G. (2000), *Interrupting Derrida* (London: Routledge).
Bennington, G. (2007), 'Foundations', in Wortham and Weiner (eds).
Bernstein, B. (1977), *Class, Codes and Control: Towards a Theory of Educational Transmissions*, Vol.III, 2nd edition (London: Routledge & Kegan Paul).
Bernstein, B. (1990), *The Structuring of Pedagogic Discourse, Class Codes and Control*, Vol. IV (London: Routledge).
Bernstein, B. (1996), *Pedagogy, Symbolic Control and Identity: Theory, Research, Critique* (London: Taylor & Francis).
Bernstein, B. (2000), *Pedagogy, Symbolic Control and Identity: Theory, Research, Critique*, 2nd edition (New York: Rowman & Littlefield).
Bernstein, B. (2001a), 'From Pedagogies to Knowledges', in Morais et al. (eds).
Bernstein, B. (2001b),'Video Conference with Basil Bernstein', in Morais et al. (eds).
Callon, M. (1986), 'Some Elements of a Sociology of Translation', in Law (ed.).

Clegg, S. (2005) 'Evidence-based Practice in Educational Research: A Critical Realist Critique of Systematic Review', *British Journal of Sociology of Education* 26:3, 415–428.
Derrida, J. (1978), *Writing and Difference* (London: Routledge).
Derrida, J. (1985), 'Letter to a Japanese Friend', in Wood and Bernasconi (eds).
Derrida, J. (1994), 'The Deconstruction of Actuality', *Radical Philosophy* 68, 28–41.
Derrida, J. (2002), 'Politics and Friendship', in Derrida and Rottenburg (eds).
Derrida, J. (2004), *Eyes of the University* (Stanford: Stanford University Press).
Derrida, J. and Rottenburg, E. (eds) (2002), *Negotiations: Interventions and Interviews 1971–2001* (Stanford: Stanford University Press).
Diaz, M. (2001), 'Subject, Power and Pedagogic Discourse', in Morais et al. (eds).
Dreyfus, H. and Rabinow, P. (1999), 'Can There Be a Science of Existential Structure and Social Meaning?', in Shusterman (ed.).
Hartley, D. (2004), 'Management, Leadership and the Emotional Order of the School', *Journal of Education Policy* 19:5, 583–594.
Hillis-Miller, J. (2007), 'Performativity as Performance/Performativity as Speech Act: Derrida's Special Theory of Performativity', *South Atlantic Quarterly* 106:2, 219–235.
Hodkinson, P. (2004), 'Research as a Form of Work: Experience, Community and Methodological Objectivity', *British Educational Research Journal* 30:1, 9–26.
Jameson, F. (1995), 'Marx's Purloined Letter', *New Left Review* Jan–Feb, 75–109.
Jasanoff, S. (ed.) (2004), *States of Knowledge: The Co-Production of Science and Social Order* (London: Routledge).
Johnson, B. (1981), 'Translator's Introduction', in Derrida, *Dissemination* (Chicago: University of Chicago Press).
Jones, K. (2001), 'Travelling Policy/Local Spaces: Culture, Creativity and Interference', *Education and Social Justice* 3:3, 2–9.
Landry, D. and MacLean, G. (eds) (1996), *The Spivak Reader* (London: Routledge).
Lather, P. (2006), 'Paradigm Proliferation as a Good Thing to Think With: Teaching Research in Education as a Wild Profusion', *International Journal of Qualitative Studies in Education* 19:1, 35–57.
Latour, B. (1987), *Science in Action* (Harvard: Harvard University Press).
Latour, B. (1993), *We Have Never Been Modern* (London: Harvester Wheatsheaf).
Latour, B. (1999), 'On Recalling ANT', in Law and Hassard (eds).
Latour, B. (2005), *Reassembling the Social: An Introduction to Actor-Network Theory* (Oxford: Oxford University Press).
Law, J. (ed.) (1986), *Power, Action, Belief: A New Sociology of Knowledge* (London: Routledge).
Law, J. (1997). 'Traduction/Trahison: Notes on ANT', Department of Sociology, Lancaster University (last revised 30 November 2003) <http://www.comp.lancs.ac.uk/sociology/stslaw2.html>.

Law, J. and Hassard, J. (eds) (1999), *Actor-Network Theory and After* (Oxford: Blackwell).
Lemert, C. (2006), *Durkheim's Ghosts: Cultural Logics and Social Things* (Cambridge: Cambridge University Press).
Middleton, S. (2004), 'Disciplining the Subject: The Impact of PBRF on Education Academics', paper presented at the Annual Conference of the NZ Association for Research in Education, Westpac Stadium, Wellington (24–16 November).
Moore, R. (2006), 'Knowledge Structures and Intellectual Fields: Basil Bernstein and the Sociology of Knowledge', in Moore et al. (eds).
Moore, R., Arnot, M. and Beck, J. et al. (eds) (2006), *Knowledge Power and Educational Reform: Applying the Sociology of Basil Bernstein* (London: Routledge).
Moore, R. and Muller, J. (2002), 'The Growth of Knowledge and the Discursive Gap', *British Journal of Sociology of Education* 23:4, 627–637.
Morais, A., Neves, I. and Davies, B. et al. (eds) (2001), *Towards a Sociology of Pedagogy: The Contribution of Basil Bernstein to Research* (New York: Peter Lang).
Muller, J. (2006) 'On the Shoulders of Giants: Verticality of Knowledge and the School Curriculum', in Moore et al. (eds).
Muller, J. (2001), 'Intimations of Boundlessness', in Morais et al. (eds).
Ozga, J., Seddon, T. and Popkewitz, T. (eds) (2006), *Education Research and Policy: Steering the Knowledge-based Economy* (London: Routledge, Taylor and Francis).
Power, M. (1997), *The Audit Society: Rituals of Verification* (Oxford: Oxford University Press).
Rose, N. (1999), *Powers of Freedom: Reframing Political Thought* (Cambridge: Cambridge University Press).
Shusterman, R (ed.) (1999), *Bourdieu: A Critical Reader* (Oxford: Blackwell).
Singh, P. and Taylor, S. (2007), 'A New Equity Deal for Schools: A Case Study of Policy-Making in Queensland, Australia', *British Journal of Sociology of Education* 28:3, 301–315.
Sobe, N.W. (2006) 'Accountability in US Educational Research and the Travels of Governance', in Ozga et al. (eds).
Spivak, G. (1996) 'More on Power/Knowledge', in Landry and Maclean (eds).
Tsatsaroni, A. (2006), 'The New Information and Communication Technologies: Ideological Uses and Misuses of 'Practice' in the Discourse of European Education Policy', *To Vima ton Koinonikon Epistemon* 48, 173–214.
Wellington, J. and Nixon, J. (2005), 'Shaping the Field: The Role of Academic Journal Editors in the Construction of Education as a Field of Study', *British Journal of Sociology of Education* 26:5, 643–655.
Wood, D. and Bernasconi, R. (eds) (1985), *Derrida and Difference* (Warwick: Parousia Press).
Wortham, S. and Weiner, A. (eds) (2007), *Encountering Derrida: Legacies and Futures of Deconstruction* (London: Continuum).

Yates, L. (2004) *What Does Good Education Research Look Like? Situating a Field and its Practices* (Maidenhead: Open University Press).

Chapter 10
'Identity' after 'The Moment of Theory'

Paul du Gay

Introduction

Is the end nigh? After many years at the top of the intellectual hit parade, are 'Identity', 'Identification' and their conceptual fellow travellers slipping down the charts? They've had a good run, no one could deny it. Those whose academic careers and publishing profits have been built upon them can attest to this. But has 'Identity' run out of steam?

At first sight this may seem an absurd question. After all, in many disciplinary fields 'Identity' work is thriving. Management studies would be a good example. But can something be simultaneously expanding its empire and losing its explanatory power? I want to suggest that in the case of Identity, indeed it can. Moreover, I want to argue that the reason for this lies at the door of what has come to be known as 'the moment of theory'. For the destiny of 'Identity' as a sociological object, and the moment of theory, I wish to argue, are inextricably linked.[1]

The first question that needs to be addressed concerns the status of this 'moment of theory'. According to Ian Hunter (2006), 'the moment of theory' refers to a series of intellectual-cultural developments taking place within the universities of central and western Europe and their colonial offshoots. Although this moment has a number of distinctive historical precedents, it can be appropriately represented as emerging during the 1960s and continuing into the present. For Hunter (2006), the 'moment of theory' signals the surfacing of a particular sort of philosophical reflection within a variety of disciplines which were thereby recast as 'empiricist' or 'pre-theoretical'. So, what exactly does this mean?

Well, unlike natural scientific theories, the theory that emerged in the humanities and social sciences in the 1960s was not defined by its object, as it arose in disciplines with quite divergent objects. Furthermore, the types of theories deployed differed in many important respects. It is therefore understandable that one might baulk at the very term 'moment of theory', given the diversity which it is meant to muster into something more uniform. If it is neither a distinctive theory in the singular, nor a particular object, that frames the 'moment of theory', then what exactly does the term refer to? For Hunter (2006: 81), the answer lies with the shared intellectual deportment or attitude that the various constituent

---

[1] This chapter is a revised version of 'Introduction: "Identity" after "the Moment of Theory"', in du Gay (2007).

developments exhibit, albeit to different degrees. The 'moment of theory', then, is characterized by a scepticism towards empirical experience, but also towards *a priori* formalism – which it regards as foreclosing a higher level experiential immediacy – and hence cultivates openness to breakthrough phenomena of various kinds. Stanley Fish (1994: 251), without endorsing it, calls this attitude/deportment 'indeterminate negativity'. Roberto Unger (1986) (with definite endorsement) prefers the phrase 'negative capability'. Hunter (2006: 81) also argues that this attitude is characteristic of a particular kind of intellectual persona, and that providing an account of this persona and the exercises associated with its formation, is central to reflection on 'the moment of theory'.

In this chapter, then, I approach 'identity' in two ways. First, I explore the shared intellectual deportment or attitude characteristic of this moment of theory, and suggest certain ways in which it creates a particular identity for the persona of the theorist. Second, I indicate how 'identity' as a sociological object has been framed by the 'moment of theory', and register some of the consequences of this framing. As will become evident, this exploratory essay is heavily indebted to the work of Ian Hunter (2006) on 'The History of Theory' and Bruno Latour (2004) on the problems of contemporary critique. As they both, in their rather different ways, suggest, 'identity' work may continue to flourish but the theoretical spirits animating it seem terribly tired.

Theoretical Personae

We can get a clearer grasp of what Hunter terms the shared intellectual attitude or deportment characteristic of the 'moment of theory' if we turn briefly to the question of 'Identity' that has figured so large in that moment, and whose own destiny is so inextricably bound up with it. In post-structuralist lines of thought, for instance, 'identity' as an object is assumed to arise from the manner in which a fixated consciousness exists by disavowing and repressing its 'other'. It is this repression/occlusion that gives the 'other', as self-manifesting being, the capacity to break through its disavowal and throw fragile identity into the flux of becoming. The notion that identity is the temporary fixing of consciousness by the occlusion of the transcendental phenomenon – the phenomenon whose ruptural appearance calls forth a higher and more fluid form of self – is endemic in poststructuralist thought, as Hunter's (2006) essay makes clear.

We can see this, for instance, in the practice of Derridean deconstructive hermeneutics, where the affirmative meaning of a text is taken to be the product of its repression or marginalization of contradictory or subversive meanings; while the recovery of these through deconstructive reading is taken to be the undoing of positive meaning. We can therefore suggest that the figure of 'the other', together with the whole architecture of occlusion and transcendence (breakthrough), is part and parcel of a practice of self-problematization and self-transformation – a spiritual exercise, in Hadot's (1995) words – through which an individual learns to inhabit a post-structuralist persona. And this persona is not without its attractions. It appears to offer its practitioners a distinct muscle of the spirit or mind whose exercise allows it to float free of the boundaries and lines of demarcation that shape consciousness – those boundaries and demarcations that disavow the other – and thus to remain forever unsettled. Unpindownable. How amazing is that!? Pretty, as Latour (2004: 239) suggests

> Do you see now why it feels so good to be a critical mind? Why critique, this most ambiguous *pharmakon*, has become such a potent euphoric drug? You are always right! When naive believers are clinging forcefully to their objects, claiming to do things because of their gods, their poetry, their cherished objects, you can turn all of these attachments into so many fetishes and humiliate all the believers by showing that it is nothing but their own projection, that you, yes you alone, can see. But as soon as naive believers are thus inflated by some belief in their own importance, in their own projective capacity, you strike them by a second uppercut and humiliate them again, this time by showing that, whatever they think, their behaviour is entirely determined by the action of powerful causalities coming from objective reality they don't see, but that you, yes you, the never sleeping critic, alone can see. Isn't this fabulous? Isn't it really worth going to graduate school to study critique?

For Latour, as for Hunter, this critical theoretical persona clearly has some purchase, and not just in the social sciences and humanities. While Latour has rather different theorists in mind to Hunter, their arguments are united in two key respects. First, they discern a particular attitude or deportment in the theorists they discuss, one characterized by opposition, not opposition in particular, in clearly specified contexts, for instance, but opposition as a principle (the 'indeterminate negativity' noted earlier). Second, for both authors, the power of theory and its 'identity' work, for instance, is proportional to the allure of the persona it allows one to occupy. Its prestige and reach should not be underestimated. This has recently extended into what many would see as more vocational areas of academe (not that it didn't permeate some of the more powerful of these early on in its march through the academy; the Critical Legal Studies Movement (CLS), lest we forget, is nearly 30 years old. See Saunders (2005), for a detailed discussion of CLS and the moment of theory).

Nonetheless, the recent emergence of a 'Critical Management Studies' movement tells us something about the dynamics of the moment of theory, and thus of the intellectual time-space of 'Identity', something I alluded to in the Introduction to this chapter. In management studies, the feeling of marginality among critical academics is often rife, and the opportunities for theoretical vengeance on the more 'instrumental' or vocational aspects of the disciplinary area therefore enormous. The theoretical persona – post-structuralist, deconstructive, whatever – clearly appears attractive to those whose pedagogic bread and butter is often represented by themselves and by other 'critical' intellectuals as less than spiritually uplifting.

Where (anti-foundational) theory (and the critical hope it expresses) is still a (relative) novelty – often related to the degree of vocational, practical, or otherwise 'worldly' purposes of the field it enters – Identity work flourishes (in management studies). Where that novelty has worn off, frequently where theory first gained a foothold – in the humanities and social sciences, say – we find 'Identity' and 'difference', and the predictable chain of theoretical signifiers running out of steam (in literary theory and cultural studies, for example).

The upsurge of interest in Identity in the social sciences and humanities, then, is inextricably linked to the 'moment of theory'. And if that moment is passing then we can expect 'Identity' to begin to lose its foothold in the upper echelons of academe too. However, this demise is unlikely to indicate any diminution in the significance of the positive phenomena to which Identity has been theoretically attached. Theoretical identity – identity as framed by the 'moment of theory' – might be running out of steam, but that does not signal a lessening in the practical import of debates – in politics, management, sociology, history – which invoke identity as a *descriptive* as opposed to distinctively theoretical term. Rather, this descriptive 'Identity' work has tended to be occluded by the very philosophical problematizations which have made theoretical Identity work such a 'big issue' in the social sciences and humanities. What I want to suggest is that more descriptive 'identity' work loses its kudos, appears considerably less exciting – boring, even – when untouched by theory's epochal wand. Can you really be seen to be 'where it's at' if the work on identity that you perform remains unconnected to the 'moment of theory'? As Latour (2005: 136), has argued, though, '[N]o scholar should find humiliating the task of sticking to description. This is, on the contrary, the highest and rarest achievement'.

Some Sociological Consequences of 'The Moment of Theory'

In the social sciences, for instance, theoretical 'Identity' has frequently been bound up with something called 'social constructionism'. And social constructionism, as Fish (1999) and Hacking (1999), in their rather different ways have shown, has often ended up akin to an all purpose, across the board formula, and, as such, has frequently evacuated that which it purports to analyse of any of its positivity.

How so? Well, in its distinctively 'theoretical' mode the social constructionist formula often takes two forms. First, and most frequently, as Fish (1994) suggests, it is deployed as critique: 'Aha! You may think your agenda, project, object, self is somehow obvious, free-standing, natural, but actually it is socially constructed!' The post-structuralist capacity to treat identity as arising only from the manner in which it represses its other is regularly deployed in this move, to chide an object, agenda, project, or person for its failure to understand and/or encompass the symbolic (or actual) violence it does to that which it represses in order to be itself. This is a powerful move, as the quote from Latour (2004) above suggests; it can destabilize, undermine, induce feelings of guilt and all the sorts of affects that the critical mindset wishes to bring about. But really, why? What exactly does this achieve? Well, a frequently stated aim is precisely to indicate that the existence or character of something is not determined by the nature of things. It is neither natural nor inevitable. Not only this, and here is the second move, once its 'constructed' character is revealed, it can be re-imagined and/or radically transformed. In other words, once you have shown that something is socially constructed as opposed to obvious, there, natural, whatever – you are by dint of this insight, it is argued, better able to revise that thing, or turn it into something altogether different, something more radical, open, less exclusionary, perhaps. You can offer to return to it – as the otherwise fulsomely 'anti-social' constructivists Callon and Muneisa (2005) have recently suggested doing to the market – a politics its current theorization emits, represses, marginalizes, and occludes.

These moves raise a number of questions, though. First, do we actually learn anything positive about that which is subject to this theoretical exercise? Or is it the case that the social constructionist move is precisely designed to take away self-evidence from that which forms its object? Second, given that the same moves can be made on anything – robots, death, corporations, fish – what exactly is the status of the critical claim being made? Thirdly, why does deployment of the mantra 'socially constructed' (or even the more pragmatic term 'constructivist') give the theorist any sort of advantage in the practice of revising something, compared with those who do not buy into the social constructionist programme; those who maintain a belief in 'objectivity', for example?

This sort of social constructionism, like the moment of theory more generally, emerges from a work of philosophical problematization and transformation performed on a variety of positive knowledges. As Foucault (1971) indicated in *The Order of Things*, linguistics, sociology and the 'psy' disciplines can be seen to emerge from a certain kind of interrogative work performed on the positive knowledges of classificatory language studies, political economy and biology. According to Foucault, the space in which this interrogation took place, and in which the human sciences emerged, is a field formed by three poles: mathematical formalization, the positive knowledges themselves, and a specific use of Kantian critical philosophy. The latter in particular performs a special role in enabling theory to approach the positive knowledges not in terms of their objects, but in terms of the a-positive structures or relations that make knowledge possible for a subject (Hunter 2006: 93). This then begs the question: what drives this philosophical problematization of positive knowledges?

As we have already seen, Ian Hunter's (2006: 81) answer concerns the forms of self-problematization that informs the activity of theory. He points in particular to the influence of Kantian and Husserlian techniques of self-problematization – means of acting on oneself with a view to suspending one's commitments to one's thoughts, perceptions, desires etc – through which the theorist learns to problematize an object by interrogating his or her commitment to the positive knowledge in which the object resides. As Hunter (2006: 87) argues

This applies to all the founding moments of theory; for example, when it is said that meaning is never present and is only accessible in a deferred way through a chain of signifiers; or when it is said that historical time is only an appearance generated by a-temporal concepts unfolding themselves in the human sensorium; or when it is said that speech is the manifestation of deep structure, or a generative grammar. Each of these moments of doubt is contingent on an act of suspension of commitment performed on oneself with a view to becoming another kind of person.

This philosophical or metaphysical problematization of positive knowledges is therefore precisely designed to rob them of their self-evidence, and to effect a shift in the theorist's existential relation to those knowledges as a mode of inner intellectual conduct.

If such problematizations are not part and parcel of a detached investigation into a particular discipline or form of positive knowledge, but rather function as vehicles for the formation of a distinctive persona, what exactly are we to make of the critical claims made on behalf of this persona? For instance, the thesis that meanings are not freestanding and natural but are socially constructed, takes many forms. In certain Lacanian psychoanalytic or deconstructive moves, for instance, we learn that meanings are produced by a system of articulation from which we, as speakers or hearers, cannot distance ourselves, because we are situated within it. Since that system (the unconscious or *différance*) is the unarticulated ground within which specification occurs, 'it' cannot be specified and always exceeds – remains after, escapes – the specification it enables. What this means, of course, is that any knowledge cannot be in possession of itself. As knowledge it cannot grasp, or name the grounds of its possibility, and whenever it thinks it's done so, those grounds actually appear somewhere other than they appear to reside (Fish 1994: 235–236). Ignorance, the forgetting of the enabling conditions of knowledge (conditions that cannot themselves be known), is thus deemed to be constitutive of knowledge itself. It follows from this, then, that if ignorance is the necessary content of knowledge, knowledge is not something that should be allowed to settle, since in whatever form it appears it will always be excluding more than it reveals; and indeed it is only by virtue of the exclusions it cannot acknowledge that it acquires its 'identity'. As Fish (1994: 236) asks, does this practice hold out the hope of anything beyond its continuous unsettling of whatever claims us in the name of positive knowledge? One crucial thing it does do, as we have seen, is offer the theorist a prestigious persona, one which can look down on the positive knowledges as vestiges of a lower, less elevated self (Hunter 2006: 29).

Thirdly, why does deployment of the term 'socially constructed' give someone any sort of advantage in the practice of revising something, compared with those who do not believe in the social constructionist hypothesis? After all, the impulse to revise – markets, curricula, accounting standards – has been experienced and acted upon many times before the advent of a constructionist programme in the intellectual field. As Fish (1999: ix) has remarked, 'the work of revision isn't furthered a whit by declaring it possible'. Neither the critic nor those who s/he manages to persuade of the analytic power of the social constructionist perspective will find themselves in a better position to revise anything than those who do not buy into the creed, or those who have never heard of it. In other words, the practical work of revision cannot be undertaken by simply announcing the thesis of social constructionism. More banally, what exactly can we learn about particular practices by making this move; by deploying the metaphor of social constructionism? If the social constructionist thesis simply prefigures a philosophical attitude to phenomena which simultaneously robs those phenomena of their positive (non relational) content (Hunter 2006), we might usefully ask: what's the value added?

What I want to suggest – as Hacking (1999) and Latour (2005) in their different ways have done already – is that such a move can hamper understanding of the ways in which particular objects, persons, things are put together, assembled, or constructed in the plain, literal sense of the term (i.e. how their identity is organized). It does so because the theory deployed doesn't suit such a purpose. Rather, it substitutes philosophical, preponderantly metaphysical, argument for empirical description. Let's take an example. It is one that was for a time very popular in social constructionist circles but which has, recently, like the hypothesis it represents, simply got tired. The example concerns authorship.

During the 1980s, it became fashionable to talk of the 'death of the author'. This claim was often referenced in relation to the work of Roland Barthes (1977) and Michel Foucault (1984). This claim did not usually appear as part of a descriptive empirical investigation – an historical argument concerning the construction of particular authorial statuses in legal argument, say (Saunders 1991). Rather, as Fish (2003: 396) has argued, the claim functioned to call into question – as a philosophical truth – the very notion of a singular voice that owned its utterances. As such its paradigmatic status within social constructionist discourse is self-evident. However, its usefulness for empirical debates about authorship (and copyright, one of its favourite preoccupations) appears somewhat limited, and for the reasons outlined above. If it only makes sense to enter a debate about the authorship of something if you believe, in principle, that there are facts the discovery of which could settle the matter one way or another, then it appears somewhat pointless to get into such a debate with the conclusion already arrived at. In other words, if what you believe is that the attribution of a work to a single author will always be a mistake – not an empirical mistake, but a metaphysical mistake – because the idea of an individual voice is a myth and/or an artefact of bourgeois culture, or because authorship must always and necessarily be seen as multiple, that belief can have no significance or weight in relationship to empirical questions it renders meaningless (Fish 2003: 396).

Such 'metaphysical' preformatting does not of course begin and end with the question of authorship. It is to be found applied to a diverse range of objects and propounded by a wide range of theorists within the social sciences and humanities. Jurgen Habermas, for instance, would not be everyone's idea of a prototypical participant in the 'moment of theory', especially given his famous attacks on post-structuralism and deconstruction in *The Philosophical Discourse of Modernity* (1986). However, seen historically, Habermas's social theory appears as a central and influential example of theoretical world view, involving as it does a philosophical (basically phenomenological) problematization and transformation of a particular disciplinary field, in this instance sociology (Hunter 1994; 2006). By representing society as an entity that evolves with its theorization, Habermas (1991) is able to present his theory of social communication in the form of a chain of hermeneutic problematizations of the work of the great sociologists (Marx, Weber, Durkheim et al.)

> [T]his hermeneutic chain is envisaged as a progressive refinement of man's capacity for rational self-determination ... In keeping with the Husserlian model, each stage in the process takes place in the form of a brief but fundamental breakthrough to the intuitions of the life-world – Marx's grasp of the importance of productive relations, Durkheim's conception of society as the social form of religious and philosophical categories, Weber's understanding of the rationalisation of society – which is then occluded through the elaboration of formal theorisations finally themselves complicit with society as "system" (Hunter 2006: 109–110).

The comparative strengths and weaknesses of these sociologists and sociologies, indeed their very purposes, are benchmarked against this goal; the possibility of a final breakthrough to the domain of the life-world, evidenced in Habermas's notion of the 'ideal speech situation'. In effect, it is this possibility that provides the entire hermeneutic chain with its *telos*.

The normative conditions furnishing this ideal speech situation are clear enough: 'Entrance into moral discourse demands that one steps back from all contingently existing normative contexts. Such discourse takes place under communicative presuppositions that require a break with everyday taken for granted assumptions; in particular it requires a hypothetical attitude toward the relevant norms of action and their validity claims' (Habermas 1997: 164).

Because there is somewhere that has to be got to, there has to be a route, and ultimately Habermas holds the key. Here it is: the universal perspective we must rise to if the ideal speech situation is to be realized is already implicit (but occluded) in the activities we perform in the contexts that are ultimately to be transcended. Thus, without knowing it, by making the simplest of statements, we effectively buy into the strongly idealizing, context transcendent claims of reason.

How this move works repays some attention. It begins like this: 'anyone acting communicatively must, in performing any speech action, raise universal validity claims and suppose they can be vindicated [or redeemed: *enlösen*]' (Habermas 1991: 2). As Fish (2003, 399) indicates, this is a 'must' independent of anyone's conscious intention. The intention belongs to the communicative context in general. By entering that context, one is, as it were, committing oneself to everything that communication as a universal form of action implies, including, the goal of bringing about 'an agreement (*Einverständnis*) that terminates in the intersubjective mutuality of reciprocal understanding, shared knowledge, mutual trust, and accord with one another' (Habermas 1991: 3).

> Whoever makes use of a natural language in order to come to an understanding with an addressee about something in the world is required to take a performative attitude and commit herself to certain presuppositions; ... natural language users must assume, among other things, that the participants pursue their illocutionary goals without reservations, that they tie [the possibility of] their agreement to the intersubjective recognition of criticisable validity claims, and that they are ready to take on the obligations resulting from consensus and relevant for further interaction ... That is, they must undertake certain idealizations – for example ascribe identical meanings to expressions, connect utterances with context-transcending validity, and claims, and assume that addressees are accountable, that is autonomous and sincere with both themselves and others (Habermas 1997: 4).

For Habermas, then, as Fish (2003: 403) has indicated, a claim to universal validity is presupposed by every mundane act of communication. The programme of making good on this claim produces the project of discourse ethics that, if followed correctly, will instantiate the ideal speech situation participated in by discourse partners wholly committed to the universal norms now filling their consciousnesses. For Habermas, this claim to universal validity is unavoidable. For Fish (2003: 404), though, it appears entirely avoidable by everyone except the few, but prestigious, philosophical practitioners of discourse ethics, for whom it is a baseline assumption from which to launch their project. Habermas's 'must' of communicative action, reported above, therefore belongs entirely to one particular practice – that of critical philosophy; it is not a necessary component of every particular act of assertion, communication, or debate, in every conceivable context. It may provide the discourse ethics philosopher with a certain metaphysical persona, but it is not a universal form of life to which all categories of person need or could aspire, or ever seek to comport themselves according to its requirements (by giving reasons for everything, by regarding their interlocutors as free and equal, by self-consciously seeking a shared intersubjective form of understanding) (Fish 2003: 403–405).

In *Between Facts and Norms*, Habermas (1997) draws a moral distinction between two communicative orientations. One, to understanding within the values, norms and practices given to you by a particular 'context' (without your assent, or deliberation), the other to understanding within norms and values so general as to be applicable and appropriate no matter what the context might be. The former orientation, he argues, is preponderantly that of the 'self-interested' actor, for whom situational features are 'transformed into facts that they evaluate in the light of their own preferences'. Actors oriented to 'understanding, in general', however, 'rely on a jointly negotiated understanding of the situation and interpret the relevant facts in the light of intersubjectively recognized validity claims' (Habermas 1997: 27).

The possibility of different categories and practices of personhood requiring and expressing distinctive ethical comportments irreducible to common underlying principles appears quite foreign to Habermas's mode of moral reflection, whereby a common or universal form of ethical judgment is seen to reside in the capacities of the self-reflective person. His assumption that 'self-interested' conduct is unitary and continuous – that 'self-interest' can only be one thing – selfish adherence to one's own preferences – and that thing is always and already the enemy of the common good or ideal speech situation, is a telling instance of such a worldview.[2] A brief historical genealogy of 'self-interested' conduct – like that undertaken by Albert Hirschman (1985), for instance – suggests something rather more complex. The 'self' of 'self-interest' is put together differently – normatively and technically – in relation to particular 'local' purposes (du Gay 2005). In contrast to Habermas's a-historic uni-dimensionalism, Hirschman points to the ways in which early modern conceptions of 'self-interested' conduct were viewed in context as far from selfish and egotistical. Rather than presaging society's ruin, as Habermas would have it, early modern conceptions of 'self interest', for instance, were aimed precisely at society's salvation, by seeking to offer a mechanism that might help to bring about an end to the ruinous religious civil wars besetting Europe at the time. Rather than interpreting 'self-interest' as intrinsically involving a mean spirited repudiation of the public interest or common good – as the bad other to the good, reflective, deliberative, full human being – it is better to look to the particularity of the circumstances and to the business of descriptions. Then we might be able to trace how different forms of self-interested conduct are put together and thus what they enable the agents they bring into being to 'do' in particular circumstances.

If we do so, we quickly see that Habermas's distinction/struggle between self-interested understanding and a general orientation to understanding is a wrestle between two phantoms. As I have just suggested, human capacities are too positive and too various to be tied to a general 'communicative' form. It might therefore appear difficult to avoid Fish's (2003: 405) conclusion that '[I]f an

---

2 Critical philosophy of the sort practiced by Habermas seems constitutionally incapable of distinguishing two quite different senses in which 'values' might be 'personal'. Values might be personal, for instance, in the sense of deriving – *comme* Habermas – from processes of moral reflection that individuals (rightly or wrongly) identify with their own inner conscience. But values might also be personal in the sense of simply providing a focus for individual moral commitment and ethical action. Clearly these two senses of 'personal' are not the same. Individuals can and do find a (personal) focus for moral life in ethoses that derive from impersonal ethical institutions, rather than their own individual moral reflections. It is in this sense, as Minson (1993) and Latour (2002), for instance, indicate that bureaucrats and judges can and should be personally committed to the ethos of their distinctive office even though that ethos lies outside of their 'personal' moral predilections or principles.

orientation to understanding as such is not built into every communicative act and thus cannot function as a bridge to itself, if intersubjective norms name a desire but not a possible human achievement, then there is no Habermasian project, nowhere to start, nowhere to go, and no possible payoff except the employment of a few rationalist philosophers'. Such a conclusion has certain attractions and yet, as Hunter (1994: 117) suggests, such outright condemnation might be less interesting, sociologically and ethically, than seeking to describe the comportment of the would-be universalist critical philosopher in its own terms. Seen in this light, the most suggestive part of Fish's critique concerns the institutional status of the critical philosopher: how a certain prestige – academically, spiritually – gets attached to this persona. More prosaically, how – in the plain literal sense of the term, is the identity of this persona organized?

> Through what intellectual-technical devices does this personage achieve the spiritual problematization of other intellectual domains – of law, government, the empirical sciences – by positioning them as deficient in moral ends and theoretical reflexivity? And, if this problematization forms part of an ethic of 'world flight', then from what intellectual and institutional sources does this flight from mundanity gain its not inconsiderable authority, reverence and prestige ...? (Hunter 1994: 117).

Concluding Comments

The approach suggested by Hunter (1994) to what we earlier termed 'the organization of identity', or the material-cultural making up of 'persons', involves a shift away from general social and cultural theoretical accounts concerning the formation of 'subjectivity' and 'identity' towards an understanding of the specific forms of 'personhood' that individuals acquire as a result of their involvement in, or subjection to, particular normative and technical regimes of conduct.[3] In other words, instituted norms and techniques of conduct are regarded as instruments for the cultivation of particular 'personal' deportments, whose historical circumstances, purposes and distribution are matters of sociological and historical investigation and description (Saunders 1997). Alongside this emphasis comes recognition of the importance of not routinely or carelessly abstracting or divorcing the properties of particular 'persons' from the specific regime or milieu in which they are formed and make sense, particularly when such an exercise is

---

3   This is very much Max Weber's programme as argued by Wilhelm Hennis (1988; 2000). Weber's contemporary, Paul Honigsheim (quoted in Hennis 1988: 108), recalls how Weber 'presented himself to the world as fragmented, and at each opportunity declared himself to belong to a particular sphere rather than presenting himself as a totality'. He concluded, rather dismissively, that 'You can't make a lively tune out of that'. Quite so. How refreshing. We have far too many lively tunes as it is.

undertaken under the auspices of mining 'the' concept of a person. As Amélie Rorty (1988: 31) has argued

> there is no such thing as "the" concept of a person. This is so not only for the obvious historical reason that there have been dramatically discontinuous changes in the characterization of persons, though that is true. Nor for the equally anthropological-cultural reason that the moral and legal practices heuristically treated as analogous across cultures differ so dramatically that they capture "the concept" of personhood only vaguely and incompletely, though this is also true. [T]he various functions performed by our contemporary concept of persons don't hang together: there is some overlap, but also some tension. Indeed, the functions that "the" notion plays are so related that attempts to structure them in taxonomic order express quite different norms and ideals. Disagreements about primary values and goods reappear as disagreements about the priorities and relations among the various functions the concept plays, disagreements about what is essential to persons. Not only does each of the functions bear a different relation to the class of persons and human beings, but each also has a different contrast class.

Why then does there appear to be such a strong – one might say permanent – metaphysical desire for one concept? Perhaps it has something to do with the unifying functions that the concept plays: 'the subject of right', 'the locus of liability', 'the autonomous, reflexive self'. Since these various functions appear to be unifying functions there is often a strong temptation to look for their unifying source. This, Rorty argues, is an elementary error. 'A desire for unity', she writes, 'cannot by itself perform the conjuring trick of pulling one rabbit out of several hats: a transcendental unity of the concept of person, unifying the variety of distinct, independently unifying functions that each regional concept plays' (Rorty 1988: 45).

Rorty's preference is for what she describes as a strongly contextualist approach, with its privileging of description rather than theoretical colonization or (social) reconstruction; an approach which refuses to provide a general answer to the question: how are entities identified across contexts? Instead it accepts that since questions and contexts are particular 'all the way up and all the way down' (Rorty 1988: 8), questions about identifying entities across contexts are themselves given their sense and direction by the context within which they arise. 'The question, "How are contexts identified and individuated?" is answered by the counter-question, Which contexts?' (Rorty 1988: 8).

Latour (2004: 231–2) would appear to concur – though without using the terms 'context' and 'contextualist' which he abhors (see Latour 2005: 215) – suggesting that such a descriptive enterprise gets us closer to the objects – in this instance, persons – we seek to understand, treating them with a degree of care and concern that more elevated theories simply cannot because they set out their co-ordinates too far in advance and leave no way out from their terms of reference. This latter tendency has the effect of rendering certain extremely important but often (seen from the heights of grand theory) rather banal details insignificant or even invisible.[4] Only by under-describing persons is it possible to make them conform to 'the' – illicitly decontextualized – concept of a person. To get closer requires description, and through such proximity concern for the qualities of particular personae can be registered. If nothing else, overhasty attempts to reconstruct, modernize or otherwise transform persons – human and non-human (states, corporations) – under the auspices of universalist or epochalist theories can then be seen for what they are, and the costs of such an exercise can be better appreciated.

References

Barthes, R. (1977), 'Death of the Author', in *Image-Music-Text* (New York: Hill and Wang).
Callon, M. and Muniesa, F. (2005) 'Economic Markets as Calculative Collective Devices', *Organization Studies* 26:8, 1229–1250.
du Gay, P. (2005), 'Which is the Self in "Self-Interest"?', *Sociological Review* 53:3, 391–411.
du Gay, P. (2007), *Organizing Identity* (London: Sage).
Fish, S. (1994), *There's No Such Thing as Free Speech ... and It's a Good Thing Too* (Oxford: Oxford University Press).
Fish, S. (1999), *The Trouble with Principle* (Cambridge, MA: Harvard University Press).
Fish, S. (2003), 'Truth but No Consequences: Why Philosophy Doesn't Matter', *Critical Inquiry* 29 (Spring), 389–417.
Foucault, M. (1971), *The Order of Things* (New York: Pantheon Books).
Foucault, M. (1984), 'What is an Author?' in Rabinow (ed.)

---

4 In *La Fabrique du Droit* Latour (2003) finds the jettisoning of deep philosophical and moral justifications for the work of law personally quite difficult to achieve. Only by rigorously focusing on description of the law, and making it compatible with the practice of the judges does the 'philosophically minded' enthnographer begin to answer his own despairing question : 'sera-t-il jamias *assez superficial* pour saisir la force du droit?'.

It may seem churlish, but one could wish that Latour (2004) had exhibited the same stoical self-restraint in his essay on theory and critique. After offering a brilliant dissection of the philosophically inclined 'critical persona', Latour (2004: 239) is unable to resist the pull of this persona himself. When he writes 'Although I wish to keep this paper short ... ' and then continues, the alarm bells should be ringing. Shortly thereafter, we arrive at what, to this reader's eyes, at least, appears to be a classic 'moment' of theory: 'The solution lies, it seems to me, in this promising word "gathering" that Heidegger had introduced to account for the "thinginess of the thing"'. The extent to which Latour, and indeed, ANT, more generally, is part of the 'moment of theory' is an interesting question. For one balanced answer (largely in the affirmative, despite some important reservations) see Zammito (2004).

Habermas, J. (1986), *The Philosophical Discourse of Modernity* (Cambridge: Polity Press).
Habermas, J. (1991), *Communication and the Evolution of Society* (Cambridge: Polity Press).
Habermas, J. (1997), *Between Facts and Norms: Contributions to a Discourse Theory of Law and Democracy* (Cambridge: Polity Press).
Hacking, I. (1999), *The Social Construction of What?* (Cambridge, MA: Harvard University Press).
Hennis, W. (1988), *Max Weber: Essays in Reconstruction* (London: Allen & Unwin).
Hennis, W. (2000), *Max Weber's Science of Man* (Berks: Threshold Press).
Hadot, P. (1995), *Philosophy as a Way of Life* (Oxford: Blackwell).
Hirschman, A. (1985), *The Passions and the Interests* (Princeton, NJ: Princeton University Press).
Hunter, I. (1994) 'Metaphysics as a way of life', *Economy & Society* 23:1, 93–117.
Hunter, I. (2006) 'The History of Theory', *Critical Inquiry* 33:1, 78–112.
Latour, B. (2002), *La Fabrique du Droit: une ethnographie du Conseil d'État* (Paris: La Découverte).
Latour, B. (2004), 'Why Has Critique Run out of Steam? From Matters of Fact to Matters of Concern', *Critical Inquiry* 30:1, 225–248.
Latour, B. (2005), *Assembling the Social* (Oxford: Oxford University Press).
Minson, J. (1993), *Questions of Conduct* (Basingstoke: Macmillan).
Rabinow, P. (ed.) (1984), *The Foucault Reader* (Harmondsworth: Penguin).
Rorty, A.-O. (1988), *Mind in Action* (Boston: Beacon Press).
Saunders, D. (1991), *Authorship and Copyright* (London: Routledge).
Saunders, D. (1997), *The Anti-Lawyers* (London: Routledge).
Saunders, D. (2005), 'The Critical Jurist and the Moment of Theory', Seminar presented to the Centre for the History of European Discourses, University of Queensland, November.
Unger, R.M. (1986), *The Critical Legal Studies Movement* (Boston, MA: Harvard University Press).
Zammito, J. (2004), *A Nice Derangement of Epistemes* (Chicago: Chicago University Press).

Chapter 11
Concluding Thoughts: Reconfigurations of Social Theory

Andrew King and Ruth Rettie

Each chapter has contributed, in different ways, to the book's key themes of sociological objects and the reconfiguration of theory. They have done this through discussion of a disparate collection of objects – arithmetic, money, queues for example – but also through active engagement in the process of reconfiguring both existing theories and ideas about the role that theory should play. Moreover some common sources, notably Durkheim, have been subject to some very different reconfigurations. In this concluding chapter we draw together some of the strands running through these different treatments, and consider several key issues that have emerged: changing conceptions of sociology and sociological objects; the way in which social theory is transmitted, reconfigured and transformed; and the relationship between social theory and its spatio-temporal, empirical context.

Sociology's Object(ive)

In Chapter 1, Cooper observes that reconfiguration and reflection on its objects of study are characteristic features of sociological discourse. He suggests that there is a normative element at work within these processes of reconfiguration, as is evident in debates within the discipline on its goals and boundaries, on appropriate analytical approaches and methods, and on the relationship between the sociologist and the objects of sociological knowledge. Each chapter in this book raises questions about the remit of the discipline. They do this not only by directly addressing the issue, but also indirectly, in the analytical perspectives they adopt and the topics they cover.

Pyyhtinen explicitly discusses sociology's quest for a subject matter of its own, and, noting a change of focus from 'social facts' (Durkheim) to 'social forms' (Simmel), highlights the way in which key aspects of current discussions have been prefigured within classical sociology. He relates the need for a distinctive focus for sociology to the distinction between what is, and what is not, social. Pyyhtinen contends that Simmel's work shows that the inclusion of material objects in sociological investigations does not render them non-social, but forces us to broaden our conception of the ontology of social things.

Inglis and Robertson also consider the significance of classical social theory for contemporary sociology, given the current 'global turn', and move away from society as the focal point for sociological analysis. They identify elements of an incipient global sociology in Durkheim's works, although they locate these in texts that have not traditionally been viewed in this manner. There are similarities between their reconfiguration of Durkheim and that of Rawls, who also writes about the role of sociology in a context of globalization. Rawls claims that sociology is being left behind because it continues to focus on shared beliefs and norms which, whilst highly significant for traditional societies, have been superseded by practice, which now takes a central role in social formation. Rawls argues that, *contra* the predominant perception of Durkheim, he emphasized the importance of the details of communities of practice, as subsequently exemplified and elaborated in Garfinkel's ethnomethodology.

The ethnomethodological turn in sociology is approached rather differently by Lynch, who deliberates on Garfinkel's use of Durkheim's aphorism, which holds that the objectivity of social facts is sociology's basic principle (or phenomenon). The aphorism implies that social facts are a central topic or object for sociology. However, for Garfinkel, the objectivity of a social fact is a *produced* phenomenon, an achievement of everyone involved, rather than something to which the professional sociologist has privileged access. Ethnomethodology changes not only the nature of social facts and therefore the objects of sociological analysis, but also the nature of this analysis and the relationship between the sociologist and the object of her knowledge. Greiffenhagen and Sharrock also adopt an ethnomethodological approach, considering whether mathematical equations are social facts and consequently amenable to a sociology of knowledge. They conclude that mathematical equations such as '$2 + 2 = 4$' are *rules* in our 'default' system, which are necessarily true if considered from within a system where they apply, but contingent (or meaningless) if viewed from outside that system. If we extend Greiffenhagen and Sharrock's conception of social facts as rules beyond mathematics, the 'rules' of communities of practice become a topic for sociological inquiry. Although the rules of situated practices are enacted by those involved, they take these rules for granted and can rarely articulate them; their formulation, therefore, can be regarded as a task for the sociologist, and an object for analysis.

Although Rafanell is not explicitly concerned with the borders of the discipline, she also explores Durkheim's concept of social facts, using a model of performativity derived from Butler and Barnes, to challenge his classification of the social as ontologically *sui generis*. She endorses Durkheim's emphasis on the collectivity of the social, but argues that this collectivity does *not* function independently of individuals' activities. Taken collectively, individuals' activities are *performative*, and thereby constitutive of objective social phenomena. Greiffenhagen and Sharrock's concept of a 'default system' can be related to Rafanell's performative explanation of social objectivity. The 'default' system, that includes social categorization, language and norms, constructs and constitutes social life; its objectivity arises from consensus and the collective acceptance of these rules. The 'default system' can be narrowly defined and based on the traditional concept of society usually associated with Durkheim, or alternatively, interpreted more broadly and associated with the communities of practice described by Rawls.

While Rafanell outlines a performative approach to social categories, Mik-Meyer explores these categories from a different perspective, considering the two-way flow of categories between professional sociologists and the actors they study; Mik-Meyer's research suggests that theoretically loaded sociological categories are embedded in lay discourse. She argues that, in contrast to the ethnomethodological position which eschews the use of theoretically derived categories, the presence and influence of dominant social theoretical discourses in everyday practice provide an important warrant for the use of theory in sociological research. Whereas the framing of the phrase 'sociology's object' might suggest that sociology is outwith its topic, Mik-Meyer's chapter recognizes that sociology is situated within its own field, complicating the relationship between the discipline and its subject matter.

If Mik-Meyer's chapter focuses on the ways in which academic discourse can shape everyday practice, du Gay's chapter interrogates the place and significance of theorizing within the academy. Du Gay follows Foucault and characterizes the human sciences in terms of a particular *kind* of interrogation rather in terms of the objects it interrogates. Moreover, for du Gay, social theory's subject matter and analytical approach define not only the discipline within which they are formulated, but the persona of the theorist. In 'the moment of theory', both critique and 'indeterminate negativity' boost the prestige of the sociologist, building his (sic) persona and identity. Du Gay's chapter returns us to the theme of the historical specificity of social theory that Cooper introduced in chapter one. The concept of a 'moment of theory' challenges the assumption of an absolute evaluation of theory, suggesting a normative assessment of the value of theory, both from within and beyond the discipline, which changes over time. Presumably, however, the theory that there are 'moments of theory' itself has its moment, and this moment is amenable to analysis? Tsatsaroni and Cooper's chapter could be taken as just such an analysis, their argument beginning with a consideration of the place of theory today in what some regard as an uncongenial cultural context. However, they go on to argue that since translation is a constitutive feature of theory, simple valorizations of theory as, for example, a source of resistance to external threats must be rethought. Whilst each of these two chapters pursue a different line, and indeed provide resources for critically reading aspects of the other's argument, they share the view that since theory is embedded in time any ahistorical assessment of its role is inadequate. Perhaps we might say, to paraphrase Goffman (1967: 3): Not, then, theories and their moments. Rather moments and their theories.

Overall, many of the chapters in this book exemplify Pyyhtinen's assertion that sociology tends to overlook *things*, focusing instead on actors and their communities, practices and personae, or at a more philosophical level, on conceptual abstraction, linguistic categories and meta-theory. Generally they do not follow Latour's (2005) call for a deflationary use of the term 'social', although several chapters explore the distinction between social and natural (or material) objects and the coherence of 'social' as a category. For instance, Tsatsaroni and Cooper contrast Bernstein's unproblematic treatment of the social as a separate domain with Latour's rejection of the purification that divides natural and social. Pyyhtinen also draws on Latour, claiming that despite Simmel's recognition of the interdependence of social and material phenomena, he retained an asymmetric priorization of the social. Although Rafanell uses Barnes' distinction between social and natural kind terms, her performative view is not dependent on this distinction, which she describes as idealized and not a reflection of an empirical division. In fact, Rafanell argues that social phenomena 'acquire a material status as artefacts, as it were: phenomena constructed by humans but perceived as objective materiality' (Rafanell, this volume: 71). Ethnomethodology also avoids a natural/ social dichotomy: Lynch notes that Garfinkel's 'methodology is indifferent to natural/social distinction, except when that distinction is locally and constitutively relevant' (Lynch, this volume: 114).

Reconfiguring Social Theory

Throughout this book both classical and contemporary theories are interwoven. All of the authors use existing social theory, and their usage stimulates several related questions. In what ways are earlier social theories used in the production of new theory? When authors and social theory are cited in general terms (e.g. 'Durkheim') is the reference to an essentialist distillation of his oeuvre, to the author's intentions (or even persona), or to common (or accepted) understandings of the author's works? Are there correct or preferred readings of social texts, so that it makes sense to identify misreadings and lack of fidelity to the original sources? What is the effect of taking social theory out of its historical context? To what extent can classical theories develop and change within new contexts, while still retaining their authenticity?

In this book the names of authors have often been used to invoke and denote either the general tenor of an author's oeuvre, or a theoretical perspective associated with the author, rather than in reference to a specific theoretical claim: for example, Durkheim, Garfinkel, etc. This usage is characteristic of, but not exclusive to, sociology. In the sciences key concepts or theories are often referenced more directly: gravity rather than Newton, for example. Bernstein's (1999) distinction between hierarchically and segmentally organized knowledge structures illuminates this practice. For Bernstein, sociology is segmentally organized and therefore consists of a series of specialized and largely incommensurate languages: what counts and what is transmitted is the author's perspective and the 'acquirer's gaze' rather than any one particular theory. Bernstein notes that 'in these conditions, it is likely that canonical names will be a useful resource. Later, the names will be associated with languages or, in some cases, the language will come before the exemplars. Thus, managing names and languages together with their criticisms becomes both the manner of transmission and acquisition' (1999: 164).

One role for existing theory is as a resource for the production of new theory. Bernstein argues that in disciplines such as the sciences, theory develops by becoming 'more general, more integrating than previous theory' (1999: 163), but that this is not generally possible in a discipline with a horizontal knowledge structure such as sociology. This is because its different discourses are not mutually translatable. At first glance Pyyhtinen's chapter, to take one example, would seem to fit Bernstein's model: his chapter is an exposition of Simmel's perspective, making it more accessible and helping the reader to acquire the relevant 'gaze', rather than a development of Simmel's theory. Pyyhtinen is critical, commenting on merits and flaws in Simmel's approach, and positioning it within the current field by drawing parallels between Simmel and more recent theorists. In this, his contribution exemplifies the transmission of theory in changing contexts discussed by du Gay. However, Pyyhtinen also identifies Simmel as a precursor of Latour[1] and implies that actor network theory (ANT) is a *theoretical development* of Simmel's perspective. This suggests that theory development may be more relevant in sociology than Bernstein's model would indicate. Inglis and Robertson make a similar theoretical move and show how theory can be adapted for later contexts, adapting and developing Durkheim's theory to make it more relevant to a globalized world. Similarly, Rafanell explicitly aims to develop and extend Durkheim's theory. Although her chapter discusses Durkheim, Butler, and Barnes among others, her objective is not simply the elucidation of these perspectives, but the extraction of elements which she uses in the development of her performative approach to social reality.

In the 'Social Practices' part of this book, Bernstein's notion of theory as a specialized language or distinctive perspective becomes more pertinent, as does the issue of authenticity. The authors in this section are all overtly concerned with interpretations (and misinterpretations) of Durkheim; consequently, the fidelity and accuracy of the theory they expound is as relevant as its validity. Rawls complains that Durkheim has been mis-interpreted and offers a radical interpretation, tracing continuities between Durkheim's work and Garfinkel's ethnomethodology. Lynch challenges her reading, and in doing so, argues that Garfinkel is not following but deliberately 'misreading' and thereby respecifying Durkheim. His chapter shows how a new perspective can use theory as a resource *without* reconfiguring or developing it: Lynch contrasts the use of previous theory to legitimate or provide heritage, with Garfinkel's deliberate 'misreading' of Durkheim's aphorism. Rather than giving an exegesis, or developing Durkheim's approach to social objects, Garfinkel uses it as a 'take-off' point for reorientation and the creation of a new path. Lynch's chapter neatly illustrates the difference between exposition and new theory; he is clearly concerned with the explication of Garfinkel's perspective,

---

1   Note that the relationship is partly analytical rather than historical and therefore not disproved by Latour's own identification of Tarde as his precursor (Latour 2005).

but he argues that Garfinkel is not concerned to explicate Durkheim. Lynch's discussion of Garfinkel's situated tutorials and their use to 'retune sensibilities' is one pragmatic solution to the acquisition of an authentic perspective or 'gaze'. Greiffenhagen and Sharrock bypass the issue of authenticity in their comparison of 'inflationary' and 'deflationary' readings of Durkheim, and focus instead on the implications of theory. Their chapter accepts that there are alternative readings of Durkheim, but rather than trying to identify a 'correct' reading, they advocate choosing a preferred reading on the basis of its consequences. Their focus is on the theory and its implications rather than on authentic exegesis.

A focus on the path of theory as it is read, translated, developed and transformed can overlook the complex relationship between theory and context highlighted by du Gay. Tsatsaroni and Cooper suggest that theory is not a passive resource, but part of an active process: theory is stabilized, defined and developed through its transmission and transformation in new contexts. For Tsatsaroni and Cooper the translation of theory is not a secondary, derivative process; theory is always partial and provisional. This challenges the concept of a faithful reading, and the distinction between appropriation and misappropriation. Theory is configured, rather than reconfigured, by transmission.

If the transmission and transformation of knowledge is the point of issue here, it is worth exploring how these processes might differ in the natural and social sciences, and Latour's (1987) use of the concept of black boxes provides a useful resource for such a comparison. Latour contrasts the way in which the theory that DNA is a double helix was treated in 1951 with its use in 1985. In 1951 it is controversial and debatable, and assessment of the theory is not independent of its context. However, in 1985 the theory has become routine and is seen as factual; its black box has closed and it has become an 'immutable mobile' that can be imported and used in new contexts in the construction of new scientific theories. Scientific facts go through a process of transmission, translation and transformation, during which controversies are resolved. The theory that forms the strongest unified network is eventually deemed to have been determined and accepted as factual. Black boxed facts (or theories) are useful for theory building in science, because they are incontrovertible elements, with established networks that act in unison. Consequently, they can be treated like machines, mobilized in new areas and used to build networks for new theories. For Latour, scientific theory is configured by its network, but the process of transformation and configuration ceases when the black box closes. Latour's description of the development of scientific theory is consistent with Bernstein's claim that scientific theory develops by becoming 'more general, more integrating than previous theory' (1999: 162).

Latour explicitly restricts his account to scientific facts (and technological artefacts). Once the black box is closed, theory is treated as factual and not subject to transformation, so it is relatively unproblematic to import it as a resource. In contrast, sociological theories are rarely settled empirically or by consensus. They retain their indeterminate status and do not become facts, and consequently, they remain susceptible to transformation in transit.[2] Nevertheless, some aspects of Latour's black box metaphor still seem to be relevant. The name of a sociologist can be inserted into a text and used to stand for a perspective without going into any detail; for instance, 'Garfinkel' identifies an ethnomethodological perspective quickly and easily and avoids the need to define the perspective more precisely or to consider the effects of its recontextualization. This approach is essentialist insofar as it assumes that a theoretical perspective can be treated as a bounded, internally consistent entity, which can be recontextualized unproblematically. However, the connotations associated with a named sociologist can, like the contents of Latour's black boxes, be transformed by their networks during transmission. Rawls argues, for instance, that the strong positivist connotations that Durkheim has acquired are the result of a misinterpretation; in turn her arguments may serve to remove or reduce this association, transforming the perspective identified by the 'Durkheim' label. The use of the names of well-known authors disseminates, revitalizes and transforms their work, building associations and sustaining their networks; as Latour notes, being ignored is worse than being criticized. At the same time, naming sociologists adds credibility to the works of those that cite them, enlisting support from their established networks.

The book illustrates a variety of ways in which theory is reconfigured by sociological texts. These include: drawing attention to neglected aspects of social theories; drawing attention to connections or similarities between distinctive perspectives; correcting or refining interpretations of social theory; illuminating a perspective by contrasting it with a different perspective; extending or developing a perspective; and building a new perspective which is derivative of one or more perspectives. The chapters in this book also raise more general questions about theory, and its relationship with a range of other entities which include description, the persona of the author, ontology, research, practice, society, and its temporal and spatial context. We now consider the last of these in a little more detail.

Reconfiguring Geosociology

In the opening chapter Cooper, under the heading geosociology, sketched a number of events and conditions that form part of the socio-historical context of contemporary sociology, including globalization, transformations in the flow of information and changed strategies of governance; many of the authors in this book examine these events and conditions in more detail. In this section we extend the discussion in order to explore some further aspects of the temporal and spatial contexts of theory, sociological objects and their reconfigurations. We begin by considering the notions of orientation and tempo, before considering the complex relationship between politics, theory and empirical research.

---

2   This may help to explain the emphasis on authenticity in sociology, and consequent disputes about interpretations.

In reflecting upon the relationship between theory, sociological objects and their temporal-spatial contexts, Ahmed (2006) argues that how we orient to an object alters both the object and the work that it does. For instance, by sitting down at a table with paper and pen (or laptop) we 'turn' (orient) the table into a desk for writing. The repetition of this action, over time, alters the meaning of this action and the objects involved. The table becomes a writing desk, the act of sitting at the table orients the person to become a writer. However, Ahmed also notes that these orientations are not always taken through choice; they are taken in 'specific directions' in relation to wider socio-cultural understandings and forms of power (Ahmed 2006: 112).

Applying Ahmed's (2006) work here, we could view a particular theory as a sociological object and note how orienting to it in certain ways and not others over an extended period of time alters both its meaning and how it is 'read'. As noted above, the question of fidelity, or otherwise, to certain theorists has been significant to a number of the chapters in this collection. The process of theorizing, of orienting to theory and orienting theory to objects, can transform theory; yet certain 'readings' become fixed whilst others may become marginalized or disappear altogether to be resurrected and transformed at a latter point in time and space. Durkheim and Simmel are two classical theorists who are subject to this process of transformation in this collection. There are, however, two significant points to note here: first, orientations or transformations are 'political' – as Ahmed notes they are not neutral actions since any process of inclusion and exclusion is an act of power. Secondly, orientations or transformations have a tempo; to orient is to act and to act is to move at a certain speed.

The politics of sociology are indirectly raised in du Gay's chapter with its focus on academic personae. This aspect of disciplinary focus was broached by Cooper in chapter one, which considered the audience to whom the discipline is addressed. Tsatsaroni and Cooper focus more directly on the political context of sociology, and use the 'audit culture' as a starting point to consider how social theory can be transformed by its changing socio-political contexts. Their chapter notes that an 'audit culture' can shape the direction of sociological research and reduce the scope for theorizing (even if they go on to point to some problems with the ways in which these phenomena are often formulated). In this sense, some theoretical orientations are more valued, more frequently taken, than others and subsequently they may become *almost* obligatory within a given discipline. Hence, the type of 'misreading' noted above provides a means of subverting or realigning orientations, leading to a reconfiguration of social theories. However, there is another way in which orientations and reconfigurations are political: they are undertaken in relation to the tempo of contemporary social life; or perhaps more accurately, the tempo of contemporary social life and the means by which theory is produced have implications for the possibilities of reconfiguration.

Gane (2006) contends that contemporary social theorists are responding to, and grappling with, the problem of speed because changes in the flow of information and the acceleration in the pace of social life have altered the context in which they work. Theorists, he suggests, offer two responses in terms of their own practices: speeding up or slowing down. The former, which he suggests is espoused by writers such as Lash and Lunenfeld, involves utilizing new forms of technology and (for Lash especially) developing new styles of writing. The implication here is 'keep up or die!' Alternatively, Gane suggests, others, notably McLuhan, Virilio and Baudrillard offer the opposite response: contending that in an age of fast moving information, theorists need to decelerate their pace; to take time to respond.

Gane notes, however, that there are problems with both of these approaches and he argues that it may be advisable for theorists to adopt variable speeds, depending on context. The challenge, therefore, might be to examine the speed of social processes, events and objects and orient one's theorizing to bring it into alignment with these. Suggesting that the future of social theory lies in theorists 'taking stock' of and reacting to the tempo of social change does not mean that one can or should disengage theory from its context of production, as a number of authors in this book have emphasized. For example, Tsatsaroni and Cooper argue that it is impossible, whilst Greiffenhagen and Sharrock, and Rafanell deny that an objective analytical 'space', or context, external to its social production can be located.

Consider, for example, the following hypothesis. It is the late 19th Century; Durkheim is central in establishing sociology as an academic discipline with a specific scientific focus: the analysis of social facts. Using modern print technologies he publishes a book, which comes to form part of a sociological canon. The book is translated, read and interpreted by others throughout Europe and North America, again by means of print technology. A 'preferred reading' emerges and is contested and reinterpreted at a later date by others. Now picture a contemporary theorist; she works in what we might call a global educational environment and her work proliferates across a range of media. It is read by a variety of personae, both academic and non-academic. The rate of diffusion and consequently the speed of interpretation and reinterpretation of her work is accelerated, condensing the process of transformation, since the internet offers her and others the possibility of ever faster 'readings'. Simultaneously, the spaces for reading and reconfiguring her work have proliferated. She produces more works, in more places. Again, the internet appears to offer a pluralization of spaces and domains, which may be beyond the political control and governance of the author, and of established disciplinary practices, such as peer review, opening the possibility of transforming her theory into different objects.

Perhaps this reflects Gane's point? Theorizing in this context does require a consideration of speed; a contemporary theorist cannot evade it. Of course, this concern with change is not new; sociologists have always been working in relation to change. Durkheim himself was concerned with the cumulative effects of social changes, even if his work has primarily been read as being concerned with social order (Giddens 1986; Turner 1999). Perhaps, therefore, Gane can be understood as pointing at a new 'moment of theory'? A moment marked by contingency in meanings, objects, times and space. Wherever we locate this moment, and whatever we call it – globalization, cosmopolitanism, post-modernism – the speed of theory and theorizing are altered, new reconfigurations are manifested in this context.

Rather than considering theory and context it may be more useful to conceptualize the relationship in terms of theory/context. This does not negate the significance of speed, but it draws attention to the question of whether theory can ever be considered to be external to context rather than a constitutive part of that context that it is theorizing. This is problematic for empirical research, threatening validity. Perhaps, adopting an ethnomethodological approach, the separation of theory from context should be seen as a local accomplishment. Several writers claim that changes in temporal-spatial context have altered the relationship between sociologists and their empirical data, changing the relationship between theory and empirical research. These authors stress that the relationship between theory and empirical research is challenged by temporal-spatial transformations, such as changes in how and where data is collected and disseminated. For Savage and Burrows (2007) this means that sociological research methodologies, formerly a significant marker of the discipline and the basis of its unique claims to investigate and comment upon 'the social', have become both pluralized and problematized. Commercial research organizations, transaction data analysis gathered as part of commercial practices, social networking sites, geodemographic technologies, all provide extraordinarily rich data, often de-contextualized from academic sociological discourse (Burrows and Gane 2006). Therefore, for these writers, sociologists are being forced to come to terms with a rapidly changing empirical context; one that, in many ways, mirrors concerns about changing theoretical contexts. Indeed, Savage and Burrows (2007) suggest that this new climate further troubles the role of theory within sociology, since commercial organizations are not necessarily interested in theorizing their data sociologically; on the contrary, they may be more interested in its practical (and commercial) applications. Hence, the sort of theorizing that Savage and Burrows suggest has traditionally been a hallmark of sociology, a form that provides an overview of social change without recourse to empirical validation, may preserve sociology's public profile whilst failing to avert a decline in its analytical value. Savage and Burrows propose a renewed connection between theory and practice; a form of sociological description and classification and one with political intent: a reinvigoration of the project of sociology to take part in a changing world, in public engagement, not one that becomes mired in internal conflicts. We believe that this book contributes to this process. Its contributors certainly demonstrate that theory is not ossified or in terminal decline; moreover, they indicate that theory is not necessarily separate from empirical practice. As we noted above, social theory is changeable, subject to transformation and reconfigurations that contribute to the vitality and reconfiguration of the discipline itself.

Concluding Comments

Social theories, as sociological objects themselves, and social theorists, as the figures who practice theorizing, face a number of challenges, which are both within and external to the academy. Being sensitive to new conceptual, theoretical, methodological and historical developments, while simultaneously resisting the urge to overstate radical disjunctures of modes of theory, method and analysis are important. Social theory has too often fallen into the trap of self aggrandizement, focusing on causality and prediction. This book demonstrates that the reconfiguration of social theory means doing things with theory, whether that is contemplating the nature of the objects of sociology or transforming the meanings of existing theories.

Any theory is inescapably *of* its time, but its meaning and significance are not wholly reducible *to* its time: indeed, meaningful reflection upon the changing significance of theories and forms of sociological practice, in which the contributors to this book have been engaged, would not be possible if the latter were not true. We therefore hope that this book has a value that goes beyond the particular time and circumstances of its production; but we recognize, and welcome, the fact that it will itself be subject to further reconfiguration.

References

Ahmed, S. (2006), *Queer Phenomenology: Orientations, Objects, Others* (Durham: Duke University Press).
Bernstein, B. (1999), 'Vertical and Horizontal Discourses', *British Journal of Sociology of Education* 20:2, 157–173.
Burrows, R. and Gane, N. (2006), 'Geodemographics, Software and Class', *Sociology* 40:5, 793–812.
Gane, N. (2006), 'Speed Up or Slow Down: Social Theory in the Information Age', *Information, Communication and Society* 9:1, 20–38.
Giddens, A. (1986), *Durkheim on Politics and State* (Cambridge: Polity).
Goffman, E. (1967), *Interaction Ritual: Essays on Face-to-Face Behavior* (New York: Doubleday Anchor).
Latour, B. (1987), *Science in Action: How to Follow Scientists and Engineers Through Society* (Cambridge, MA: Harvard University Press).
Latour, B. (2005), *Reassembling the Social: An Introduction to Actor-Network Theory* (Oxford: Oxford University Press).
Savage, M. and Burrows, R. (2007), 'The Coming Crisis of Empirical Sociology', *Sociology* 41:5, 885–899.
Turner, B.S. (1999), *Classical Sociology* (London: Sage).

Index

Abstraction, misplaced 91–2
Adorno, Theodor 18
Ahmed, Sara 198
Appropriation of concepts 162–5, 172–3
Arendt, Hannah 10
Assemblages 54–5
Audiences for sociology 7
Audit culture 159–62
Auge, Marc 4

Ball, Steven 160–1
Barnes, Barry, performative theory of
    social institutions 60, 65–73
  collective, significance of 66, 71–3
  individual inferences as collective
    accomplishments 68–71
  social life as 'self referential
    bootstrapped induction' 66–8
  social and natural kinds distinction 66–8
Beck, Ulrich 8, 28–9
Bennington, Geoffrey 172
Bernstein, Basil 165–9
  horizontal and vertical discourse
    165–7, 194–5
  recontextualization 165–8
  the social 168
Bloor, David 69, 71, 72
  on mathematics 120, 124–33
Body
  being overweight 143–4
    in Denmark 146–53
    personal responsibility for 151
  sociology of 139, 143–4
  see also Butler
Bourdieu, Pierre
  criticism of Durkheim 61
  habitus 166
  on practice 92
  scientific and everyday consciousness
    139–40
Burrows, Roger 200

Butler, Judith
  construction of materiality 63–5
  performative model 62–5
  misreadings of 65
  neglect of collective in 65, 72–3

Casey, Edward 4
Communities, traditional vs practice 81–99
Conversation analysis 139–40, 153–4
Coulanges, Fustel de 36
Critical management studies 179
Critique 12–13, *see also* Hunter, Latour

Deconstructive hermeneutics 178
Deleuze, Gilles 4
Derrida, Jacques 170–173
  auto-immunity 8
  performativity 171
  theological translation 170
Durkheim, Emile
  conscience collective 33
  debt to Plato and Aristotle 30
  Division of Labour in Society 34, 81, 90
  Elementary Forms of Religious Life
    34–8, 88–9, 90
  global society 35–8
  global sociology 25–39
  international sociology 31–4
  moral culture 34
  organic solidarity 34–5, 90
  positivism of 103–106
  practices 87–91
  pragmatism 92–3
  Professional Ethics and Civic Morals
    33–4
  religious universalism 36–7
  Rules of Sociological Method 90,
    101–6
  social objectivity 60
  society 29–31
  theory of meaning 93–4

world culture 38
world patriotism 32–4
see also social facts

Economy, sociological studies of 6
Edgerton, Samuel 112–3
Educational policy 162–5
Educational research 160–2
Ethnomethodology 81–7, 101–116, 119–20, 139, 153–5
   members' tutorials 113–4
   situated tutorials, perspicuous phenomena 112–5
   see also Garfinkel

Feminism 2, 8
Fish, Stanley 180, 183–7
Foucault, Michel 181, 183
Fuller, Steve 12

Gane, Nicholas 198–9
Garfinkel, Harold 81–7, 91–6, 119–20
   constitutive organization of phenomena 103, 110–12
   documentary method of interpretation 106–7
   and Durkheim 11–12, 81, 82, 93–5, 101–12
   indexical expressions 108, 141
   and Parsons 103
   on queues 110–11
   respecification
      of 'social facts' 108–16
      of theorists and philosophers 106–7, 109, 115–6
   seminars and tutorials 107–12
Gasché, Rodolph 13
Geosociology 4–8, 197–200
Gibbons, Michael 6
Globalization
   reliance on practices 82–4
   and sociology 4–5, 9, 25–42, 81–99
Glocal norms and values 34
Governance, neo-liberal forms of 144–53
Greco, Monica 143

Habermas, Jurgen 183–7
   Between Facts and Norms 185–6
   ideal speech situation 184–5
Hacking, Ian 139, 141, 180, 183
Heidegger, Martin 5
   Building, Dwelling, Thinking 48–9
   the thing 109
Hirschman, Albert 186
Hunter, Ian 177–9, 181–2, 184, 187
Husserl, Edmund 45, 103

Identity 177–189
Information and communication technologies 5

Jones, Ken 164

Kusch, Martin on platitudinal knowledge 70–72

Lash, Scott 2
Latour, Bruno
   black boxes 196–7
   co-production 169
   on critique 12–13, 178–80, 188–9
   deflation of theory 169–70
   on Durkheim and Tarde 10–12
   on Heidegger and the thing 109
   reformulation of social 48, 169
   on Simmel and Marx 50
   sociology of translation 169–71
Law, John 142
Lofgren, Orvar 52
Lukacs, Georg
   on reification 2
   on Simmel 45–6
Lury, Celia 2
Lynch, Michael 112–3

Martins, Herminio 27
Marx, Karl 7, 29, 90
Material and social 43–4, 48–9, 55, 71–4
Mathematics, sociology of 119–33
   conventions 127–8
   two forms of sociological explanation 129
   see also Bloor, social facts, Wittgenstein
Mauss, Marcel 31–2
Methodological nationalism 27–31
Middleton, Sue 161
Modes of knowledge production 6–7, 200

'Moment of theory' 177–189, 199
National sociologies 27–8
Neo-liberalism 6, 142, 164
   see also governance
Nowotny, Helga 5, 6

Objects
   different senses of 1–4
   objectification 3
   sociological neglect of 193
   see also Heidegger, Latour, Simmel

Parsons, Talcott 103
Performativity 59–74
   of methods and theories 142
   see also Derrida
Practices 81–96
   in classical sociological theory 89–90
   reduced to concepts 84–7, 91–2, 94–6
   scientific practices 88–9
   see also appropriation of concepts, Durkheim, globalization, performativity
Pragmatism 92–4
Professional sociologists
   expertise of 105–6, 128–33, 177–89
   sociological discourse frames everyday life 139–55

Reisman, David 81
Religion and technology 7
Risk 8, 140, 142, 148–53
Rorty, Amélie 188

Sacks, Harvey 7, 108, 120
Savage, Mike 200
Scheff, Thomas on 'deference-emotion system' 70–72
Schutz, Alfred 122–3
Serres, Michel 48
Simmel, Georg 43–55, 90
   asymmetry of humans and non-humans 52–4
   Bridge and Door 47–9
   concrete philosophy 45
   objects 43–58
      autonomy of 51–2
      neglect of their materiality 47

   psychological effects of 51
   Philosophy of Money 46–7
   social totality 45–6, 48
   sociology of the meal 53
   subject and object 49–55
   things 44–6, 54–5
   tragedy of culture 51, of the spirit 45
Sobe, Noah, W. 164
Social constructionism 180–3
Social facts 10–12, 30–1, 61–2, 72–4, 105, 107–12
   Garfinkel's respecification of 108–16
   inflationary and deflationary readings of 119–23
   mathematical equations as social facts 119–33
Social order
   at all points 85
   disruptions of 86
   local order and professional discourse 140–43, 148, 153–5
   stigmatizing 152
Society as problematic concept 9–10, 26–9, 46
Suchman, Lucy 82
Symbolic Interactionism 141, 153

Tarde, Gabriel 10–11
Theory
   development of 195
   in everyday life 139–55
   orientation and tempo 197–200
   theoretical personae 178–80
   translations of 106–7, 109, 115–6, 159–73, 196–7 *see also* Bernstein, Garfinkel, Latour
Trust 82, 91

Urry, John 4, 142

Vattimo, Gianni 13
Vergés, Françoise 8

Wagner, Peter 9
Weber, Max 29, 90, 187
Whitehead, Alfred North 91–2
Wittgenstein, Ludwig
   approach to meaning 94

on mathematics 124–5, 128–9, 133
moving away from theory 133

Woolgar, Steve
social and material relation 53